Amazing Grace

Amazing Grace

A Life of Beauford Delaney ———————————

DAVID LEEMING

NEW YORK   OXFORD

OXFORD UNIVERSITY PRESS   1998

Oxford University Press

Oxford New York
Athens Auckland Bangkok Bogota Bombay
Buenos Aires Calcutta Cape Town Dar es Salaam
Delhi Florence Hong Kong Istanbul Karachi
Kuala Lumpur Madras Madrid Melbourne
Mexico City Nairobi Paris Singapore
Taipei Tokyo Toronto Warsaw

and associated companies in
Berlin Ibadan

Published by Oxford University Press, Inc.
198 Madison Avenue, New York, New York 10016

Oxford is a registered trademark of Oxford University Press

Library of Congress Cataloging-in-Publication Data
Leeming, David.
Amazing grace: a life of Beauford Delaney / by David
Leeming.
p. cm.   Includes bibliographical references and index.
ISBN 0–19–509784–X
1. Delaney, Beauford, 1901–1979.   2. Painters—United States—
Biography.   3. Afro-American painters—United States—Biography.
I. Title.
ND237.D339L44 1997   97-1645   759.13—dc21

Writings by Richard Long are reproduced with his permission.

9 8 7 6 5 4 3 2 1

Printed in the United States of America
on acid-free paper

For

Ogust and Imogene

contents

n the living room of the Delaney house on Dandridge Avenue in Knoxville, an elderly woman sits at the old piano and in a gravelly and surprisingly deep voice sings:

> Amazing Grace! how sweet the sound,
> that saved a wretch like me!
> I once was lost but now am found,
> was blind but now I see.

She sings by rote and seems unconscious of her audience of three. I have the feeling of being at a personal seance rather than a performance. The woman's gnarled hands know where to go on their own, her eyes look straight ahead at the empty music rack. This piano has been hers since she took command of it and began playing, as if by magic, at the age of two.

At this moment and, for that matter, at any given time Imogene is only partly with us; she spends most of her day in what seems to those around her another space entirely. Yet almost mechanically she answers questions and can remember details about her family that others have long forgotten. Imogene especially remembers "Uncle Beauf," and her "Amazing Grace" reminds those of us in the room of his rendition of the hymn—deep and soulful. Her separate space, too, is like his, and like him she comes into our mundane world most fully, usually with bright laughter, when we speak of food or tease her about her love life. As Imogene sings, Ogust, Beauford's other niece, leans over and whispers to me, "Beauford's here, isn't he?" and he is. And now, church people all—Ogust, the visiting social worker, and I—we join in, singing with Imogene and Beauford, whose voices are both there in profound understanding of the journeys each has taken:

> Through many dangers, toils and snares,
> I have already come;
> 'tis grace that brought me safe thus far,
> and grace will lead me home.

I remember Beauford through Imogene's face, through the sure movement of her hands on the keyboard—the instrument of her art—through her beatific aloneness.

I met Beauford Delaney in the summer of 1966. I was sent by James Baldwin, for whom I was working at the time, to bring him from Paris to Istanbul. My meeting with Beauford, the ensuing journey, and the weeks with him in Turkey changed my life and made this biography somehow inevitable. It was impossible to spend time with Beauford Delaney without becoming aware that his was a profound and complex story. Like his "spiritual son," James Baldwin, Beauford was a "case" to be studied; his philosophic ramblings, characteristic facial and hand gestures, his unpredictable behavior, and general Buddha-like demeanor made him always the central figure in any group. When you were with Beauford Delaney you watched, you listened, and you learned. Henry Miller recognized this in his 1945 essay, "The Amazing and Invariable Beauford DeLaney." And James Baldwin acknowledged it when in answer to my questions about his old friend he said, "He's a cross between Brer Rabbit and Saint Francis of Assisi."

After the Istanbul experience in 1966 I saw little of Beauford. We corresponded during the late 1960s and the early 1970s. For a birthday present in 1967 my wife and I took him to one of Josephine Baker's farewell concerts at the Olympia in Paris. That was it. But Beauford has remained an important part of my life through my memories of time spent with him, my connection with James Baldwin, and through his paintings.

Baldwin and I talked about Beauford—sometimes on tape—a great deal in the 1980s as part of the preparation for my 1994 biography of the writer. Whenever members of the "Baldwin circle"—for example, Mary Painter, Lucien Happersberger, Bernard Hassell, and David Baldwin—were together, the subject of Beauford came up and developed into a mythology: the drive to Istanbul, the "escape" from the hospital in the south of France, the ill-fated journey to Greece, the days in St. Anne's Hospital for the Insane in Paris.

But most of all, memory of Beauford lives on in his paintings. For me certain ones are particularly important. There are the brightly abstract yellow and red landscapes of St. Paul de Vence in the Baldwin house there, the huge abstractions and the exquisite and mysterious yellow nativity scenes at the home of a Delaney friend and patroness in Paris, and the terrifyingly perceptive portraits of his and sometimes my friends, including one of a bespectacled, purse-lipped me as a twenty-nine year old, or another, more abstract one of James Baldwin, whose face has become that of one of his lovers. Then there are the self-portraits and Greenwich Village scenes that have now surfaced in various museums and exhibits in the United States and Paris. And there is the romanticized portrait of a nude black youth seated on a daybed surrounded by exotic plants—a painting that turned up recently in a suburban New York attic with the title *Dark Rapture* scribbled in Delaney's hand on the back. Among the most exciting works for me are the early portraits now being unearthed by the Delaney Estate and others of W. E. B. Du Bois, Ethel Waters, W. C. Handy, the fifteen-year-old James Baldwin, and many other cultural giants or giants-to-be whom Beauford captured in pastel, quickly and expertly, to preserve what he saw as significant aspects of African American history in the 1930s and 1940s. And there were the other pastels that defined and gave permanence to friendships, or those drawn on Greenwich Village street corners to earn money for a much-needed meal.

In all his works one feels Beauford Delaney struggling to find the right balance between two sides of his art: the subjective analysis—psychological and philosophical—of which he was so fond, and the strongly felt obligation to use form and light to create works of art that would transcend individual subjects and speak for themselves as paintings or drawings. This struggle was reflected in his personal and life-threatening battle with the "voices" within himself that all too often escaped his inner world and took form as tormentors in the world around him. They whispered softly to his mind in adolescence and got a bit louder in early manhood. They were beside him in the train and the ship as he took a long-planned trip to Greece in 1961. They were sitting with him at the cafes of Montparnasse through most of the 1960s and early 1970s, and they finally smothered him in his last days at St. Anne's Hospital in Paris. It was through his art alone that Beauford could contain and transcend those tormenting voices, the way human misery is transformed into a celebration of living in the art of the blues. So Beauford held onto his brush for as long as he possibly could until the voices took it away from him and left him blank.

Who was Beauford Delaney? people ask. Those who knew him all say he was a joy to be with, that he loved life—food, wine, sun, and especially light. They say he was dedicated to his painting, but they wonder when and how someone who spent so much time in the cafes of Greenwich Village and later Paris had time to do all the work he did. Everyone remembers Beauford's philosophizing—his ability to listen and give wise if sometimes confusing counsel. Many friends speak of his deep serenity. The same people and others remember his bouts with acute paranoia. In all my research I have never met anyone who disliked Beauford Delaney.

But who was Beauford Delaney? The art world is now recognizing him as a major African-American and American painter—one of the great modernists. Gallery owners, universities, museums, and collectors argue over the ownership of his once unwanted works. Paintings that went unsold now sell for prices that would have amazed an often hungry Beauford. But this is an old story in the world of arts and letters. Who was Beauford Delaney? Beyond the point of general agreement and what seems to be the emerging judgment of the art world, there are radical disagreements and a great deal of mystery. There were the voices, but what did they say, and why were they there? Was it because he was black, because he was gay? He certainly was African American and homosexual. But does his painting say anything about his racial or sexual history? Was his childhood particularly painful in a racist border state? Did he leave America to escape racism? Were there any significant lovers? For the most part Beauford was a very private man who had hundreds of friends, most of whom knew little or nothing about his past, his private life, his voices, or even his other friends. His own family knew nothing about his psychological problems until the very last years of his life. There are those who speak of premature senility or Alzheimer's disease and others who say that Beauford's "problem" was alcoholism, pure and simple. Some of his friends claim that Beauford did not concern himself with racial or sexual issues, that his whole life was his painting.

In this book I have attempted to discover the man behind the paintings and have sometimes used the paintings as clues. This is not a *catalogue raisonné* or an analytical study of the works of Beauford Delaney. It is, however, the story of a life of an artist and it will, therefore, consider the challenges taken up in particular paintings and the relation of those challenges to the artist's life. The book grows naturally out of my earlier work on James Baldwin, who spoke often of Beauford as his "spiritual father." In a sense, then, this work is a continuation of the Baldwin biography, one aspect of which, after all, is the story of a committed artist's lifelong attempt to understand his father and fatherhood. Baldwin found both in Beauford Delaney.

Finally, I do not concern myself in the main body of this book with the worth of Beauford Delaney's work. It is enough to say that I agree with James Baldwin when he wrote:

Perhaps I should not say, flatly, what I believe—that he is a great painter—among the very greatest; but I do know that great art can only be created out of love, and that no greater lover has ever held a brush.

— *acknowledgments*

I wish to thank the following people and organizations for their moral or financial support and information regarding the life of Beauford Delaney and for permission to quote documents or reproduce paintings and photographs: the scholars and critics whose works are listed in the Bibliography, the late James Baldwin, the late Bernard Hassell, Richard Long, my children, my mother, David Craven, Don Belton, Florence Ladd, Henry Louis Gates, Jr., Houston A. Baker, Jr., Arnold Rampersad, Leon Edel, Hazel Rowley, Richard Powell, Richard Newman, Edward Naughton, Jennifer Klopp, Ernest "Dixie" Nimmo, Cecil Brown, Philippe Bebon, Cindy Spangler, James and Pamela Morton, Krysia Jopek, Dalia Kandiyoti, Ernie Bynum, Dennis Costin, Dorothy West, Ed Grayson, Michelle LeGros, Bill Belli, Judith Bledsoe, Shirley Jaffe, Nidra Poller, Carolyn and Sarah Wells, the late Mary Painter, Richard Olney, Myron Heise, the late David Baldwin, Gordon Boggs, Birgitta Stig-Boggs, Joanne Sitwell, Al Hirschfeld, the late Ollie Harrington, Ed Clark, the late Selma Burke, Herbert Gentry, Robert Blackburn, Gregory Masurovsky, Helen Bishop, Arnold Newman, Ann Freilich Schutz, Robert Wasserman, Leslie Schenk, Gene Davis, Joe Wood, John Ashbery, Amy Hill Hearth, Rose Piper, Dante Pavone, Shirley Suttles, Barbara Chase-Riboud, Mary Schmidt Campbell,

Vincent Smith, Gloria Jones, Mara Weissman, Darthea Speyer, Ted Joans, Joe Downing, Lois Jones Pierre-Noel, Joe O'Reilley, W. F. Lucas, Ruth Ann Stewart, Eva Arvonio, Margaret and Patrice Higonnet, Corrine Jennings, Joe Overstreet, Barry Gaither, Camille Billops and Jim Hatch at the Hatch-Billops Collection, Robert Booker and the Beck Cultural Center, Barry Tompkins, Elizabeth Maguire, Beryl Wright, Richard Gibson, Jack Neely, Burton Reinfrank, Paul Jenkins, Lucien Happersburger, George Sugarman, Addie Herder, Ann Weber, Bill Rivers, Edward Field, Robert Dubliner, the Estate of Larry Calcagno for the Calcagno–Delaney letters, Frank Carner, for the Irene and Billy Rose/Dorothy Gates–Dealaney letters, the Beinecke Rare Book and Manuscript Library for the Wallrich-Delaney letters, The Research Library at the University of California at Los Angeles and the Henry Miller Estate for the Miller– Delaney letters, Ida Balboul at the Metropolitan Museum of Art, the Museum of Modern Art, the Brooklyn Museum, the Smithsonian Institution, the Library of Congress for Harmon Foundation records, Diana Lachatanere and Tanimi Vance Lawson at the Schomburg Center, the Schomburg Center for Delaney letters, Sedat Pakay for Delaney photographs, Valerie J. Mercer at the Studio Museum in Harlem, Thomas Burke at the New York Public Library, Tina Bunkley at Clark-Atlanta University, Joe Pierce, Elwood Peterson, Thomas Gibson, Nancy Roden and Thelma Golden at the Whitney Museum of American Art, Nancy Mollog at the Archives of American Art in New York, Judy Throm at the Archives of American Art in Washington, the University of Connecticut Research Foundation for research and travel grants, and the Florence Gould Foundation for a grant to support the reproduction of paintings in color.

Most especially I want to thank Charley Boggs, Jim and Bunny LeGros, Solange du Closel in Paris, Sam Yates and the Ewing Gallery at the University of Tennessee, and Michael Rosenfeld at the Michael Rosenfeld Gallery in New York for their help on and enthusiastic commitment to this project. My primary research assistants have been Betty Kaplan Gubert in New York and Katie Drowne in Knoxville; their work has been invaluable, as have the support and encouragement of my agent Faith Childs and my editor Susan Chang and the research assistance and suggestions of Allison Singley and Pamela Leeming.

I wish to thank the Delaney Estate for its permission to quote from Delaney's writings and reproduce his artwork. Hardy Liston, Tammy Kaousias, and Andy Davis have all been supportive.

Most of all I am grateful to the late Beauford Delaney himself for the weeks we spent together and the worldly and otherworldly conversations we had and to his nieces Ogust Mae Delaney Stewart and the late Lois Imogene Delaney for all they have contributed to this project in the way of information and loving encouragement.

Amazing Grace

Amazing grace! how sweet the sound,
that saved a wretch like me!

one

Knoxville

Beauford Delaney's early life was dominated by the powerful figure of his mother, Delia Johnson Delaney, a strict, proud woman who upheld what she saw as the Christian virtues. She punctuated lessons on forbearance, patience, self-control, and turning the other cheek with songs. In later life Beauford often talked of and sang the songs she taught him: "My Good Lord Done Been Here Blest My Soul and Gone Away" was one, along with the more traditional spirituals and the ever popular "Amazing Grace" that became Beauford's favorite hymn. His mother and he especially liked the verse that reads: "Through many dangers, toils, and snares, I have already come; 'tis grace that brought me safe thus far, and grace will lead me home." And there were secular lyrics such as "She never told her love, but let concealment feed on her damask cheek . . . smiling, smiling at grief." From the 1930s these and words like them are copied out over and over in Beauford's journals as if they had the power, through connection with his mother's strength, to ward off the inner voices that in the early years only teased him but later gradually took over his mind.

Delia Johnson was born into slavery in Richmond, Virginia, on February 1,
1865. Her mother was Susan Johnson, possibly a descendant of the free black set-
tlers who, in 1651, had formed the Johnson settlement on the banks of the Pun-
goteague River in Northampton County. Northampton County is just across the
bay from Norfolk, where Susan was said to have been born in the 1840s. Susan
Johnson's father had been black, her mother a Cherokee Indian. The father of her
children, Delia and Philip, and a younger daughter, was a relatively recently
arrived African slave with whom she lived in Richmond and later Abingdon, Virginia, as a slave herself. Like many of the Northampton Johnsons, Susan was by
trade engaged in fishing, and after the Civil War returned with her husband to
the Chesapeake to make a living gathering and selling oysters. The Delaney family remembered that Susan said certain words in the way peculiar to the people of
the Northampton peninsula, and they remembered, too, that she was inexplicably in possession of some old silver. She guarded that silver carefully but would
lend it out to people on special occasions, warning them that if they stole or lost
it she would take them "out the shoye [shore]" and push them in. The Delaneys
always assumed that the silver came from the household of her former "owners,"
who, it was said, had treated Susan with some kindness, but it might also have
come down from prosperous free black Johnsons of Northampton County.

Whatever her social situation, Susan Johnson did not have the demeanor of
the downtrodden. And she transferred a sense of dignity and self-esteem to her
children. Delia was to be known later in Knoxville and nearby towns as a woman
of special qualities with strong views. She never learned to read and write, but
she kept a picture of Sojourner Truth in her bedroom and preached to her children about the indignities and injustices of racism and the importance of education. And she sang the old songs and loved telling stories she had heard from her
mother about plantation life and the Civil War days. A particular favorite was one
about the death of "Old Massa," told here in Delia's words as remembered by
Beauford in his journals.

> The reason for telling this tale is that it's unique from slave times in America.
> One of the villainous slave owners died and his crimes upon his slaves had
> been so heinous that his wife who survived him was literally afraid to have the
> local pastor attend to the funeral rites. So she turned her attention to Uncle
> Marsten, a devout slave who was respected by all the whites as possessing true
> humanity and love for all mankind. But when Uncle Marsten was asked to
> officiate at the funeral such was his confusion as to completely upset his usual
> calm. Nevertheless, it was a command and to ignore the order meant death.
> So up comes Uncle Marsten to the vast parlor of the mansion home where

Massa is laid out in state. The funeral was held, and after songs and words by other notables, it was Uncle Marsten's turn. After much hemming and hawing and fear of going on, Uncle Marsten said a few things and then said them again. Then Old Miss said, "Yes, you've said that three times, now get on with the sermon. After a bit more of his hemming and hawing the old lady became adamant and lost all patience: "Marsten, get on with the sermon; we haven't got all day." And old Marsten answered straight away, "Well, Ole Miss, Ole Massa is daid, and I'm mighty 'fraid Ole Massa is gone whar I hope he hain't. Amen."

Delia took in laundry and cleaned the houses of white people, but she was never obsequious. In appearance she was stately. She wore long dresses and high buckled shoes until the 1930s, when she returned from a visit to sons Beauford and Joseph in New York dressed in the latest fashions.

Delia was naturally artistic. Not only was she a talented singer and storyteller, she was a fine seamstress and quilt-maker. Her grandchildren remember her working on a quilting frame, creating works of unusually intricate and imaginative design. They most admired a quilt that was decorated with hundreds of images—Indian fashion—of her own right hand. The children had watched with fascination as she first traced the hand onto paper, then used the tracing as the pattern for cutouts made from odd bits of colorful material.

Delia could be imperious and morally arbitrary. The neighborhood children loved being in the Delaney house, but when Delia had had enough of the noise created by her children's or later her grandchildren's friends she would come into the room, wave a hand slightly, and the guests would scatter. One day she found Beauford in early adolescence kissing a girl on the cheek and scolded her son in such a way as to make him—to repeat his own words—"afraid of sex forever." She liked to make up or quote pithy comments with a moralistic tinge. "A child out of wedlock's a woods colt," she would say or, in the first years of the miniskirt, "The women don't wear enough clothes these days to make a mouse a jacket." When her son Joe showed her a portrait of a nude woman he had painted, she told him the woman was beautiful but that he should put some clothes on her.

At her husband's funeral it was said that she shed no tears but that when she arrived home she collapsed in despair. To the world at large Delia Delaney never revealed her sufferings. She passed this quality on to her son Beauford. Delia died in 1958 at the age of ninety-three. For seventy some years she had been the much deferred-to matriarch of the Delaney household.

Beauford's father, John Samuel Delaney, was born on September 18, 1859, in Bristol, Tennessee, just across the border from Bristol, Virginia. He was brought up by his mother, whose ethnic background was Creek Indian, African American, and perhaps white. According to family tradition, the father of John Samuel, his brother, Henry, and his sister, Mary, was a light-skinned man, probably of at least part Irish descent. And there were said to be other, very light skinned brothers, or possibly half brothers. One ran a sugar plantation in Hawaii, one became a judge, and the other operated a brothel. John, or Sam, as he was called by his family, and Henry and Mary lived very simply with their mother in a small house on a large farm. It seems likely that the mother had been freed from slavery by a Mr. Delaney and that she and the children took his name. The Delaneys were share-croppers, but there was a small garden next to the house where they could raise their own vegetables. Sam's mother, a quiet and gentle woman, who died in late 1885, was revered by her children and her daughter-in-law.

John Samuel met Delia Johnson when, as a young man of twenty-five, he vis-ited Abingdon on church business. He was already a preacher in the Methodist Episcopal church at that time, and he fell in love with the nineteen-year-old Delia, who was a member of the congregation in Abingdon. Sam and Delia married on April 9, 1885.

Samuel Delaney was a man committed to his religion; he was especially dedi-cated to the ministry to his people, who had suffered and continued to suffer so much after the war. He was called Brother Delaney by all who knew him and he spent much of his adult life as a circuit-riding preacher, finding black communi-ties that lacked a Methodist Episcopal church, helping them to construct church buildings, then moving on. Even when he was established at various periods as the pastor in charge of churches in Knoxville and Jefferson City, he could often be seen being carried off by a horse and buggy to places as far afield as Harriman, Strawberry Plains, or Mascot, Tennessee, or Pulaski, Virginia, where he would stay for months doing his mission work for the church. Because his minister's salary, even when supplemented by his wife's housework for others, was too small to support a large family, Brother Delaney learned to be a barber, a skill he practiced professionally until his death. His was not an easy life, and he would die thirty-nine years before his wife, a man exhausted by his mission.

After their marriage, Samuel and Delia settled in Knoxville, where Brother Delaney accepted a call as assistant minister at the Methodist Episcopal church. Their first child, Carabelle, was born on April 8 of 1886, but died of a childhood-disease complication two years later. This fate awaited several of the Delaney children born in Knoxville, as well as one born in Jefferson City. Percy, born on June 4, 1893, lived for only four months. Clifford Henry, born the next year on August 22, survived for six years until his tragic death, probably as a result of

The Delaney family, 1909. Top, left to right, Samuel Emery, John Samuel, Delia; *bottom, left to right,* Joseph, Ogust Mae, Beauford, Naomi.

pneumonia, on October 11, 1900. Marion was born on October 27, 1899, but died at a little over a year's age on March 16, 1901. Later the Delaneys would lose daughters Ogust Mae, born December 15, 1896, and Naomi, born September 20, 1908. Beauford Delaney was the eighth of the ten children of John Samuel Delaney and Delia Johnson Delaney. Three of his bothers survived into adulthood; Ogust Mae lived to be nineteen.

Sterling, born on June 14, 1889, was a proud, handsome, and somewhat aggressive young man. He spent some time at Morristown College before being expelled for "womanizing," and, in some disgrace with his parents, moved to Virginia, where he became a highly successful maitre d' at a resort hotel in Natural Bridge. Sterling rarely returned home after that and Beauford hardly knew his oldest brother.

Easily Beauford's favorite brother was Samuel Emery, born on August 15, 1891. Always called "Em" as a child, and later "Emery," he was also sent to Morristown College, where he excelled as a student and a leader. Highly musical and possessed of a fine bass voice, he was a member of a jubilee quartet that traveled around Tennessee and Virginia singing the songs that grew out of the traditions of the black churches and colleges of the South. The quartet sang the old spiritu- als like "Didn't My Lord Deliver Daniel," "Jacob's Ladder," and "Swing Low Sweet Chariot," but also performed some of the newer "witness" gospel songs like "I'm a Soldier in the Army of the Lord" or "Jesus is on the Mainline."

Emery met his contemporary, the concert tenor and collector of spirituals, Roland Hayes, at the home of the Knoxville Colored High School principal and black leader, Charles Cansler, who was so fast with numbers that it was said he had once outadded an adding machine in his head in a race. Cansler enjoyed telling how in earlier days he, then a railway clerk, had seen Hayes working as a shoeshine boy in Bristol, Tennessee. For Emery these successful men were exam- ples of what could be done with time and perseverance.

Emery enlisted in the army during World War I and so impressed his some- times barely literate white superiors with his combination of humility and learn- ing that they frequently asked him to write letters home for them. He always said he was "paid" for his work by being made a noncommissioned officer. After the war Emery took a position as a teacher in Virginia and on March 18, 1919, his father officiated at his marriage to Gertrude Harris, whom he had met and fallen in love with at Morristown College. Gertrude was also of Native-American and African-American descent.

Although Emery was Beauford's favorite brother, his sister Ogust Mae—"Sis- ter," as everyone called her—was almost a mystical presence in his life. A slight figure with a very serious face and beautiful singing voice, she was relatively close to him in age and was his best friend. Ogust Mae's early death on July 11, 1915, left a permanent emotional scar on the whole family, but especially on Beauford. The family remembered Sister as the prime example of the generosity and good nature that they particularly valued and that found other notable expression in the characters of John Samuel, Emery, and Beauford Delaney.

Two children were born after Beauford. Joseph Samuel came on September 13, 1904. Called "Joe" or sometimes "Kokomo," his fame as a painter would later rival that of his brother. From an early age Joe was the most rebellious and difficult of the Delaney children. When it came time for middle school, he was so undisci- plined that his father sent him to a private school in Knoxville run on the "English system" by a West Indian called Mr. Mayers. The school had little effect, and Joe continued to tarnish the Delaney family reputation in Knoxville until in 1925 he hopped a train to Chicago and joined the National Guard for three years before returning home. Joe did win a first prize for a pencil sketch of a sparrow at his pri- vate school and later started a black Boy Scout troop in Knoxville. But essentially he was a "challenge to community life," as he was fond of saying. Soon after his return to Knoxville, he hopped another train and began several years as a wanderer, taking jobs of any kind, finding "the easiest way to make a dollar without stealing it." In Kentucky he worked in the coal mines and then met a woman who suggested that he work for her instead, washing dishes in the hotel she ran. The relationship and the job lasted for ten days and, in terms of the relationship, established a pattern in Joe's life. He sought out women—particularly big women—to love and to draw, but never stayed with one for long, and he never married. After Kentucky Joe lived the boxcar life of the hobo, until he landed in New York in 1930, the year after Beauford arrived, and, like his brother, took up the life of a painter.

Joe was always a bit wary of his older brother Beauford, describing him in later years somewhat facetiously as always a "dutiful and attentive child," never approving of what he saw as his "art for art's sake" painting, and being particularly uncomfortable with his homosexuality. But a strong affection always existed between the brothers, as their correspondence clearly shows.

The very last of the children of John Samuel and Delia Delaney was Delia Naomi. Born in Jefferson City, she died an infant of eight months on June 14, 1909. Naomi had been sickly from the beginning. With her death and Ogust Mae's a few years later, Sam and Delia Delaney were left with four of their ten children: Sterling, Emery, Beauford, and Joseph.

Beauford Delaney was born in Knoxville, Tennessee, on December 30,1901. He was a quiet, chubby baby with a round face, and he smiled a lot. Almost from the beginning he was "Beauf" to his family. Beauford's first memory was of the family's preparations in 1905 for a move to Jefferson City from the house at 815 East Vine Street in Knoxville in which he and all his brothers and sisters through Joseph had been born. This was a one-story, green woodframe house that Samuel and Delia had moved into not long after their marriage. But the church had called Sam to be the pastor in Jefferson City.

A vignette returned frequently to Beauford's mind years later in Paris after his father and mother were both dead. It was of the front room in the evening, in the late fall or early winter. A fire was lit in the stove to keep off the cold. The children were there—Em trying to be helpful, Sterling looking cross, Sister coughing, holding baby Joe, and Beauford himself, as he put it, blubbering quietly. The children knew they were leaving a way of life, the only one they had known. Delia, teary-eyed, was in the center of the room, working with boxes, some already packed. Around her were several women friends, all crying.

Life in Knoxville had been relatively good for the Delaneys. They were poor and had lost several children, but church work had been rewarding, and social life in what was a particularly sophisticated and educated black community had been active and stimulating. The Delaneys were well liked and respected.

Life in Jefferson City, a much poorer and more rural town at that time, was necessarily very different. Sam was installed as the pastor of the Boyd Chapel Methodist church. His only pay was help with the rent for the "parsonage" the family lived in near the church. The family income was supplemented by rent money from the Knoxville house, Delia's laundry and housecleaning for white people in town, and Samuel's work as a barber. Sam and Delia were determined to save money for Sterling's and Emery's education. As the children grew old enough they, too, were encouraged to find odd jobs after school and do chores around the house. The house was quite small, but it had a large vegetable garden as well as a huge front yard for the young children to play in. This would be home for five years.

The people the Delaneys socialized with in Jefferson City were almost exclusively parishioners of their church. It was a poor congregation, one representative of the rural black South in the early 1900s. Drink was a problem. As a child Beauford was fascinated by Jim Mat Watkins, a poverty-stricken, alcoholic mulatto married to a woman befriended by Delia. Florence Watkins was a washerwoman and prominent church member. She and Jim helped the Delaneys with the upkeep of the church. Jim would stagger to the parsonage from time to time to complain to Delia that Florence had had a drink and that he did not know where it would all end. The Watkins's problems were typical of those of the congregation in general. This was the first Beauford remembered hearing about the evils of drink. When he thought about the Watkins in later life he assumed that drink was their only "comfort" in the face of abject poverty.

The family rarely left Jefferson City during the days they lived there, except occasionally to accompany Samuel on his mission trips. Beauford did remember once being taken to Bristol to the movies by his Uncle Phil—Delia's brother, and his wife, Aunt Rhoda, of whom the children were all very fond. It was his first movie—a Saturday serial called *Old Clutching Hand*—and the outing was his earliest memory of a "big city."

Church dominated their time in Jefferson City; it was always the true center for the Delaneys, who were by nature spiritual people who loved and depended on their religion. Beauford describes in his journals how on Sunday the day began with church school from 9:00 until 10:30. Then the main service followed from 11 until about 2:00. There was singing, praying, the collecting of alms, and sometimes communion. And there was color and excitement that captured the attention of the young painter-to-be. Beauford loved the songs and the shades of the congregation—from mother of pearl to deep amber to "purple and egg-plant black," creating "a stained glass effect in the choral reality of their splendor." He also waited with all the other children for the inevitable and always late entry of Lulu Norman, a tall ebony-colored woman wearing a dress of many hues and a huge straw hat perched on a great deal of piled-up black hair—a hat with what seemed like hundreds of colored plumes or tropical flowers. Her coat was scarlet with white fur on the shoulders, and she "was possessed of the grace and ease of a lioness." Miss Lulu always came in as Brother Delaney was reading the devotional. The taffeta petticoats under her dress made a noticeable swishing sound, and she bowed at all the members of the congregation—but especially at the men, including the preacher—before achieving her seat just under the pulpit. And there was always a sermon, preached usually by Brother Delaney. Samuel Delaney's sermons were surprisingly intellectual for a small-town church. When Beauford visited Knoxville in 1950 he made a point of going through his father's books and was amazed at the depth of his reading, especially in the areas of philosophy and logic. As a child, Beauford had not understood his father's intellect and was understandably bored by his long philosophizing and soft-spoken sermons, but as an adult he realized where much of his own respect for learning and his tendency to philosophize had come from.

Church was not limited to Sunday morning. There was a late afternoon prayer service on Sunday and another on Wednesday evening. And on Thursday there was the board meeting at which issues of concern not only to the Methodist people but to the Baptists, Pentecostals, and Presbyterians were discussed—such issues as the effect of pool halls, dance halls, and ice cream parlors on the black community. There was discussion, too, of the role of secret lodges—Masons, Odd Fellows, and others—on their lives. And, of course, there was the ever-present theme of church finances.

The church was also a physical concern. Coal had to be bought and stored in a bin near the church stove. The oil lamps had to be tended to, and the cleaning was done by the pastor and his family, with the volunteer help of the Watkins and others. Roof repairs and other maintenance work also fell to the pastor. If he lacked the money for the work, there were fund-raising potluck suppers and musical events to be arranged. And, of course, there was the missionary work that took so much of Sam's time when he was not working at Louis Ingraham's barber shop.

Louis Ingraham was a tall good-looking African-American man whose shop, near the railroad station, was reserved for white men. Blacks had their hair cut at another barber shop on the other side of town. Beauford loved going into the shop on summer evenings when he was eight or nine to pick up his father from work. He would greet Mr. Ingraham, who was at the first chair, and Roy, who was at the third. The second chair was his father's. Beauford especially enjoyed being teased by Hop Peck, the shoeshine boy. The white men in the chairs always asked about school and what he was going to do when he grew up. "I'm going to be a singer," Beauford would reply.

Because the barber shop closed late and Delia sometimes had to cook for her employers, the family had late dinners. When they finally came together at the end of the day, there was much to talk about—school, the church, bits of the white world overheard in Delia's "white houses" and in the barber shop. Money matters were sometimes discussed; there was emphasis on the need to save. But Sam and Delia, although strict, were nothing if not loving and compassionate; the children returned those feelings to their parents and each other. And despite the demands of their working lives, Samuel and Delia encouraged a sense of fun. The family loved singing together and continued to do so over the years. They all sang well, and people loved passing by and hearing them sing spirituals, gospel songs, and even Delia's favorite secular songs of unrequited love. From the time they were little more than toddlers Delia recognized that Beauford and Joseph had drawing talent, and encouraged them to make copies of Sunday school cards and pictures from the family Bible. The Delaney family life together was, as Beauford put it later, "very close: passionate and dramatic."

The late family dinners were often cooked by a child, Ogust Mae, and it was around her and her sister Naomi that most of the passion and drama attached itself in the years between 1906 and 1915. Sister was in some ways the center of the family. From the age of eight, in addition to her schoolwork, she did most of the housework. Ogust Mae helped bring up her younger brothers as well, and for the short eight months of little Naomi's life was the baby's surrogate mother. Beauford had developed a seven year old's possessive love for the baby, and her sudden passing from his life left him confused and unsettled. He remembered that it was Ogust Mae who most helped him through this confusion.

At about the age of fourteen Sister, always fragile, began to show signs herself of serious illness. After a mental breakdown in the 1960s, Beauford tried to recapture Ogust Mae; the sense of her loss oppressed him all those years later. These are his own words in a 1961 journal:

Sister was older than me and we were very close. As we grew older there were ever increasing needs for money and Mama began to go out in service cooking, or nursing, or being a general housekeeper which meant that Sister with our help had to carry on at home. She was very bright and good natured, although her health was frail, and we were devoted to her and tried in our clumsy way to save her, but we did not know how, we were all so young and so unaware of the pain and unspoken intensity of our home and community life. Sister was full of fun and in no way pretentious—she sang beautifully—it was a joy to hear her. Mama being away from home, all her chores fell upon Sister who never complained— but she was always sick. We became alarmed because [from] the first time the doctor came it was always something the matter with Sister. Mama would quit her job and come home, the house became very quiet and we were awake late at night [talking] in hushed voices in fear for Sister's recovery. She was strong willed and survived most difficulties and would seem to be well and we would rejoice. So much of the sickness [Ogust Mae's and others] came from improper places to live—long distances to walk to schools improperly heated—a walk twice a day [they came home for lunch]—too much work at home—natural conditions common to the poor that take the bright flowers like terrible cold in nature. . . .

Ogust Mae died in 1915 of severe respiratory disease in Pulaski, Virginia. She was nineteen years old and weighed what she had weighed at age ten.

When John Samuel Delaney was called to Knoxville in 1915 to once again become pastor of the Methodist church there, they moved back into the house on East Vine. The family was now reduced to Sam and Delia and the two boys at home, Beauford and Joseph. The boys had attended school in Jefferson City, and later in Harriman and Prendergast, Tennessee, and Pulaski, Virginia, as their father moved from church to church. Emery, now a fully grown young man who had graduated from Morristown College and was teaching in Virginia and who would soon go off to the army, had always been a brilliant student. Beauford, too, aged fourteen, had done well in school, and entered Mr. Cansler's Knoxville Colored High School. The eleven year old Joe, a less serious student, was sent off to Mr. Mayer's private school.

For the next four years life was relatively tranquil for the Delaneys. Samuel was much loved as a pastor, and Delia enjoyed being with her boys when she was not at work for people downtown. Emery was happy. Sometimes on weekends he came home and worked with his father at a barbershop at Central and Vine until he went off to the army during World War I. Joe was at least settled, and Beauford, always overly sensitive and still grieving, as was the whole family, over the loss of Ogust Mae, was much pampered by his mother's women friends— Mollie Evans, Mrs. Brabson, and others—who loved him for his gentle nature and the interest he took in their lives. His peers loved him, too. He was famous for his ability to mimic people and could entertain his friends and relatives for hours by playing the ukulele (and later the guitar) and singing the old songs. He seemed to be enjoying school well enough, too. His teachers liked him and he liked them. As Joseph would say after his brother's death, "Scholars of all grades in school as well as teachers and professional people of high rank gave Beauford time and understanding." Mr. Cansler would invite him to his house; it was a great honor for a boy of fourteen to be asked to a house where such notables as Roland Hayes and the James Weldon Johnsons were entertained. He took algebra, Latin, English, history, and manual training and a Mr. Hugh Tyler gave him some lessons in drawing. But what he enjoyed most was singing; as his voice changed it developed into a beautiful baritone, and when asked what he wanted to do, he still told people he wanted to be a singer. He also continued, like Joseph, to draw, and when he could afford the material, to do pastels and watercolors.

After school both Beauford and Joseph had jobs cleaning up tables and floors at the Vine Street Cafe. Beauford also occasionally worked as a leatherwork/shoemaker's apprentice and shoeshine boy at Mr. Willis's shop in Gay Street. And he had a job for a while in a Gay Street sign painting shop. While he was shining shoes, perhaps in 1916, he forgot his sketchbook at work and Mr. Willis found it. Impressed by what he saw, he demanded a painting for his house. Beauford undertook the commission—for a nature painting in oil—and Willis bought him the necessary materials. The painting was to be a seascape, but Beauford had never seen the sea, and had never painted in oils. Somehow, however, with the help of his newly acquired large canvas and blue, red, white, and yellow paint, a "very individual seascape emerged." Willis liked it so much that he introduced Beauford to the white painter Lloyd Branson, who was also impressed.

Branson was a Knoxville celebrity and a dandy in dress. Now seventy and an impressionist of some reputation, as a young man he had attracted the attention of an older artist who admired his sketch of Ulysses S. Grant on a cigar box. Branson had made the sketch during the general's visit to Knoxville in 1863. Branson was a promoter of his hometown and a nostalgic patriot of the Confederacy; he had been greatly influenced in his youth by the well-known Confederate Civil War doctor, John Mason Boyd. He designed the Knoxville flag and the soap model for the "Soldier at Rest" on top of the Confederate Monument in Bethel Cemetery. It was said that he carried on a liaison with Catherine Wiley, the popular impressionist painter, and he was much admired for his portraits of famous Tennesseeans and his impressionistic Tennessee country landscapes.

Apparently the promise indicated by young Beauford Delaney's work was sufficient to make him put aside the prejudices inherent in his politics and point of view. He offered to give the boy art lessons in his studio on the second floor of the Tennessee Theater Building on Gay Street in return for work as a "porter." Beauford's job was to clean up, move canvases around as instructed, and stoke the coal stove. During the several years of his sporadic work under Branson, Beauford did landscapes in watercolor and oil, several portraits of Knoxville blacks—in pastel, oil, and watercolor—including watercolors in 1922 of his mother and his brother Joe, and one of Mr. Cansler. Branson himself did a portrait of his protégé. The works—especially the landscapes—that Beauford did under the influence of Branson were representational rather than abstract and revealed the older man's concern as an impressionist with light (see Color Plate 1). All painting, he told the boy, should be studies in light; the subject could be interesting in itself, but it was the interaction of the subject with light that made painting as opposed to mere representation.

Branson encouraged Beauford to commit himself to his painting and continue his studies in Boston. Branson made the necessary arrangements for Beauford to leave Knoxville in 1923 and helped him financially. It is strangely coincidental that Branson, like Beauford, would end his life in a mental institution.

The tranquillity in the Delaney family life had come to an abrupt end on April 30, 1919. Soon after Emery's return from the army, his marriage to Gertrude, and his taking of another teaching position in Virginia, John Samuel Delaney died of a heart attack. Emery immediately gave up his teaching career, returned home to Knoxville, and took up what he saw as his natural obligation to support his mother and two younger brothers—Beauford and Joseph—who were all that was left of her family. He opened a barber shop in the front room of the old family house on Vine Street, partitioned the building so that his mother and the two boys had half, and moved in behind the barber shop with Gertrude. As soon as he could he installed indoor plumbing and a coal furnace. He became a church and Sunday School leader and spent the rest of his long life giving financial and emotional support to his family and anyone else he could help. This was a very different Emery from the nineteen-year-old boy who had shocked his parents by announcing his intention to move to Hawaii to make a living with his rich and almost legendary "white" uncle there. They had hoped he would become a minister, and in spirit if not in fact he did.

Coinciding with the loss of his father in Beauford's mind was the Knoxville race riot of 1919. This event was ever present in Beauford's memory and something he talked about often. It marked the end of the old Knoxville way of life as well. Knoxville had prided itself on its relatively pro-Union and pro black stance during the Civil War and the period immediately after. This is not to say that the town was a model of race relations. There was no question as to which race was in control, and blacks, however fortunate in their education in comparison to other border state and southern African Americans, were seen by whites as distinctly a servant class.

The center of the riot was at Vine and Central, the dividing line between white and black Knoxville and also, on the day of the riot, a barrier between the workplaces of the Delaneys and the home they were desperate to get to.

It seems that Maurice Hays, a talented, well liked, and handsome light-skinned African American, who was rumored to be the illegitimate son of Knoxville's white mayor, John Macmillan, had the reputation of being attracted by and attractive to white women. Rumors were particularly rampant in connection with one Berdie Lindsay, the wife of a railwayman who was often out of town. The sheriff had warned Hays that when he caught him there would be trouble. Trouble there was when Berdie was murdered in her bed by a person her female cousin, who was sharing her bed that night, described as a "nigger." The sheriff leapt to the conclusion that the "nigger" must be Hays and promptly arrested him for first-degree murder. It was not long before a white lynch mob formed to teach Hays a lesson and marched on the city jail, breaking down the door, stealing what weapons could be found, and drinking the confiscated moonshine whiskey stored there. Fearing trouble, the sheriff had spirited Hays off to protective custody in Chattanooga, but the mob freed any white prisoners who were in the jail before beginning a drunken night of looting and black-baiting. From here on rumor takes over. According to the most prevalent story, certain blacks who had returned from the war with weapons defended themselves with a machine gun from the roof of a building at Central and Vine. Remarkably few people were killed that day or in the two days of "troubles" that followed. But the races were kept separate for several months, and two years later Hays was executed for the murder after vehemently pleading his innocence and writing heartrending poems and pitiful letters to the Knoxville black newspaper from jail.

The Delaneys had a terrible time getting home on the day of the riot, and young Beauford was particularly horrified by what he saw. In support of the gun on the roof story is an incident that occurred years later when in an acute paranoid attack, Beauford inexplicably threw himself onto the floor of a car I was driving and shouted, "Get down, they're shooting from the roof."

The Delaneys, like most of the Knoxville African-American community, attended the elaborate funeral for Hays at Logan AME (African Methodist Episcopal) Zion Temple. The people did not believe in his guilt, and by then he had become an honored martyr and symbol of their collective plight as the victims of racism, however relatively benign.

After the riots and John Samuel's passing, it was only a matter of time before the Knoxville period would end for Beauford. In 1923 his apprenticeship with Branson had gone about as far as it could go. As for home, he was really too old to be living in the somewhat crowded conditions on East Vine in his mother's half of the house. Joe had already moved to his own place, and Emery was busy running his barbershop in the front room and, with Gertrude, starting a new generation of Delaneys in the rooms behind the shop. Samuel Emery, Jr. (often called Junior) had been born in 1921, and Ogust Mae and Lois Imogene would follow in 1924 and 1926.

Beauford was much loved at home and leaving was emotionally almost impossible for him. But by now the call of his art was overwhelming. There were already the inklings of disturbing voices within—nagging doubts about Sister's death, the loss of Naomi, and about the skin color of which he had been taught to be proud but which in the world seemed to threaten his advancement. And there was the voice that laughed at his other difference—one that he could not yet define but was at the root of his being, made him radically unlike his father, Emery, and Joe, and rendered any kind of family life of his own quite impossible. The only defense against these whispering voices was his art. He would give up the idea of being a singer and would make his music on canvas and paper, with chalk and paint and what he had learned from Branson about light. Beauford left for Boston, beginning his long journey away from Knoxville and, he hoped, from the voices of despair.

Boston and Harlem

Beauford's departure for Boston in September 1923 was in every sense difficult. His mother, with Emery and Gertrude and Joe, saw him off at the train station. Lloyd Branson, wearing white spats, a beret, and leaning on a silver-headed cane, was there too, as Beauford's sponsor and patron, and this made the good-byes more awkward. Beauford found himself torn between his emotions in regard to his family and his need to be grateful and strong in the presence of Mr. Branson, since it was Branson's money that made the trip possible. This conflict between feeling and manners, between the man he was and the man he wanted people to think he was would plague Beauford for the rest of his life, especially as it applied to his relations with his black friends. Saying good-bye to his mother was particularly painful as she had always been the dominant force for stability in his life. She alone seemed to sense the inner conflicts that had already taken root in his mind. But when they embraced it was with a formality bred of long years of not wanting to display "weakness" in front of whites.

The train ride was long and tiring. Delia had packed food, but Beauford felt guilty and gave a lot of it away to fellow passengers. The benches were hard for sleeping, and Beauford arrived in Boston feeling confused, hungry, and tired. Traveling would always be difficult for him; his tendency toward disorientation was kept under control best when he was in familiar surroundings. He had the little money Branson had given him, some small savings, and a few letters of introduction from Branson, Charles Cansler, and the pastor of his church in Knoxville and from a church official who was a relative in Nashville.

Boston seemed overwhelming. The pace outside South Station was much faster than what he was used to in Knoxville; people did not seem to hear when he asked for directions, and the weather was rainy and cold. It was with difficulty that he found a boardinghouse near the train station; he had heard that Boston was liberal in regard to blacks, but the owners of boardinghouses did not seem to know this.

The records of Beauford's years in Boston are sparse, but in the 1960s he did make a list of Boston memories and out of that list and his comments to various people during his New York and Paris periods a misty but significant picture emerges of his activities between 1923 and 1929. The picture will be particularly surprising to those who have long maintained that Beauford had no "racial consciousness."

Through church people and the Canslers, Beauford had Boston "society" contacts, and quickly went about establishing relationships that were to dominate his years in Boston. The first home he called on with a letter of introduction was that of a Mr. and Mrs. Bryant, who were in some way related to the poet William Cullen Bryant. The Bryants had strong literary connections, and Beauford met Edna St. Vincent Millay at their home in Braddock Park. Although white, the Bryants, in keeping with the older liberal Boston tradition of the late nineteenth century, were also well acquainted with members of the black upper middle class. Mr. Bryant's father's portrait, for instance, had been painted by the African-American painter Edward Bannister. The Bryants were of "blue stocking" abolitionist–womens' rights Boston Brahmin stock and played an important role in directing what could be called Beauford's sociopolitical education during his Boston years. This was an education dominated by questions of race relations in America and, despite the tea party formality of the atmosphere in which it was presented, it was surprisingly activist in nature.

Mrs. Bryant was the first of many formidable women who would be important in Beauford's life. It is tempting to say that these women took the place of the dominant influence represented by Delia Delaney. In any case, in Mrs. Bryant's distinctly liberal salon a pattern was established. During all his years in Boston, New York, and Paris, Beauford took advantage of the intellectual nourishment he could find in such homes. He also took advantage of the physical nourishment and to a significant extent was willing to play a role to get it. Beauford always loved food and usually lacked the funds to buy it; for good food he would make what he called "good nigger" compromises, telling his mother's stories of the old South, avoiding any indication of anger at white people, occasionally singing a spiritual, and making people laugh at his mannerisms and witticisms. In a brief journal entry from those days he writes:

> Have located about myself an amazing capacity for creating laughter among innumerable people with whom I have nothing in common. Observing this spontaneous [reaction] without having done anything to induce it for [a] while caused me much irritation. However observing my inability to understand it or prevent it, I have decided to make friends with it and include it in the general flotsam and jetsam of my very complex existence—the very complex conditions so beautifully blended with various degrees of development culturally speaking.

At the Bryants and elsewhere Beauford often saw another important Boston hostess, Mrs. William Shakespeare Sparrow, born Cawlyn Stanford. The Sparrows were a church connection through the Canslers. Mr. Sparrow was First Vice President of the Negro Tailors' Dressmaking and Pressers Association of America and he and his wife were active AME Zion members. Their home was on Massachusetts Avenue. At his first dinner there Mrs. Sparrow told Beauford of her mother's friendship with Julia Ward Howe and they discussed the importance of Mrs. Ward's most famous work, "The Battle Hymn of the Republic" and her support of abolition and women's suffrage. White people of the "right sort" came to Mrs. Sparrow's parties. In fact, Beauford met Maud Howe Elliot, a daughter of Julia Ward Howe there. He also met important African Americans.

The cast of characters was impressive and could not help influence the thinking and aspirations of a penniless southern black man in his twenties. These were members of the group referred to in the 1920s as the Boston radicals. They were financially successful, culturally sophisticated lawyers and journalists who were pioneers for what would become the civil rights movement of later years; they were Boston's political equivalent of the Harlem Renaissance. Mrs. Sparrow's living room was often full of "black firsts," people who were rightly celebrated in the Colored Who's Who and are now all too often forgotten.

A frequent guest was Butler Wilson. For a time Wilson had been a partner of the then best-known black lawyer in America, George Ruffin (1834–86), friend of Frederick Douglass, active abolitionist, first black graduate of Harvard Law

School, first black judge in Massachusetts. Judge Ruffin's wife, Josephine St-Pierre Ruffin, leader in the womens' club movement, early supporter of the activist Boston chapter of the NAACP, adamant fighter for women's rights, civil rights, and the ideas of the young W. E. B. Du Bois in her journal, *The Courant*, had long been the grande dame of Boston black society. A society white woman once commented that she was committed to helping Mrs. Ruffin's race. The very light-skinned Mrs. Ruffin replied, "Which one?" Like her friend Mrs. Sparrow's mother she had been close to Julia Ward Howe. Her home on Charles Street, where she was ably assisted by her daughter, Mrs. Florida ("Birdie") Ruffin Ridley, had been the center of black social life at the turn of the century. Beauford met Mrs. Ruffin and her daughter just before the older woman died in 1924.

Another partner in Judge Ruffin's firm was Archibald Grimké, whom Beauford also met at the Sparrows early in his Boston stay. Grimké was the second black graduate of Harvard Law. He founded the black newspaper, *The Hub*, was active in the NAACP, and served for a time as Consul General in Santo Domingo. Beauford particularly liked Grimké's daughter, Angelina, whom he met once or twice at the Sparrows', she was a writer and teacher who would respond to W. E. B. Du Bois' call for black theater for and by black people with her strongly anti-racism protest play, *Rachel*. "Nina," as she was called, shared Beauford's interest in books and ideas. He felt more comfortable with her than with the more formidable men of the group. In later years Beauford often gravitated to women rather than men in social situations, yet he admired the Boston men, too.

Butler Wilson particularly impressed Delaney. He was active in NAACP affairs in Boston and was on the National Board at the time Beauford knew him. He wrote regularly for *The Hub*, and was a supporter of W. E. B. Du Bois and the Niagara Movement as opposed to the more moderate civil rights approach taken by the opposing camp, led by Booker T. Washington. Beauford went with Wilson to a meeting in 1924 in which Wilson spoke out against the legislature's attempt to ban mixed marriages in Massachusetts. Wilson was a militant protector of black rights, in the courts, in newspapers, and at public meetings.

One of the most notable figures Beauford met at Mrs. Sparrow's was William Monroe Trotter. It could well be argued that Trotter, in earlier days the most militant of the Boston radicals, was the ancestor of Martin Luther King's nonviolent black civil disobedience. By the time Beauford met him, Trotter had drifted into a state of some disillusionment and depression over the demise of his wife, Geraldine Pindell, and the gradual breakdown of the Boston tradition stemming from the days of Frederick Douglass and the abolitionist movement in which successful blacks were accepted by white society. Trotter, who had grown up in comfortable surroundings in the Hyde Park section of Boston and was active in church work and in the city's polite black society, had turned his attention early to the plight of the less fortunate. He had helped Du Bois found the Niagara Movement in 1905 and later broke with him on personal grounds. In his autobiography, Du Bois spoke of the difficulties within the movement associated with Trotter's "dynamic personality" (D. Lewis, Chapter 5). He also wrote about the elitism among the upper class Boston blacks with whom he associated during his Harvard days. He seems to have felt some class-based resentment in connection with "Deenie" Pindell, an extremely light-skinned college-educated woman whom he describes as technically African American and "a fine, forthright woman, blonde, blue-eyed and fragile," whom he had "no chance to choose . . . for she married Monroe Trotter."

The Niagara Movement had in effect merged with the NAACP, and by the time Trotter and Du Bois had their falling out Trotter had decided that the NAACP was too moderate and founded the National Equal Rights League. He had long advocated nonviolent but active protest against the denial of rights to blacks. He saw as a primary enemy of black rights what he considered the complacent optimism of Booker T. Washington and his followers. He had spent time in the Charles Street jail for his vociferous part in the so-called Boston Riot of 1903, in which a speech of Washington's was disrupted at the Negro church on Columbus Avenue. A prominent member of the Democratic Party, he argued so vigorously with Woodrow Wilson about segregation in government jobs that he was ejected from the president's office. In 1915 he was arrested again for protesting and leading a march against the opening of the film *Birth of a Nation* in Boston. Trotter had founded *The Guardian*, a more radical journal than *The Hub*, to serve as a place for his views and those of other activists. He had been ably assisted in this venture first by George Washington Forbes and later by his wife. Beauford had been told much about Trotter by the Bryants and Mrs. Sparrow; he was surprised to find a very quiet man who seemed essentially broken in spirit.

Beauford made a particularly close friend of Judge Ruffin's son, George. George was an operatic tenor, an organist, and the first black member of the Handel and Haydn Society, and a soloist in the choir at Trinity Church. George took Beauford to concerts at the Boston Symphony, the Boston Pops at the Esplanade along the Charles River, and at Trinity Church. Beauford referred to Trinity as "Philip Brooks' church." Brooks, who had been Episcopal Bishop of Massachusetts for a time and had died in 1891, had been famous for his sermons preached at Trinity and his liberal ideas regarding race. He had preached a sermon on Lincoln as he lay in state in Philadelphia and was much admired by the Ruffins, the Bryants, the Sparrows, and their circle.

The Roscoe Conkling Bruces took a liking to Beauford when they met him at Mrs. Sparrow's and he to them. Roscoe Conkling Bruce was descended from a postwar Mississippi senator. His family had generally been supportive of the Booker T. Washington approach to race matters, but had retained social contacts with the Boston radicals and had joined Du Bois and Trotter in their fight against segregation in government jobs during the Wilson administration. Mrs. Clara Washington Bruce was Howard and Radcliffe educated. A women's rights advocate, now in her forties, she attended Boston University Law School between 1923 and 1926 and in 1926 became the second black woman to pass the Massachusetts bar exam. When Beauford met her she was the editor-in-chief of the *Boston University Law Review*. Bruce's daughter, Clara, was at Radcliffe; their son, Roscoe, Junior, was at the Boston Latin School. Beauford sometimes visited the family at their home on Parker Street in Cambridge.

Through the Bruces, Beauford met the young Countee Cullen. Cullen studied for his M.A. at Harvard in 1925–26, a year after the celebrated publication of *Color*, his first book of poetry, for which he won a national college poetry award. Beauford knew of Cullen from his poems in the two black cultural magazines, *Crisis* and *Opportunity*. He warmed to him, finding in him a kindred spirit. There was a common interest in the arts as well as something deeper and more personal that he was not yet able to describe or face. Cullen talked to Beauford of his hope to go to Paris, something he would do on a Guggenheim grant two years later. At the time, Beauford was fascinated by Cullen, by his somewhat flamboyant style, and by the idea of Paris. The two men maintained a friendship during the 1930s and 1940s, and Cullen collected a few of Beauford's paintings. After the demise of the Harlem Renaissance, of which he was an important part, and his return from Paris, Cullen would become a schoolteacher. It is of coincidental interest that he taught beginning French to a junior high school boy who would become one of Beauford's closest friends—the young James Baldwin.

Music was always a primary interest in Beauford's life, and in Boston he found a great deal of it. There were the concerts at Trinity Church, the Pops concerts, and, through Ruffin, tickets to the Boston Symphony concerts at Symphony Hall. He particularly remembered two concerts because they involved African Americans who had Knoxville connections through Charles Cansler. Since childhood, Beauford had heard stories of the singer Roland Hayes and the writer-diplomat, rights activist James Weldon Johnson, both visitors at the Cansler home. He admired both men for their accomplishments. Hayes represented the possibility of success in the arts for a poor boy from the South. Johnson's success as a lawyer, as executive secretary of the NAACP, as a diplomat in Nicaragua and Venezuela, as the writer of the "Negro National Hymn" "Lift Every Voice and Sing," and as compiler of *The Book of Negro Spirituals* was legendary. In 1926 Johnson's African-American dramatic musical version of the *Creation* was presented by Serge Koussevitsky and the Boston Symphony Orchestra to enthusiastic audiences in New York and Boston. Beauford was at a Boston performance and he introduced himself to Johnson afterward. He had done the same thing with Hayes in 1923 when he had attended one of several concerts the singer had performed with the Boston Symphony. Beauford particularly loved Hayes's renditions of spirituals and black folk music in general. He always said he wished he could have been a singer, and he loved singing for friends, sometimes to the accompaniment of his guitar, the songs Hayes sang. If he could have changed places with anyone in 1923, it would have been with Roland Hayes.

Early in his Boston stay Beauford attended a musical event that he talked about for years. It was Noble Sissle and Eubie Blake's *Shuffle Along* starring the teenaged Josephine Baker. Beauford admired Baker and followed her career closely. In 1968, when asked what he wanted for his birthday, he would request that he be taken to one of Baker's many farewell concerts at the Olympia in Paris. He would be as thrilled by her that night as he had been by her performance some forty years earlier.

Beauford seems to have reveled in the sociopolitical and cultural life of Boston. During his first months there he wandered all over the old city, admiring the Public Gardens and Boston Commons and the old homes on Beacon Hill, especially on Louisburg Square. He looked with pleasure at the Paul Revere Monument, the State House, and was particularly moved by Augustus Saint-Gaudens' great statue of Robert Gould Shaw and the Civil War soldiers of the black 54th Massachusetts Regiment. The statue, which stands in front of the State House on Beacon Hill, had been unveiled in 1897 and honored in speeches by Booker T. Washington and the philosopher William James, among others. Mrs. Sparrow had told Beauford how a column of black veterans had marched up Beacon Hill on the day of the unveiling to honor those who had given their lives to the Union cause. The statue was a symbol of the old collaboration between black and white abolitionists in Boston. Shaw himself, who with many members of the 54th, was killed during the 1863 assault on Fort Wagner in Charleston, South Carolina, was from a prominent white Boston family. The regiment became famous not only for its heroism but for its insistence on equal pay to that of white soldiers. During the months and years that followed, Beauford listened to speeches and lectures in front of the Wendell Phillips Memorial Statue in the Public Gardens, at the Women's Service Club, at the Ford Hall Forum on Ashburton Place and later on

Boylston Street, where young African Americans (including painter Lois Mailou) and liberal whites gathered on Sunday afternoons. He read a great deal in the Copley Square Library. He stood in the street with thousands of others to watch the passing of the Sacco and Vanzetti funeral procession in August 1927. In the same year he followed with interest the story of Lindbergh's crossing of the Atlantic and was thrilled to shake hands with Nobel Prize winner Sinclair Lewis in the Public Gardens. He attended black and white churches that emphasized liberal causes and/or black musical traditions—the Boston Community Church and especially the Charles Street AME Meeting House, which, as the Tremont Temple, had been the first truly integrated church in the United States, breaking away from the Charles Street Baptist Church where segregated seating had prevailed. At the Charles Street Church he once heard a lecture by "Lady" Frances Hope, the mother of Morehouse College president John Hope on the plight of southern blacks. At the Community Church on Carver Street, known for its pacifist, left-wing positions, he heard a sermon by John Haynes Holmes (1879–1964), pastor of the New York Community Church, one of the founders of the Boston church and also of the NAACP. Holmes was a socialist particularly committed to black civil rights.

Beauford enjoyed a bit of the "low" life, too. He went to baseball games at Fenway Park and to Revere Beach with some art school friends and people he met in and around his boardinghouse, mostly white young men—Barney Dombrowsky, Tom Philips, Louis Applebaum, and others. He was somewhat shocked by Scully Square, where with some of the same friends he saw burlesque performances at the Old Howard Theater. And he had his first "intimate experience" with a young man in a swan boat in the Public Gardens. One can only wonder at the nature of the experience in so public a place. Beauford was always very shy and even puritanical about sex.

To earn money during the Boston years he worked the midnight to 8 A.M. shift as a janitor for the Western Union Company on Congress Street. In a journal note describing his work there—work that contrasted strangely with the social life he found at the Bryants' and the Sparrows'—he remarks, "Nobody knows my face," and then, rather mysteriously, "The other face. What must be done? Time runs out." Beauford knew that people did not know who he really was, and he was not sure that even he did. He lived several lives: the life of the poor but polite black man in elite living rooms, that of the black janitor in an unseeing white world, and the life of something seething within him but that he was not yet ready to face or to accept—the "other face" that had perhaps appeared briefly in the swan boat incident. In all this his plight resembled one that would plague his future friend James Baldwin in his early years. Baldwin was born at about the time of the swan boat incident and would one day entitle an early book of essays *Nobody Knows My Name.*

Beauford knew he was in emotional trouble, that he was presenting too many faces to the world and to himself. The faces were beginning to fight with each other and they were already becoming the voices that would later haunt him. He even talked about the trouble with a Harvard psychology professor he met through George Ruffin, but apparently to no particular end. Beauford spent a great deal of time during his Boston years alone in his boardinghouse room listening to records on the little windup Victrola he had bought with his earnings. He loved all kinds of music—symphony, opera, jazz, the blues. His favorite record at the time was Walter Melrose's "Tin Roof Blues," first recorded in 1923 by the New Orleans Rhythm Kings. Beauford had been told about the song by a niece of Mrs. Bryant. The record fed a lingering homesickness for the South, but somehow also lifted his spirits, and he loved singing it:

> I have seen the bright lights
> Burning up and down old Broadway,
> Seen 'em in gay Havana,
> Birmingham, Alabama, and say—
> They just can't compare with my home town,
> New Orleans.
>
> There you'll find the old tin roof cafe,
> Where they play the blues to the break of day,
>
> . . .
>
> Lawd, I've got those tin roof blues.

Even in his early childhood, Beauford Delaney knew that he was somehow different and that although he could make others happy, with his mimicry, his music, his stories, he was not necessarily happy himself. He also knew from the beginning that creating images with his hands helped. At first it was copies of Sunday School cards and the molding of Knoxville red clay. Later it was his free drawings and then the impressionistic work on paper and canvas with Lloyd Branson. Whatever form it took, his art increasingly became a means of salvation, a defense against the many conflicting faces, a place where he could somehow reconcile them.

Beauford had come to Boston to study art and as much as possible pursued this mission. The mission was not simple for a poor black attempting to enroll in art classes in the 1920s. In several places he was offered the chance to serve as a live model in return for some opportunity to paint, but a deep sense of physical mod-

A Boston Man, 1926. Charcoal on paper, 25 x 19 1/2 in. Courtesy of the Delaney Estate and the Ewing Gallery, University of Tennessee.

esty made that impossible. He did manage, with the help of the Bryants and letters from Lloyd Branson, to enroll informally in several classes. What he concentrated on was portraiture and basic academic techniques. He worked on his drawing by copying from antique statuary and the great masters at Massachusetts Normal Art School. At the Copley Society he took life study classes. He also took classes at the South Boston School of Art and the Lowell Institute. He sometimes sketched copies of paintings in the various Boston museums. From time to time he saw Lois Mailou Jones doing the same thing. She was in Boston at the time studying at the Boston Museum School. When he emerged from the Boston experience, Beauford Delaney could no longer be called the "self-taught" or "primitive" painter that commentators have so often assumed he was. The portraits of the late 1920s were classically representational and demonstrated a sure sense of line and perspective.

Beauford was a good draftsman, and he greatly admired the traditional and famous representational paintings—especially the portraits—that he saw on his frequent visits to the Fine Arts Museum, the Huntington Art Museum, the Fogg

A Young Boston Man, 1928.
Charcoal on paper, 25 x 20 in.
Courtesy of the Delaney
Estate and the Ewing Gallery,
University of Tennessee.

Museum in Cambridge, and his "favorite place in Boston," the Isabella Stewart Gardner Museum on the Fenway. Beauford said he had once met Mrs. Gardner at the museum, where he often went for concerts. When asked why he was doing something he liked quoting her famous remark, "C'est mon plaisir."

Although he was a student of the classics in art, in the 1920s Beauford was already flirting with a more abstract approach to painting. Several influences can be pointed to in this connection. There were ample selections of European early modernist work in the museums he frequented, but at first Beauford was attracted to the work of the impressionists, who shared his concern with light and its use in composition. A particular favorite was Monet, who died in 1926 and in whose honor an exhibition was held at the Boston studio of another favorite, John Singer Sargent, who had died in 1925. Beauford attended this show and was enchanted by what he saw.

In Monet Beauford found a serious attempt to understand the effects of different stages of daylight on color and form. Monet's late paintings, the water lily series, point to the direction Beauford's work would take in his New York street scenes of the early 1930s and his still more abstract paintings of later years. Moving from his earlier concern with the effect of light on representational subjects, Monet makes light and its fluctuations almost the subject itself, an approach that suggests a later abstract expressionism such as Beauford's.

John Singer Sargent's influence involved the use of light in portraiture to define form. While essentially realistic, portraits such as his *Madame X*, painted in 1884, present surfaces of color that take us away from a sense of line to an appreciation of form defined somewhat fuzzily by light and shadow. The approach is realistic, but the paintings suggest the painterly concerns of a more abstract approach. Beauford clearly took note of this, and his transitional portraits of the 1930s that were done after the purely figurative works in Boston and before the much more abstract ones that would come later are somewhat reminiscent of Sargent's approach.

While in art school, Beauford met a painter who would became a friend for a while and later would be associated with the American Southwest. Alfred Morang spent a part of the 1920s in Boston working on a technique that owed something to Van Gogh in its modernist celebration of brush strokes and paint on canvas even as it represented particular scenes. Morang's pallet was heavy and he was fond of swirls of paint that would lead to a more abstract approach. All of this fascinated Beauford, who often visited Morang's studio in 1925, and by the time he left Boston in 1929 he was himself experimenting with Morang-like cityscapes and portraits that articulated a painterly interest in paint, light, and forms rather than a desire to convey external likeness. He did this even as he continued both traditional portraiture and landscape.

By the spring of 1929 Beauford felt he had done all he could in Boston. Everyone he knew suggested that to succeed in the world of art he must go to New York. He said his good-byes to the friends and happily gave up his Western Union job and the drab boardinghouse. The few clothes he had he could fit into a not very large bag and he carried his Victrola in a separate box and his paintings—all on paper, because he could not afford canvas—in a large portfolio. He had earlier sent home to Knoxville a few of the drawings.

Despite poverty and developing psychological problems, Boston had been in most ways a rewarding experience, one Beauford talked little of later but looked back on with general pleasure. The Boston period was primarily educational. He learned what he called the "essentials" of classical techniques on which he could build as a modernist painter. Of his representational sketches for portraits and landscapes he always said, reminding his listeners of the example of Picasso, "You

Beauford in New
York City, 1929.

have to draw the lines before you can paint the subject." He felt that in Boston he
had learned how to "draw the lines." He had also received a "crash course" in
black activist politics and ideas, having associated socially with some of the most
sophisticated and radical African Americans of the time.

His arrival in Harlem, in early November of the year of Martin Luther King Jr.'s
birth, was exciting. This was the Harlem of the 1920s "renaissance." Associated
with it were such figures as his friend Countee Cullen, Langston Hughes, Zora
Neale Hurston, and Claude McKay. And there were the famous restaurants—
Johnny Jackson's on 135th and Seventh, the Marguerite nearby on 132nd. There
were the churches, too, and the music in them—St. Mark's AME on 138th and
St. Nicholas Avenue and the Abyssinian Baptist just over from there between
Lenox and Seventh. There was the fast life as well—at the Cotton Club, Cairo's,
Small's, Connie's Inn. Most important, ideas were everywhere, and black culture was being addressed. Hurston and Sterling Brown were actually celebrat-
ing black language and folklore. Du Bois and Marcus Garvey and Alain Locke
were talking about racial pride. Locke was writing about the "New Negro" and
"the Legacy of Ancestral Arts." Beauford, directed by Countee Cullen, was
reading these people. Harlem was the very center of black life in America.
Beauford felt he had to live there. But the dream of Harlem did not fit the reality he discovered.

What happened on that day of arrival shocked and humiliated him and left him, for the moment, disillusioned; he experienced all too directly the submersion of the legendary Harlem and its renaissance in the realities of the Great Depression. The description in note form that follows is from his own journal.

> Went to New York in 1929 from Boston all alone with very little money—went directly to Harlem—found modest street—130th St.—and looked at rooming houses—suddenly there was a sign in a window—ROOM FOR RENT. Naturally I went in immediately—rang the bell, a very pleasant woman answered the bell—asked very friendly what I wanted—I said I would like a room for two weeks—She answered I should pay in advance and to come right in. I walked in with my baggage—paid two weeks rent and then before leaving told her I would be back in about 2 hours—She said take your time—so I took the number of the house and went downtown to look for work—Looking about I found it was later than I thought and decided to go back to the room—I found the number, rang the bell—the same woman answered the door and asked me in a chilly voice what I wanted. Of course I answered somewhat surprised, Madam I would like to go to the room I paid for 2 hours ago—She called a certain young man by the name of Bob to come here an throw this guy out—he looking for trouble talking about a room—I never saw him in my life. Naturally this immense young man gets ready to go for me in no uncertain terms. There was nothing for me to do but beat it at once, which I did, leaving behind my scarce belongings—alone—near night—my first night in N.Y.C. I was discouraged and knew not what to do—so I take a bus and go down to Greenwich Village.

Very quickly Beauford had lost his clothes, his precious Victrola, and, most important, his portfolio of paintings from the Boston years.

He got off the bus at 14th Street and walked west. "Tired and confused," he came to Union Square, sat down on a park bench, and found himself experiencing visually the reality of the Great Depression, which was emerging from the crash of the stock market only days earlier. He

> lit a cigarette, and somewhat collected myself. This was the . . . depression, and I soon discovered that most of these people were people out of work and just doing what I was—sitting and figuring out what to do [for] food and a place to sleep.

A man asked Beauford for a cigarette and explained that the police allowed sleeping in the park and that there was a nearby cafe where the owners let people stay for long periods of time if they bought something simple to eat or drink. The man offered to go there with him. They managed to find a table and order coffee and rolls. Then,

> being tired and a stranger suddenly with nothing but a few dollars in my pocket and knowing not a soul I embraced in my mind the idea of the enormous difference among the great masses of people with nothing—the camaraderie and immediate understanding which can sometimes happen by chance.

Beauford was warming to his seemingly difficult situation. The cafe in Union Square was a long way from the living rooms of the Sparrows and Bryants, but the episode in Harlem had landed him by chance in another place, one where he almost immediately sensed that he belonged. He was among

> a multitude of people of all races—spending every night of their lives in parks and cafes and seeming very much in a good mood.

These people were communicating openly with each other and surviving on next to nothing. There was a genuine community of interest. Beauford felt exhilarated; he

> felt a new kind of stimulation growing and sending out curious fancies. . . . somehow someway there was something I could manage if only with some stronger force of will I could find the courage to surmount the terror and fear of this immense city and accept everything insofar as possible with some calm and determination—the determination among the young [in the park and cafe] was contagious and quickening to my state of shock and after two cups of coffee and rolls I began to find things to talk about other than myself.

These people and their outdoor city life would become the subject of some of Delaney's greatest New York period paintings. He listened carefully to his new friends and through them learned something of the bohemian life. He realized that if they could survive he could—if only he could learn from them: "These were natives of N.Y.C. and among millions to whom every day was a challenge of how to exist through it." So began Beauford Delaney's twenty-three-year stay in New York.

-- *three*

New York: The Early Years

Beauford spent that first New York night, in November 1929, on a Union Square park bench, and someone stole his shoes while he slept. In the morning he made his way, shoeless and self-conscious, to a store on 14th Street and spent precious money on footwear. The exhilaration of the night before was gone, and the thoughts in his head were spinning; they seemed to be laughing at the presumption that he could survive in New York. He decided to go back uptown to Harlem and began the trip on foot. By the time he reached Central Park the blisters on his feet were painful and he sat down to rest. The whole New York idea seemed hopeless, and a terrible homesickness for Knoxville came over him. Then he remembered the name of an established painter in New York given him by a Boston friend. He had the address in his wallet. Learning from a passerby that the painter's apartment was not a long walk from the park, he decided to go there. Beauford had a way of asking for help that was at once genuine and not obsequious, and people usually responded positively. In this case, the painter not only arranged an immediate interview for a bellhop position at the Grand Hotel on Broadway and 31st Street but suggested someone in Harlem who could help him find an apartment. By the end of the day Beauford had a job and a barely furnished room at 241 West 111th Street.

The city that Beauford found himself in was, like the nation, in a state of turmoil. For artists it was particularly difficult because many people who once had money now lacked the means to buy paintings. For black artists, for whom it was never easy to find support or exhibition space, it was next to impossible. Yet Beauford, who would eventually benefit, like many others, from the strong response of African-American artists to the situation and the policies of the New Deal, managed to pursue his vocation with determination, finding the little corners in the world of the Great Depression that would or could be receptive to his work.

During the first months in New York Beauford looked for ways of improving and showing his painting, and during his time off from the hotel, he painted. Art schools either did not take blacks or were generally too expensive, but Beauford managed to find a regular place of work at Billy Pierce's Dancing School on West 46th Street, where he did pastel and charcoal portraits of the dancers and the society women who came there. He gained entry into this potentially lucrative position by offering to draw Pierce himself. That portrait, of "the Dancing Master of Broadway," as he was called, was published in the May 1930 issue of *Opportunity* under the words—words referring to Pierce but that could have also applied to Beauford—"He Smashed the Color Line." According to James Cannon, who did a March 27, 1930, feature article in the *New York Telegraph* about Beauford at the Pierce school, the artist found in "Pierce's tan face," the "tempo of restless feet." The *Chicago Defender*, in its April 5 edition, contained a photograph of Beauford drawing Miss Harriet Cawling at Pierce's, a "New York society girl" in a very short skirt seated somewhat provocatively with one bare leg raised above the other. In the *Telegraph* article Mrs. Kenneth Van Riper of 30 Fifth Avenue, "a young matron in skimpy plaid dancing clothes," is quoted as saying

> I'm crazy about his work. He just completed a portrait of a friend of mine, Kathryn Jordan. And I just had to have one, too. As soon as he finishes this charcoal drawing he's going to do me in oils.

Beauford, as he always did, had managed even at the beginning of the depression to gain access to an elite world whose money could keep him alive. But it was not just money that appealed to him about Pierce's. He loved the noise and action of the studio—the music, the constant movement, the chatter. The energy of New York was expressed in microcosm there. "I never drew a decent thing until I felt the rhythm of New York," he told the *Telegraph* interviewer.

New York has a rhythm as distinct as the beating of a human heart. And I'm trying to put it on canvas....I paint people. People—and in their faces I hope to discover that odd, mysterious rhythm.

The studio drawings of the early 1930s were almost exclusively representational. Beauford's subjects paid for likenesses, not for abstract impressions. The painter made good use of his academic Boston training, and he almost immediately gained a small reputation among the New York elite, even if, because he was black, he was often directed to the freight elevator to visit their apartments.

But Beauford did not only paint the socialites at Pierce's. From his very first days in New York he drew ordinary people in the streets—especially the streets of Harlem where he lived. And in time Harlem people began to come to his room to be drawn and painted. In these works, for which he was not paid, Beauford took more liberties and began to move away from mere academic representation. Especially in the oils, the outlines of the faces were less distinct, colors were applied in the interest of the overall effect of the painting rather than to convey likeness, and even some distortion was used to convey the painter's impression of character.

The breakthrough that led to the newspaper articles about his work at Pierce's came in January 1930, when, at the urging of the painter who had helped him get settled in New York, he approached Miss Mungo Park at the Whitney Studio Galleries on West Eighth Street, the forerunner of the Whitney Museum of American Art. Miss Park immediately warmed to the small soft-spoken black man who appeared so surprisingly with a portfolio of drawings. She even agreed to look at the drawings, and was so startled by what she saw that she introduced Delaney to Mrs. Juliana Force, who directed the purchasing and exhibition policies of the gallery. Mrs. Force reacted as Miss Park had and on the spot offered Beauford a place in a four person show of "Sunday painters," reflecting Force's interest in "self-taught" and "naive" painters (neither term, of course, described Delaney). The exhibit would open on February 26 and run until March 8, 1930. The only stipulation was that he produce more works. As *Opportunity* put it in its May article, the painter, "mute with gratitude" and with "a song in his heart . . . was conscious of the honor" the Whitney women "were conferring on him," and he worked hard "seven nights a week" to prove himself "worthy."

Choosing what he thought of as the more dignified spelling of his surname— one favored by his mother—B. De Laney showed three oil portraits and nine pastels at the Whitney show. The reaction of the critics was positive. The *Amsterdam News*, New York's primary African-American newspaper, proudly announced that

A Man, 1930. Charcoal and pastel on paper, 25 x 19 in. Courtesy of the Delaney Estate and the Ewing Gallery, University of Tennessee.

a black hotel worker, Beauford Delaney, "a promising artist of ability," had won first prize at the Whitney show for his drawing of Billy Pierce. The paper noted that honorable mention was given to all the painter's other pastels as well—including *Chinese Student, Harlem Boy in a Gray Hat,* and *Girl in Green Dress.* Mrs. Force herself bought two pastels. Beauford told *Opportunity* that he saw Miss Park and Mrs. Force "as being especially appointed by the Lord" to help him "get his feet upon the first rung of Life's ladder."

The women also offered Beauford a job at the Whitney as a caretaker and later, noting his "intelligence," as a telephone operator and sometimes gallery attendant, doorman, and guard. He took the job and gratefully accepted studio and living space in the basement for two years. So began his long stay in Greenwich Village.

The Whitney show and the publicity associated with his work at the Billy Pierce School led to a certain recognition and several new and important associations. It also brought a little bit of money. One of things Beauford did with the money was to buy a ticket at the Mansfield Theater for *Green Pastures,* the popular Pulitzer Prize–winning play for which black actor Richard B. Harrison won an award for his role as "Lawd." He also began going more to clubs to listen to jazz and to the Metropolitan Opera and Carnegie Hall, where from his standing room spot he was able to indulge his love of Italian opera and musical classics in general. And he bought a "new" secondhand Victrola.

Because of the Whitney success, the New York Public Library invited Beauford to do a one-man show—his first—at their Harlem branch on 135th Street and Lenox Avenue (later the Schomburg Center). The show ran for the entire month of May and included five pastels and ten charcoal drawings. The drawing of Billy Pierce was included as well as a self-portrait and portraits of several Harlem people—a stenographer, a chore woman, an athlete, and others. The pastels were at once delicate in execution and respectful of the sitters who, for the most part, look directly at us from formal seated positions like the nobility so often painted by the old masters Beauford had studied in Boston. These were Beauford's nobility—the nobility of the streets. The show attracted a large number of viewers, including Alain Locke, partly because of the drawing of Pierce in *Opportunity*.

One of the people who came to both the Whitney and Public Library shows was composer, music teacher, and janitor Luke Theodore Upshure, who lived and worked in the basement at 106 Waverly Place in the Village. Upshure was famous for his parties at 106, where he invited well-known black and white entertainers to perform. It was at Upshure's August 8 party for black aviator Colonel Hubert Julian, the "Black Eagle," on his return to Harlem from Abyssinia that Beauford met jazz pioneer and "father of the Blues" W. C. Handy. He would become close to both Upshure and Handy. At the party, according to the *Amsterdam News*, "there was no distinction as to race and rank." Among the entertainers and important guests of honor were Billy Pierce, Romare Beardon's mother, Bessy Beardon of the *Chicago Defender*, the painter Cloyd Boykin, who with his wife ran the Primitive African Art Center in the old Governor's Mansion on Grove Street in the Village, journalist George Schuyler, and James Cannon, who had written the *Telegraph* article about Beauford at Pierce's School. Not many days after that party Beauford did a drawing of Upshure and eventually a portrait.

One day at the Whitney when he was serving as the doorman, Beauford met the caricaturist Al Hirschfeld. They struck up a conversation and became lifelong friends. Beauford did a portrait of Hirschfeld, who introduced him to several people who bought his drawings and pastels. Years later, Hirschfeld would provide him with some of the funds for his trip to Paris.

The Whitney success also encouraged Delaney to approach the Art Students' League on 57th Street, one of the few art schools in America that welcomed black artists. There he took some classes with John Sloan and Thomas Hart Benton, who both stressed the importance of art with a social message. Sloan's naturalistic approach was not particularly useful to Beauford in terms of the direction his art would take, but the early "ash can" paintings were of interest to a painter concerned with depicting city life, and Beauford continued an association with Sloan—often visiting and working at his studio until the late 1930s. It may well be that Beauford's consistent Ash Can School-like use in his cityscapes of manhole covers, fire hydrants, fire escapes, and other such objects not traditionally considered subjects for art owed something to this association. As for Benton, Beauford found that he had interesting things to say about the importance of developing an American art form.

But most important, Beauford met other young artists at the League. Don Freeman, painter, printmaker, and champion in his art of the working class became a particularly close friend; he also talked with Jackson Pollock there. He met many African-American artists who either took classes or simply socialized at the League. Richmond Barthé was there early in 1930 creating sculpture based on African-American subjects. A significant presence was Charles "Spinky" Alston, a leading member of the group urging the creation of "Negro art"; he introduced Beauford to many jazz musicians who sat for charcoal and pastel portraits. James A. Porter, who would become a noted art historian with a mission to raise black consciousness and articulate the accomplishments of black artists, sometimes was there. The subjects of Porter's own paintings—one of which would win the 1933 Schomburg Portrait Prize at the 1933 Harmon exhibition—were generally African Americans.

An important arrival in New York and at the Art Students' League in 1930 was Beauford's younger brother Joseph. Joe moved in with Beauford at 241 West 111th Street at about the time Beauford was relocating to the Whitney Studio. The Whitney move was providential because the two brothers could not have lived together for long; they had very different approaches to life and art. At the League Joe took immediately to Thomas Hart Benton's ideas. Although Beauford liked Benton, he generally rejected his point of view, sympathizing more with the ideas of a Benton rival, the abstract painter Stuart Davis, who had become a friend after the Whitney show and was disdainful of artists and intellectuals who allowed theory to stand in the way of personal expression, even abstract, nonrepresentational expression.

Even though Beauford and Joe were both painting figurative portraits and cityscapes in 1930, the seeds of a basic disagreement on the nature of art were already there, and, rather than argue, the two men tended to avoid discussions of art. There were other problems, too. Beauford was offended by what he saw as his brother's promiscuity. He suggested to Joe that his excessive interest in women would "drain" his natural talent. Joe, on the other hand, began to sense Beauford's "differentness" and was wary of some of the people with whom he sometimes associated, people he thought of as "probably queer." The brothers would see each other fairly often, however, especially during their early New York years, and in March 1931 Joe followed Beauford to Greenwich Village, moving to 18 Downing Street.

After that, since they were both based in the Village rather than Harlem, the brothers were inevitably associated with the relatively small world of black artists in that part of town rather than the larger Harlem group. The fact that they were brothers with a great deal of family loyalty also prevented an outright break. Beauford painted one of several portraits of his brother in 1931.

One of the places at which Joe and Beauford saw each other was Cloyd Boykin's Primitive African Arts Center. Boykin is best known as the subject of his close friend Palmer Hayden's most famous painting *The Janitor Paints a Picture,* in which he is depicted trying to paint a black mother and child while a clock indicates the call of his custodial duties. Boykin's center was inspired by the ideas of Alain Locke, who was a friend of his. The building had very high ceilings and there was no money for fuel, so Boykin and his friends would search the streets in cold weather for boxes to burn in an old woodstove. Joe and Beauford eventually modeled and taught drawing classes there and met two painters, Ellis Wilson and Hayden, who became their close lifelong friends, forming with them a group they all referred to as "The Saints." It was Hayden, who on his return in 1932 from a long stay in Paris, helped instill in Beauford's mind the idea of a visit to France. Both Hayden and Wilson were interested in "Negro subjects," whether African American, African, or, later in the case of Wilson, Haitian. Wilson and Hayden and his wife Miriam were faithful correspondents, and even after Beauford left New York for Paris in 1953 they kept in close touch and paid several visits to him over the years.

Beauford's association with Boykin's Primitive African Arts Center and his conversations with fellow black artists about the importance of creating "Negro art" led naturally enough to his attempting to work out in his own mind the relationship between his own art and race. Beauford had read Alain Locke on the importance of African art in European modernism in *The New Negro* (1925), he knew Locke's *Art of Propaganda* (1928), and he listened to the discussions among other black artists on the subject of "Negro art," but was reluctant to commit himself at this point to any one theory. Yet, in a notebook of the early 1930s, for

Ethel Waters, 1940. Charcoal
and pastel on paper, 25 x 19 in.
Courtesy of the Delaney
Estate and the Ewing Gallery,
University of Tennessee.

example, we find this remark: "Relation of Rubens to his time versus DeLaney as representing the Negro." In another entry he notes that he has spent an entire Saturday with Cab Calloway discussing ideas for the painting of contemporary musicians and that over beers at Diamond Jim's they developed "wonderful new ideas for painting Negro subject matter" in general.

In late 1930, at the urging of W. C. Handy, Beauford began a series of pastels and charcoal drawings of African-American jazz musicians and other important figures. By spending evenings in the jazz clubs of Harlem and Greenwich Village, the painter was able to meet Ethel Waters, Duke Ellington, and Louis Armstrong, all of whom, along with Handy, he eventually drew.

Jazz was one of Beauford's passions; he wrote in his journal of his personal relation to the form—how the "experience and knowledge of this rare and wholesome field" could "release me to myself." He spent hours listening to jazz and the blues on his Victrola. He maintained his interest in classical music as well and did the first of several drawings of Marian Anderson in the early 1930s.

During this period Beauford by no means limited himself to the painting of musicians. He continued painting people on the street and at Billy Pierce's, and he worked on street scenes in Greenwich Village. Early in 1931 he began a series of sketches of black leaders, some from photographs, others from live sketches. One day, for instance, he went to the NAACP offices in New York with the idea of drawing W. E. B. Du Bois. He had admired Du Bois since his Boston days and was an avid reader of both *Crisis* and *Opportunity*, in which Du Bois's ideas were prevalent. When he approached Du Bois's secretary about doing the drawing she said she would try to arrange something. Du Bois told her Delaney could draw him if he would remain silent and allow him to go on—uninterrupted—with his work. Beauford did as he was told, but eventually Du Bois struck up a friendly if formal conversation with him, mostly about mutual acquaintances in Boston. The two men met at various gatherings from time to time after that but never became close. Writer Richard Gibson remembers walking with Beauford through Washington Square Park in the early 1940s and confronting what to Gibson was the almost mythical figure of Du Bois. The great man stopped briefly, tipped his hat, said "Good afternoon Delaney," and then walked on.

Despite the deprivation that was so common among black artists during the early depression years, Beauford did reasonably well for himself during the early 1930s. He had a place to live, a studio, a job, and was selling some paintings. Late in 1932, in fact, he felt he could afford to give up the Whitney job and moved to a simple apartment at 22 Downing Street in the Village—a few doors away from his brother. For the first time in his life he could say that he was a full-time artist.

Between May 17 and May 28 Beauford's works were exhibited at the main branch of the New York Public Library on Fifth Avenue at 42nd Street. The *New York Times* of May 22 (VIII, 7:5) commented, perhaps somewhat patronizingly, that the painter had a "knack for portraiture and a good eye for color." In a *Crisis* notice (July 1932, p. 228) in which Beauford is called "Bradford DeLaney," the reviewer notes that the "young Negro artist" displays "careful, deliberate draughtsmanship . . . with a tendency toward the academic," probably referring to the pastel portraits. A painting entitled *Harlem Adagio Dancer*, which was more abstract and more daring in its colors, is praised for its "verve and vitality."

Early in 1933 Joseph and Beauford made their first return trip to their old home in Knoxville. The family was astonished to see the brothers emerge from different ends of the train car in which they had traveled—they had had an argument in the train station in New York and did not speak at all during the long journey. Still, the Knoxville visit went well. The brothers put aside their antagonism in deference to their mother and much-loved brother Emery. And both were captivated by their nephew "Junior" and their two little nieces, Imogene and Ogust. The brothers were hailed by the local black newspaper and friends and acquaintances as heroes returned from the wars, as artists who had made the grade in New York. In church they were asked to stand up and talk about their ideas and experiences; they had become role models. At home everyone was overjoyed to have "the boys" back. Delia knew that Beauford loved the color red, so she put a red bedspread on his bed. The first morning back in Knoxville he said the color had excited him so much that he couldn't sleep all night. While he was home Beauford did a sketch of his mother and a full pastel of what appears to be a somewhat angry Joseph, perhaps forced by his mother to sit for a reconciliatory portrait (see Color Plate 2). An interestingly expressionistic touch to a somewhat painterly, rather than linear, depiction is the blue upper lip that matches the color of the subject's shirt. The blue lip gives the impression of a snarl. One senses the subject looking at the painter with a certain disdain.

Back in New York Beauford understood what a risky business it was to have given up a paying job and a free place to live. Living on painting alone was almost impossible. These were difficult years for most Americans and most painters, let alone black Americans. And black painters were, by definition, an anomaly in the white-dominated art world; for the most part it was assumed that blacks could not paint. The economic difficulties most people faced in the depression made white Americans even less tolerant than usual of those at the bottom of the economic ladder. Lynchings continued to be frequent in the South and Klan cross burnings took place in the North as well.

The position of black Americans was somehow epitomized by the Scottsboro, Alabama, trial of nine young African Americans (the "Scottsboro Boys") for the rape of two white women on a freight train. Beauford followed the trial carefully. Their eventual conviction was based on conflicting and highly dubious evidence, and the case became the source of marches and protests that would last throughout the 1930s.

The most hopeful national event of the early 1930s for blacks, including black artists, was the election of Franklin D. Roosevelt in November 1932. Roosevelt won with a great deal of black help. By most estimates he received one-fourth of the black vote in northern cities. This was a large percentage considering the fact that traditionally African Americans had been members of Lincoln's party rather than the dominant party of the South. The recognition by the new administration of the role of blacks in its victorious coalition helped boost African-American morale, as did the rise of several blacks in the New Deal think tanks. Mary McLeod Bethune, Robert C. Weaver, William H. Hastie, and Ralph Bunche were all Roosevelt advisors on race matters, and a new ally was discovered in the first lady herself. Most of all, in the years immediately following the election, policies of the New Deal took into consideration the plight of the poor—including poor blacks and poor artists, black and white.

Encouraged by what they saw as a new atmosphere, African-American artists of the depression—especially in New York and Chicago—formed organizations and alliances and joined political groups that would help them take advantage of that atmosphere. Before the Works Progress Administration (WPA) got under way, black and white artists in New York united in demonstrations demanding pay for their work. A receptive administration created the Public Works of Art Project (PWAP) in 1933, hoping that artists would support New Deal ideals in their art. Unfortunately, black artists had difficulty obtaining jobs under the PWAP because, given their lack of formal training in most cases, they were not able to supply credentials that would prove they were artists. The PWAP lasted for only four months and Beauford, whose attendance at art schools had been informal, did not receive a job through the program. Among his close friends only Palmer Hayden was hired; he did scenes of New York Harbor.

Before the problems of black artist recognition had arisen in the PWAP, the Harmon Foundation, under the leadership of Mary Beattie Brady, had tried to establish credentials by publishing biographical catalogue sketches of black artists who exhibited in the annual Harmon shows. Beauford Delaney biographies appear in the 1933 and 1935 catalogues. The problem with the generally productive support of Brady and the Harmon Foundation was that they represented white support, placing blacks once more in the position of being dependent on white judgments as to talent and advancement. It was only the association of Alain Locke with the foundation as an advisor to Brady that made its position tolerable to some blacks. Beauford knew Locke and was intrigued by his idea that African Americans should pay attention to the use by several European modernists—Picasso and Matisse, for example—of African sculptural ideas in the development of new art forms.

A leading activist in the cause of black artists taking control of their own destiny at the time was Augusta Savage, the African-American sculptress who had been trained in Europe and whose backing included such disparate forces as W. E. B. Du Bois, Marcus Garvey, James Weldon Johnson, and the Carnegie Foundation. Soon after returning from Europe in 1931 she had opened the Savage Studio of Arts and Crafts in a Harlem basement. The studio was a haven where young blacks were taught art and black artists in general met to discuss problems arising from the political and economic difficulties of the time. The studio eventually became the Harlem Community Center, where, under the direction of black and white teachers, young artists studied painting, pottery, photography, sculpture, and other arts. Active sponsors and board members of the center included Paul Robeson, Orson Welles, A. Philip Randolf (its chairman), and Bill "Bojangles" Robinson. When the WPA became established Savage came into conflict with its white administrators who unsuccessfully challenged her leadership of the center.

The Harlem Artists Guild, of which Savage became the second president, grew out of this WPA struggle. Members included, among many others at various times between 1935 and 1939, the Delaney brothers, Addison Bates, Charles Alston, Palmer Hayden, Ellis Wilson, Elba Lightfoot, Gwendolyn Knight (later married to Jacob Lawrence), Jacob Lawrence, Ernest Crichlow, Selma Burke, Ollie Harrington, Robert Blackburn, and Romare Bearden, all of whom went on to highly successful careers. Membership was limited for the most part to black artists, with the feeling that whites often dominated the deliberations of racially mixed organizations and that blacks had problems peculiar to their situation in America, which they needed to approach on their own. Savage and her followers understood the importance of providing an extra push in the WPA for black artists who, as in the case of the earlier PWAP, were often denied status as artists because of bias and credential problems. Always on guard in the struggle against incipient and explicit American racism, Savage would later form the Vanguard Club, where black artists could discuss their problems. Later, racists in Congress succeeded in branding most of Savage's projects as "communist." It was pointed out that part of the Harlem Artists Guild dues went to the purchasing of the Marxist *Daily Worker* and that "reds" came to community center meetings. Such attacks would ultimately effectively kill the WPA itself.

Beauford attended meetings at the Savage Studio, the Vanguard Club, and the Harlem Artists Guild. He also became associated for a while with the Artist's Union, a multiracial organization of which his friend Stuart Davis became president in the mid-1930s. Through the union's magazine, *Art Front*, Davis publicized the plight of black artists. Davis shared with Beauford an interest in jazz and African-American music in general and would sometimes accompany him to clubs. Beauford also spent some time along with most black intellectuals during the WPA days at "306" as it was always called—the old stable at 306 West 141st Street where Spinky Alston provided a studio for himself and one for the sculptor Henry Bannarn. Alston and Bannarn taught WPA classes there and offered an atmosphere where black artists and intellectuals could share ideas and concerns. The list of visitors to 306 includes the great African Americans of the time. Beauford saw his old friend Countee Cullen there and Langston Hughes, and he met actor Canada Lee and arranged to do a portrait of him. Other visitors were Selma Burke, the sculptress who would years later design the Roosevelt dime, the young Jacob Lawrence, writers Richard Wright, Ralph Ellison, and Claude McKay, and all the black painters from Harlem and Greenwich Village.

Although on one level such meetings interested him, political talk and race talk were not easily translated into Beauford's art. He enjoyed the black fellowship that permeated the Artists Guild, the Vanguard Club, and 306. He had long admired the ideas of Du Bois and James Weldon Johnson. He read all the black journals regularly, and understood and appreciated the ideas of Palmer Hayden, Ellis Wilson, Cloyd Boykin, his own brother, and many other black friends on the importance of developing a black art form or at least an American one. And in the early 1930s he by no means worked in isolation from other blacks and politically oriented artists. Some of Beauford's pastel portraits and early street scenes were shown in the Harmon exhibition of black artists in 1933, and he showed works in other specifically American, socially oriented, and somewhat politicized shows at the Cooperative Art Market and the Roxy Theater in the same year. Later, out of economic necessity, he would accept a position as one of Spinky Alston's assistants on the huge and controversial—"too Negro" as it was called in 1936 by anti WPA conservatives—mural in the Harlem Hospital. But Beauford, despite his closeness to painters who stressed the importance of "Negro" and "American" art, increasingly resisted the idea of being defined as a Negro artist or even as an American one. Once again, he realized that he was simply different. If he related to the work of his fellow black artists, he felt drawn as well to the European modernists and to Americans like Stuart Davis, John Marin, and Alfred Stieglitz.

In mid-1934 Beauford's 22 Downing Street apartment was condemned, and he moved up the street to 10 Downing. This address, in combination with his apparent optimism and energy, led to his being called the "Primed Minister of Downing Street" by his friend Don Freeman. That year he exhibited for the first of many times in the Independent Artists Exhibit at Grand Central Palace and the Washington Square Outdoor Exhibit downtown. In the context of these shows Beauford could be more himself. His portraits became slightly more painterly and his street scenes began to show signs of the expressionistic approach that increasingly interested him. In 1934 and 1935 Beauford showed paintings at the Jumble Shop on 8th Street and at the Poet's Inn. He also continued to show in all-black shows such as the Harmon College Art Association Traveling Exhibition of 1934–35 and an International Art Center show of 1935 at the Roerich Museum at 310 Riverside Drive.

The two years at 10 Downing were particularly hard for Beauford. The work at Pierce's dried up and he had difficulty meeting his rent. Although he was able to show his work, it did not sell well in a depressed economy. He did find some employment teaching occasional art classes at progressive schools in the Village and in 1935 at a small WPA-sponsored adult art project in Brooklyn, where he earned $23 a week. And in 1935 there was also the WPA work with Alston at Harlem Hospital. But money was always short, especially since Beauford throughout his life had a tendency to share whatever cash he had with those he perceived as needing it more. The building at 10 Downing was an old wooden house, in poor condition, and beginning in his second year, after the top floor was abandoned, he received monthly Vacate Premises orders from the city. Beauford collected these notices and pinned them to his wall. Frequently the electricity was cut off, and he had to paint by candlelight.

When Beauford was alone and not painting he tended to write in his notebooks. He would make brief sketches, noting on them planned colors for later paintings. He would also copy favorite poems, songs, or philosophical statements by others that he found important. And he would give vent to his own love of philosophizing, write drafts of letters he often never sent, or simply record in diary fashion things that had happened or thoughts that came to him.

His journal comments about his teaching job at the Adult Education Project in Brooklyn reveal something of his inner life and his approach to art at the time: "Focus on the student rather than upon the subject or academic or theoretic, and encourage the psychological interest in living fully, living creatively," he writes. The crucial word here is "psychological." The painting must reveal the inner world; it must be, above all, in the literal sense "expressionistic": "Beauty old yet ever new/ Eternal voice and inward word" was a motto he copied from the wall of the New York Public Library. He jotted down books to read: *Art and Expression* by Oscar Pfister; *Art and the Artist* by Otto Rank, books that stress the connection between psychology and art. And near this entry is a sketch of Alfred Stieglitz who had apparently recommended the books to him. The sketch has a title, *Eternal Spirit*. Scribbled near it over two pages in large blue letters we read, "Remember to realize the element of dream and to let nothing renounce the duty of the Presence." Led by Stuart Davis and Stieglitz to the European expressionists, Beauford was developing an interest in the whole subject of turning psychological abstractions and spiritual essences into art.

In his notebook he examined various abstract feelings—love, duty, hatred, and many others that he might convey in paintings. He copied the poems "Memory" by Vachel Lindsay and "Jealousy" and "Absence" by Richard Aldington. These

Abstraction, 1935. Pastel on paper, 18 x 23 in. Courtesy of the Delaney Estate and the Ewing Gallery, University of Tennessee.

three poems gave form to his own anguish in the area of intimate relationships. The memory poem seems especially to speak to his own loneliness in the context of a need for love that conflicted with the inner world of his innate Puritanism and guilt in relation to sex:

> I can remember our sorrow;
> I can remember our laughter;
>
> . . .
>
> But I cannot remember our love.

Beauford wanted to convey similar feelings in painting. The sketch for an abstract work—a series of small squares and circles connected by jagged lines and divided by vertical lines into a kind of grid—has written below it: "deep color pictures, bright glaze over the dark contain the mystery of the jewel element and remember the time, the long long time." The combination of light created by the

glaze and the deep color could bring the "mystery" and the dark memory of the
inner life to the surface. Beauford approached this problem in some of his first
abstract paintings, done in the mid-1930s.

Still another memory note has to do with childhood: "Remembrance of afternoons in Cleveland [Tennessee] by the color of light spirit with Mother, Sister, Joe
in rooms darkened by storms." The painter thinks of spirit in terms of its being
revealed by color and light. Beauford's lesson to his class must have had to do with
the problems involved in the expressionist's or perhaps any painter's need to translate the inner world into color and light, the two elements more than any others
that from this period on would occupy his thoughts in connection with his art. As
noted, he seems, for instance, to have attempted to convey anger or jealousy in the
expressionistic touch of the blue lip in the 1933 Knoxville portrait of his brother.

Beauford's journals reveal an inner world in a state of turmoil. Of the summer of 1935 he writes:

> The most interesting summer, the most trying and the most extremely diffi-
> cult I have ever lived thru—it has been a summer of decisions, of growing up,
> of accepting, of letting go, of searching for the intrinsic [value] of reminisc-
> ing. Suddenly one is aware of having reached the top of a small hill—one
> realizes one has climbed this hill by the aid of friends. Before one stretches
> mountains—behind one is the [valley] from which one sprung.

In his attempt to control the problems—psychological and material—that
faced him, Beauford constantly looked back at that valley, as in the mental sketch of
the painting never completed of the Cleveland memory. Material deprivation faced
Beauford throughout his life, but such deprivation stood merely as the reflection
rather than the cause of a much deeper pain that was always a part of his psychological being. Beauford painted to earn money to keep the landlord at bay but,
more important, he painted to remember and confront that pain, to control it in
a way he could not otherwise. At first it had been sufficient to paint portraits of a
relatively academic sort—pictures of his family and friends, people he met on the
streets, at Pierce's, and in the jazz clubs. But as his inner problems became more
complex, more urgent, Beauford needed a freer form of expression. He could
continue to draw people who would pay to have their images realistically reproduced in ten minute pastels on the street, but from the mid-1930s to the mid-1950s
semi-abstract city scenes and psychologically interpretive "expressionistic" portraits were better defenses against his inner demons.

The nature of Beauford Delaney's personal problems at this stage in his life
can only be surmised from his journals and from the very few people to whom he

opened himself. On the surface Beauford—already becoming a Village personality—was all tranquillity and wisdom. People came to him as they did all his life as to a guru who could solve their problems. And Beauford gave them wisdom and solace; he could do so not because he was above pain but because he was suffused by it. The pain was multifaceted, and Beauford could identify only parts of it. He knew that he was homosexual and that he did not approve of his homosexuality. Yet he was supportive of the many homosexuals who became part of his circle. For the most part, instead of forming erotic relationships with these friends, he depended on them to find him anonymous street boys with whom he could have sex that did not "pollute" friendship. This process depressed him, and he was often "in love" with the very people who procured sex for him. He fell in love with a young Italian merchant marine from Brooklyn, had sex with him, and then in a turmoil of guilt broke off the relationship. He went to a young eye doctor for a consultation on a minor problem, fell in love with him, and wrote passionate letters to him for weeks in his journal. The letters were never sent. And in the mid 1930s he met and fell more deeply in love than ever with a young singer named Dante, a homosexual who was everything he dreamed of but with whom he never made love.

Almost all the men with whom Beauford fell in love were white (a major exception would be the young James Baldwin, who would not come into his life for several years). The preference for white lovers—whether sexual or platonic—can be explained to some extent by circumstances. Living in the Village, Beauford had everyday associations with few blacks because few lived there. It is clear that he felt that the blacks with whom he did associate (with the exception of Ellis Wilson)—Palmer Hayden, Cloyd Boykin, and his brother Joe, for instance—would disapprove of any hint of homosexuality.

The black–white split in general was a major part of Beauford's problem. He had long "worked" the white world to survive, and he was not above tempering his feelings about politics or race relations to obtain a good meal or a gallery showing. Whites generally perceived Beauford as a "good Negro," that is, one who was no threat and was not concerned with race. Yet in his journals we find frequent comments on the pride he takes in "my people," as in the draft of a letter to Ethel Waters and Reginald Beaune about a performance of theirs that made him "proud to be a Negro." Beauford was an admirer of W. E. B Du Bois and James Weldon Johnson, a reader of *Crisis* and *Opportunity*, and he notes with sadness in his journal the death of Monroe Trotter in 1934. He participated in the black protests of early October 1935 against the Italian invasion of the African homeland of Ethiopia. Beauford was, after all, the son of Delia Delaney,

who never missed an opportunity to remind her children of the evils perpe-
trated by racists.

In short, Beauford was torn. He kept his life in compartments—sex with
whites but not with blacks, sex with temporary acquaintances and not with
friends, safe politics with most whites, strong race identification with blacks. And
Beauford compartmentalized his friends; his black friends knew little of his white
friends; his gay friends knew little of his straight ones. It is tempting to suggest
that Beauford's situation was a microcosm of a larger American one, and to an
extent it was; the schizophrenia reflected in so much of American life—in the
politics of interracial sex, the myths of black and white sexuality, the special faces
we so often wear for our black or white friends—is expressed in extreme form in
Beauford's dilemma. In his particular case, the compartments of his life began to
take more concrete form than they perhaps do for most people. Over the years,
beginning in Knoxville, they had gradually became voices that argued with each
other and taunted their host—gently at first, more harshly later.

Conditions at 10 Downing Street became impossible during the winter of
1935–36. Beauford noticed that he had difficulty walking, that his feet felt numb.
In fact, his walking became so painful that he took to going about the city with
the aid of a cane. The plumbers came early in March to inspect the pipes under
his floor and found a thick layer of ice from a severe leak in December. The
painter had been living on what was in effect a frozen lake. When the house
began to lean precariously during the early spring thaw, Beauford finally gave up
and moved to a tiny loft above the Remsen Trucking Corporation at 181 Greene
Street. It would be his home almost until the end of his New York years.

four

New York: Pre-War Greene Street

The Greene Street apartment was a single-room loft whose cracked walls Beauford covered with pieces of white drawing paper. He had developed a theory stimulated by his many visits to Alfred Stieglitz's all-white gallery, An American Place, that the whiteness was as a symbol of purity of expression. He believed the whiteness itself shed a light that could bring vitality to his painting. There was a window on the street side and the room was heated by a small potbelly stove. In the winter the studio was so cold that Beauford wore a wool ski cap, several layers of clothing, and an overcoat. Summers under the roof were sweltering. He fell into the same routine in Greene Street that had marked his stay on Downing. When he had some food he fed not only himself but derelicts he met in the street. Some money came in from his work, but it left just as quickly in the hands of needy acquaintances. There was a constant stream of visitors at all hours of the day—people he had met in the parks, in jazz clubs, and in his walks around the Village. He worked at his easel when he could and out in Washington Square Park when the weather permitted.

The Greene Street period began with a long visit from his mother. Delia Delaney had never been out of the South, and she came to New York to see how her two sons lived. It was to Beauford, as the oldest son, that most of the responsibility fell for supporting and entertaining his mother. His friends helped, finding her places to stay, since the Greene Street studio was too small, and taking her to parties and outings. Beauford took her to buy "New York clothes" so that she could go with him to the opera, Carnegie Hall, and some of his favorite jazz clubs. When she returned to Knoxville, Emery and Gertrude and the children said she was a "new woman." She walked differently—"New York style," they called it—and she wore a magnificently large hat and a beautiful silk shawl over a much shorter and more stylish dress than the one she had left in. Beauford had always been close to his mother and anxious to please her. The trip to New York showed her how popular and respected her son was among both black and white friends. His mother approved of his life. But there were elements of it that he kept from her.

During the Greene Street years Beauford's life continued to be divided. There was the bohemian world, centered in the Greene Street studio and the apartments of his mostly white bohemian friends, the more orderly but relaxed friendships among black painter associates at Boykins and at the Harlem gathering places, and the modernist art world of avant-garde painting and theory that was so important to his development as a painter.

His relationships with two particular friends are representative of Beauford's tendency to compartmentalize his life. His closest friend among the white bohemians was the singer Dante Pavone and among the black painters he was closest to Ellis Wilson. Yet he never made an effort to introduce Wilson and Pavone.

For Beauford, Ellis Wilson was a fellow southerner who understood the problems of living in New York as a black man, a homosexual, and a painter. As might be expected, the two men shared with all black painters the concerns raised by Alain Locke and others about the relationship between their ethnic background and the painting they did. Although they took radically different paths as painters, they naturally discussed the theories of Locke and Du Bois and the people at 306 and the Harlem Artists Guild. Their relationship was at once polite and easy. They enjoyed bantering in the language patterns of their border state heritage, they savored eating and sometimes cooking "down home" food together and remembering the old songs at Wilson's 18th Street studio. When they were eventually separated by Beauford's moving to Paris they corresponded regularly, and their ties and confidences became deeper and more personal, and in time Wilson

visited Beauford in France. But Beauford revealed only so much. Wilson was surprised, for instance, by the news of his friend's psychological problems in 1961
because to him Beauford had always seemed stable and very much in control.

The relationship with Pavone, on the other hand, was intense, intimate, and
sometimes stormy. Although the two men were not technically lovers, their relationship was marked by jealousy and sexual electricity on Beauford's part. Unlike
Wilson, Dante was not surprised by Beauford's nervous breakdowns because during their times together from 1936 to 1953 he watched many an evening as Beauford, after several drinks, wandered about the room in a "sweaty trance" talking
to invisible objects or people, shouting and crying. But after Beauford left for
Paris in 1953 it was ten years before he and Dante wrote to each other, and they
never saw each other again. Yet a friend of Dante's dropped in on Beauford in
Paris in the mid-1960s, found the door open, and came upon Beauford in a kind of
daze, walking back and forth in his studio talking to the portraits of Dante lined
up along a wall.

It was Dante who introduced Beauford to a group of young gay bohemians
who spent a great deal of time in the painter's studio drinking, encouraging their
host to play the guitar and sing spirituals to them, seeking advice and solace, and
sometimes procuring street sex for him. It is tempting to say that Beauford
needed Dante and the bohemian life as an outlet for aspects of himself he was
embarrassed to share with his black friends, and to some extent, as suggested earlier, this was obviously the case. He could relax sexually with these friends in
ways he could not around his brother Joe, Palmer Hayden, Cloyd Boykin, or even
Ellis Wilson. But there was also the fact that just as Beauford gradually moved
away from the idea of painting "Negro art," he actively sought a social life that
transcended race and economic background.

He liked being with Dante and his friends because they represented a kind of
release expressed in the classical music, European art, and philosophy they all
enjoyed discussing, as opposed to the understandably less cheerful African-
American and African-oriented ideas that dominated the conversation of the
black art world in this time of economic depression and social activism.

It is also true that the wealthier of the bohemians—one was the heir of a large
commercial fortune, one a medical student, future surgeon, and son of an old
New England family—gave Beauford significant financial support in very difficult
times. "The doctor," as Beauford called him, continued to send money to him
every month for years after he had moved to Paris. Finally, he was seduced by the
role he was cast in by these young white people. He sensed that they looked up to
him as a guru and, always ready with a snippet of philosophy anyway, Beauford

liked playing the part, even if, as he knew, his role was based on a passive racism—
the image of the noncombative, sexually nonthreatening black man full of "primitive" earthy knowledge. He was well aware, having been beaten up several times
by white Village toughs simply because he was "an artistic Negro"—that is, gay
and black—that it was only because he was perceived by the white people who
knew him as a "good Negro" that they came to him for folk wisdom and friendship. Sometimes he felt like a "mammy," but a part of him warmed to that role.

But Dante Pavone was a special case. The son of an Italian opera singer from
Abruzzi, he had had conservatory training in Italy before coming with his family
to the United States in the late 1920s. In 1936 he was twenty-five, heavyset, with
dark eyes, a broad forehead, and little hair. Although trained to sing opera and to
compose, he was forced to make a living by singing more popular music in the
clubs of Greenwich Village. Beauford met him at the Village Vanguard. They
spent long periods of time together—at Beauford's studio or Dante's apartment.
They sang and listened to opera recordings together, ate and drank together, took
naps together, often spent nights in the same bed. They both loved to philosophize about "life" and to discuss art and music. They laughed at the same things,
and they could talk openly about their homosexuality and the "boys" they saw on
the street. They could cruise the bars for merchant marines together. Beauford
spent a period each summer between 1936 and 1953 with Dante in his little house
on the island of Vinalhaven in Maine.

The reasons for their not becoming lovers had to do with Beauford's shyness,
his difficulty in reconciling love with sex, and Dante's sexual attraction to others
and not particularly to Beauford. Dante loved Beauford, but Beauford was in
love—albeit puritanically—with Dante. In addition to the good times there were
the inevitable negative consequences of such conflicting feelings. On Beauford's
part there was jealousy and sometimes days of pouting and not speaking. There
were evenings when he would say insulting things and purposely miss appointments with his friend, almost as if he wished to drive him out of his life. At one
point he tried—and succeeded—in coming between Dante and a young man to
whom both were attracted sexually and with whom Dante had perceived the possibility of developing a full relationship. Beauford's jealousy led him to act in a
way that was anything but characteristic of the man known by friends other than
Dante. Yet, however badly Beauford behaved, Dante resisted an open break, and
Beauford himself only made what was a *de facto* end to the relationship when he
left for Paris in 1953.

Beauford felt most at ease and in control of the situation when he was painting Dante. And, as Henry Miller noted in his chapbook *The Amazing and Invariable*

Beauford DeLaney (1945), Dante was for a while Beauford's principle subject. Miller noticed that there were several portraits of Dante in the studio. "Supposing that for the next five years he were to do nothing but Dante?" he wondered.

> Why not? Some men paint the same landscape over and over again. Dante was a wonderful landscape for Beauford: he had cosmic proportions, and his scull though shorn of locks was full of mystery. A man studying his friend day in and day out for five years ought to arrive at some remarkable conclusions. With time Dante could become for Beauford what Oedipus became for Freud. (p. 7)

Miller's remarks are perceptive. He realized that Dante was indeed Beauford's primary "landscape" for exploration, that Beauford's need was to fathom Dante's mystery because Dante was at the center of Beauford's attempt to understand himself. That is, Beauford thought that to capture what Miller called Dante's "living spirit" in paint was somehow to recognize his own essence, to understand his own mystery. The portraits reflected Beauford's developing interest in an expressionistic approach to art. There were at least five portraits of Dante, pastels and oil. In all the paintings he employed distortion to reflect the inner Dante rather than external likeness. The most extreme attempt depicts a fuzzily delineated subject with a kind of halo; Beauford called it *Dante as Christ*. One senses in the case of the Christ painting more irony than successful expression of psychological reality.

At times Beauford was so obsessed with Dante that he had difficulty painting anything else. In the spring and summer of 1938, for example, he had a crisis of sorts. He had been invited to present solo shows at the 8th Street Playhouse in New York and at Gallery C in Washington, D.C. in the fall, and he knew he must get some significant new work done. He wrote in a draft for a letter to his mother of his inability to work and his need for loved ones:

> It is really not laziness—it's a sort of neurosis that grows out of some condition—peculiar kind of preoccupation with every sort of gimcrack known to man. . . . But we know among ourselves that finally there is nothing [more] important than our keeping in constant touch with our loved ones . . . at least a letter, note, flowers. . . . Again I pray and seek forgiveness—also I try to give to whosoever is near me all and any kind of aid and assistance just in the hope of being worthy of your love.

In August, after a brief visit to Dante in Maine, he writes a draft letter to his friend saying, "You have been constantly in my thoughts and I wish I could telegraph or phone you and I might do one or both before the summer is over."

In a letter to Don Freeman, who was away from New York for a time, he writes to say he has been "unable to compel myself to do anything at all." He then speaks of the connection between his lethargy and his inner state:

> . . . there seems to be growing in me that possibility of becoming aware of the inner things deep within, but in order for this kind of inner clarity to take place I seem to have been placed within my own custody where many reorientations are necessary for me to achieve the ability and power of activity.

He goes on to describe the beauties of Washington Square in the spring. The description would take form in some of the early Washington Square scenes that would occupy him in the coming weeks:

> Never before have the leaves and grass been more beautiful—also the old houses around Washington Square seem like large out of shape flowers blooming softly thru the trees. I so wish it were possible for me to put into words the deep felt things which are so obvious and tangible . . . and real like great alive forces working thru the deep unconscious tracts of our inner consciousness.

If Beauford was inactive because of his preoccupation with Dante, the letter to Freeman indicates the continuing process of discovering his own kind of expressionism by which he could reveal his inner self in the city surroundings he loved so much.

Primarily in the company of Ellis Wilson, Beauford did continue in the late 1930s to have a social life among fellow African Americans. A person he enjoyed in a somewhat ambiguous way was the sculptress Selma Burke. He had met her at the Artists Guild and at 306 and was fascinated by her. Selma had some money and was able to help Beauford and other needy African Americans in the arts at the time. Under a quotation by Anna Webb, "In truth there is no loneliness and no separation," Beauford describes in his journal an outing in 1938 with Wilson and Burke. He tells how on July 3 in the evening he went to Wilson's studio and they fixed sandwiches for a "glorious 4th of July with Selma on board her palatial yacht." Beauford stayed overnight at Ellis's and the next morning they met Selma's boat—captured by Beauford in his sketchbook—at a Harlem River dock. The day was in fact glorious.

Beauford loved "coming down the Harlem River speaking with Selma about the Rhine, the Rhone, the Seine, and the Danube as per our ambitions." There were several friends on board and "for music we have the sea and the beautiful scenery of Long Island Sound." The outing led him to "reminiscences of D. H.

Lawrence's *Women in Love*." Perhaps it was the lighthouse, he suggested. Or was it the "rhythm" of the sea, conveying some elemental "source," bringing "glimpses of [the] conception of the energy of the infinite." During the night, rocked by the maternal swells in a little inlet, "One dreamed continually of home, home, and home sweet home."

Beauford enjoyed Selma Burke's company, but he was wary of her. The word he associates with her in his journal is "enchantment." He loved hearing her talk of Europe—of the places she had been, places he wanted to visit. And he notes that he has "exchanged many confidences" with her, that she has "universal appeal to all kinds of sensitive people," and that they tend to become "enmeshed in the silky coils of her charm." Beauford felt threatened by women—by their sexuality: "Women are particularly impossible in many of their attitudes," he writes. Yet he preferred social situations in which he was not isolated by his own particular difference: "mixed groups, while very complex, somehow are the most bearable."

At the end of July Beauford had a financial crisis and had to borrow money to pay his rent. It embarrassed him to borrow, and he dreamed in his journal of selling whatever paintings he had to one friend "en masse." Homesick and disjointed letters to his mother alarmed her and she wrote at the end of the month to Joseph asking him in what seems more than a perfunctory way, to "take care of your older brother." She reminds her younger son that his differences with his brother are destructive: "Together you'll stand, but divided you'll fall."

As it turned out, the autumn of 1938 was the highpoint of Beauford's first ten years in New York City. Not only did he have the two one-man shows—primarily of portraits—at the 8th Street Playhouse and Gallery C in Washington, but in its October 3 edition, *Life* magazine ran an article on black Americans, noting that black artists were rarely shown in major galleries and that their problems dwarfed any problems faced by white artists. On page 54 a large photograph of Beauford Delaney was featured. The painter is seated before several of his portraits at the 1938 Washington Square outdoor show, and the caption suggests that he is "one of the most talented Negro painters," who "combines a direct approach with skillful hand."

Beauford was thrilled by the article and the photograph. Alexander King, an editor at *Life*, gave him fifty copies of the issue in which they appeared. As Beauford was about to carry them away King stopped him: "Wait, we'll get a boy to carry them." Beauford smiled and said very softly, "You'd be surprised at what I carried that didn't have my name on it." The article made a big hit in Knoxville. The *News-Sentinel* interviewed "Aunt Delia" about it. She reminded the interviewer that she

Beauford at the Wash-
ington Square Outdoor
Show, 1938

had *two* sons who were painters in New York City. The paper described the
Delaney house with "Brother Sam's" barber shop in the front room: "Some day it
may become a shrine as the birthplace of two famous Negro artists."

Despite his resistance to thinking of himself as a Negro artist, Beauford seems
to have felt no resentment against *Life* for casting him in that role, and he was
pleased to contribute a work to the Exhibition of the Art of the American Negro
(1851–1940) in the summer and fall of 1940 at the Tanner Art Galleries in Chicago
and later at the Library of Congress. Alain Locke wrote the catalogue introduction for this show, which brought together some of the most important black talent ever assembled in one show. There were works by Edward Bannister, Henry
O. Tanner, Jacob Lawrence, Romare Bearden, Hale Woodruff, Robert Blackburn,
Ernie Crichlow, Selma Burke, Norman Lewis, Richmond Barthe, and both
Delaney brothers, to mention only a few of the hundred artists represented.

In October and November 1941 Beauford contributed to another show of black
painters at the New York offices of the McMillens, the well-known decorators.

Mark Lane, in the October 15 issue of *Art News,* commented that the show proved that "the farther removed the Negro artist is from copying a white man's style or subject matter, the better he is." Yet he makes favorable note of one of the first shown of Beauford's modernist cityscapes, a painting called *Central Park* "which is like Van Gogh in brushing, but like Cézanne in *fête-champêtre* spirit."

In fact, Beauford's move toward European modernism, which Lane so rightly spotted, should not be confused with any denial of racial heritage or lack of interest in racial subjects if they could be made *his* subject. Beauford had a tremendous pride, for example, in black achievement in jazz and tried to find ways of expressionistically conveying in his own art what he found in that achievement. Throughout his life Beauford went to jazz clubs whenever he could, and he continued his project of painting jazz musicians well into the late 1930s.

Soon after it was formed in the mid-1930s Beauford heard the Benny Goodman trio for the first time, and it was Teddy Wilson, the first black to become a part of a popular white group, who held his attention that night. Later he would get to know Wilson and sketch him. Returning from a club late one evening during the days of the boogie-woogie craze he conveyed his enthusiasm—as an artist—for that mode and for blues and for Wilson and other black musicians.

> Boogie Woogie playing [his friend Handy's] St. Louis Blues. Tonight my course in art started. For the first time I have really felt the enormity of the jazz idiom. Of course . . . it most certainly takes light suffused with pink and smoky atmosphere.

But more important, perhaps, than his seeing jazz in the context of color and light is the constant reference in his journal to the form as a "Negro" idiom. He speaks of the ability of the black musician as an artist to "move by compelling, strong . . . African rhythm integrated with American primitive life made poignant by sorrow and sustained by an irrepressible sense of humor."

Beauford pursued something similar in his own art. In the portraits and cityscapes that would emerge in the late 1930s elements of the stark city scene, the world of the street people—manhole covers, lampposts, hydrants—is given color and prominence and juxtaposed in a lyrical but abstract and even humorous way that resembles the tone of the blues and boogie woogie and renders them celebratory instead of merely melancholy. He sometimes spoke of his "blues mode." He liked the black jazz artists in part because, like him, they were "enigmatic"; they were able to make him "sense so much from their music which defies . . . [ordinary] powers of penetration." On a page near the boogie-woogie journal entry he writes, "Art is the authority to induce what we cannot perceive."

About Teddy Wilson he says that his music is "enchanting and especially adapted to augment the vibrancy of the Boogie Woogie atmosphere." A singing group he heard represented "the amazing grace, care, and coordination of Negro singing complete with the emotional intensity." The young Lena Horne, whom he also heard, "combines feminine charm with wonderful interpretation of the wronged woman finding her melancholy consolation in singing the Blues."

There are sketches in the notebooks of Wilson, Horne, as well as of Count Basie and one white musician, Benny Goodman, whom Beauford saw as "a man of virile power and iron will." But it is the soul of the music he heard, the inner world that it conveyed rather than portraits of the players or paintings of smoky nightclubs (although he did some nightclub scenes as late as 1953) that finally interested Beauford. He ends the series of notes and sketches with the comment that "downtown cafe society has the authentic atmosphere of real Negro jazz—warm, vibrant, and conducive to dreaming and romantic musing."

When Beauford speaks of "Negro questions" in his journals and letters it is almost always in this somewhat idealized way. His emphasis is on the essence of his ethnic experience, the *feeling* of being a black man, the love of black lifestyle, rather than on sociopolitical questions surrounding race and race relations or economics. As a poor man with many poor friends he was, of course, concerned with economic and other social problems, especially of his fellow blacks. In a March journal entry of 1940 he notes, for instance, that he has spent the day before "ambling from one relief station to another, meeting the great mass of urban people caught in the imponderable wheels of economic dominance," all looking for some way to regain their self-respect. But when Beauford visited Harlem, he preferred walking along Lenox Avenue or stopping in at one of the clubs rather than joining the serious discussions at 306 or the Guild. In a letter to his friend Al Hirschfeld he talks about listening to a new Billie Holiday recording—"feeling . . . fine and mellow"—and suggests that "if at any time you should like to go to Harlem . . . I would be most happy to take you along the street where we can find real local color and also enjoy it."

It was not that Beauford was not interested in serious issues or that he did not enjoy discussing them. In addition to his life with Dante and their bohemian friends and his close associations with Ellis Wilson and those involved with "Negro art," he had a third life that centered around questions concerning the aesthetics and development of modernism in Europe and the United States. This was Beauford's intellectual subject of choice. This third life, centered on the strong influence of the ideas of his friends Alfred Stieglitz and Stuart Davis and paintings of the European modernists, most affected the development of his art from the late 1930s.

Beauford had known Davis since his first days in New York and had been encouraged by him to study the works of Cézanne, Gauguin, Matisse, Picasso, and Van Gogh, all of whom had influenced his own development. By 1939 Beauford's cityscapes showed signs of Davis's influence and that of the Europeans. In the first Greene Street paintings we find a Cézanne-like distortion of forms and perspective to convey a below-the-surface reality. And although Beauford's painting is gentler and more lyrical than Davis's, there is the same lack of concern for realism in the abstract use of familiar shapes as primarily geometric or cubist planes that can serve as vehicles for color and ideas.

Stieglitz, through his photography and his showing of European and American modernists at his galleries—first the Little Galleries of the Photo Session (called "291"), then the Intimate Gallery, and from 1929 An American Place—was a champion of the avant-garde in the arts. Beauford read Stieglitz and went to his lectures at An American Place. Stieglitz showed Rodin, Matisse, Cézanne, Picasso, and Americans John Marin, Arthur Dove, and Georgia O'Keeffe, among many others. Through Stieglitz Beauford was introduced to photographer Edward Steichen, as well as Marin, Dove, and poet Dorothy Norman and to their works. He met O'Keeffe at the home of their mutual friend Mary Callery, for whom he was posing, and they sketched each other. Eventually O'Keeffe did a small portrait of Beauford.

Steichen was important to Beauford because of his interest in light. Long passages in Beauford's journals are devoted to the advances in photography in the work of Stieglitz and Steichen. Steichen's early work especially interested him because its soft-focusing paralleled the experiments with light that characterized the impressionists and postimpressionist painters. In Marin and Dove— both among the first generation of American modernists—Beauford also found a concern for light and the possibility of using light and color abstractly to express the true "reality" of a subject. "Composition is order composed of mass, line, plane, and color," he wrote in his notebook (adding as an afterthought: "Keep balance between social forces and individual"). Beauford especially admired the Marin paintings of the Maine islands that were shown at An American Place. He knew the islands from his visits to Dante in Vinalhaven and he found in Marin's paintings, rather than in the many representational seascapes for sale everywhere, the successful depiction of the "inner essence" of Maine. Near the description of a Marin painting in his journal, Beauford copied a poem by Dorothy Norman called "Art Is an Easter" that became for him a manifesto of sorts—a statement of the expressionistic power of art to bring the inner world to life. The poem defines art as "the Resurrection of Crucified Concepts Defying Mortality."

Beauford also copied a long excerpt of a letter by Picasso written in 1926 in which the painter speaks of the ability of Cézanne to "penetrate" reality and of his own realization that "painting had an intrinsic value independent of the real representation of objects. I asked myself whether one should not represent facts as one knows them rather than as one sees them . . . art is a lie which allows us to approach truth." Through Picasso's words—written down as if they were his own, Beauford seems to move definitively away from the idea of painting in the interest of social justice: "We are painters. Do they want us to be coiners of virtues and maxims, watching over the markets as well?"

At the end of this segment of the journal in March 1940, as if having absorbed the lessons of the modernists, Beauford adds his own personal lesson. In a sense it is a "blues" lesson developed in part out of his experience as a black man and homosexual in the 1920s and 1930s in America. He suggests that success as an artist is not measured by publicity or influential friends but by "how many disappointments [the artist] has withstood." The real questions for the artist in New York City in 1940 are "How shall one live and what one shall do?" Beauford's answer is "study art," and to study art means to "learn to see," to "learn to be conscious," and "to learn to be conscious one must learn to love." One must, like Billie Holiday and Bessie Smith and Lena Horne and Teddy Wilson, through love, turn pain into celebration.

We begin to hear in these journals the lessons the young James Baldwin would hear a year later when he appeared on Beauford Delaney's doorstep—lessons Baldwin would make the center of his own message: "The human stimulant of love," writes Beauford, "is the great mover to growing consciousness." And in an introduction to a Delaney show in 1964 Baldwin would write of his friend: "I do know that great art can only be created out of love, and that no greater lover has ever held a brush."

Beauford went on to say in the 1940 journal:

> Love when unimpeded realizes the miraculous, the genius of glowing purification. But when muddled by sentimental moralistic hands its noble purpose is dragged into error by ignorance of its boundless orbit. Love is pure—it's only through love that we approach the portal of greatness; in no other way is it possible to comprehend . . . wholeness.

Beauford applied this lesson to his life as well as to his art. But it was difficult to equate love with sexuality. For himself, at least, he meant a kind of love that allows spiritual entrance to the being of another. He describes it as "gentle and friendly intercourse with human beings for whom we care and respect." To be an

artist one must, he says, "learn the great secrets of nature and . . . your own enigmatic nature," and to do so one must learn to love. And like the blues and boogie-
woogie performers he so admired, Beauford knew that learning to love meant
learning to have fun. As we have seen, he spoke in his journals of the sense of
humor conveyed by the black musicians he was sketching. Beauford's paintings—
especially as they became more abstract in the Greene Street period, always convey humor and pleasure. This combination of humor and love—an essential
combination in the blues and of jazz in general— was the African-American
secret at the soul of Beauford's paintings, even if the vehicles he used to reveal it
resembled those of Cézanne and Van Gogh and Matisse rather than his black
contemporaries.

And it must be pointed out, too, that in one sense at least Beauford had found
in the modernist approach—particularly in the cubists, who were so interested in
African sculpture as an inspiration—a peculiarly African way of seeing that was
in line with the ideas of Alain Locke and other adherents of an African modernism. Writing in the Autumn 1994 issue of *Race and Reason*, Geoffrey Jacques
uses the 1942 portrait of African-American actor Canada Lee as an example of
Beauford's black modernist vision:

> What is striking . . . is the way the artist is able to capture the angles of the
> figure, making the eye almost pay more attention to the lines and shapes than
> to the figure as a representative one. This is an aspect of what might be called
> an "African" sensibility: the ability to see an object in terms of its essentialist
> shapes and forms rather than being trapped in the struggle to render the
> figure by the tyranny of narrative. (p. 37)

It was in 1941, after a brief Christmas visit to Knoxville, that Beauford Delaney
revealed himself publicly as a modernist. From January 18 to February 2, his latest
works were exhibited in a one-man show at the Vendome art gallery at 59 West
56th Street. It was difficult for blacks to obtain midtown gallery exposure, and
with this show Beauford made a definite mark in the art world. The exhibition
was introduced by Don Freeman, who would also do a short "local color" article
on Beauford in his monthly magazine *Newsstand* in April (1,2,) complete with car-
icatures of a decidedly "good Negro" with a mischievous look holding up a bot-
tled candle for light and working by his potbelly stove, corncob pipe in mouth.
The Vendome show was widely reviewed.

There were the portraits that had become his trademark, including a pastel of
his mother and a fine large oil of his friend W. C. Handy that was used for the
announcement poster. Don Freeman wrote of the portraits in a catalogue note that

Canada Lee, 1942. Oil on canvas, 28 x 36 in. Photograph by Joe O'Reilly. Courtesy of the Delaney Estate.

Beauford De Laney's work always reflects his own vital and personal reactions to his subjects. It is never out of a set mold or style. His moods change but his essential humanness comes thru.

The portraits exhibited were relatively representational, but less so than his earlier work: the brush strokes—almost Van Gogh-like—were more evident, color was used more freely to achieve a particular formal composition rather than likeness. And the portraits expressed a tenderness of feeling that suggested Beauford's expressionistic and psychological interests. The *New York Sun* reviewer, Melville Upton, spoke of his "personal and peculiarly understanding way" of treating Handy and a portrait of a "Negro girl" (January 25, 1941).

But what attracted most notice were the new cityscapes such as the large oil entitled *Greene Street* and the more expressionistic paintings with titles such as *The Wave* and *Inner Glow.* The *New York Times* reviewer, Howard Devree, whose comments were somewhat patronizing, found these works "quite personal and effective" in spite of "rawness of color and an occasional French adumbration" (January 26, 1941). Upton criticized the painter for leaning "rather heavily upon Cézanne." The *Art Digest* reviewer recognized that the painter's "color has some of

Greene Street, 1940. Oil on canvas, 39 x 27 in. Courtesy of the Delaney Estate.

the emotional intensity of Van Gogh" and noted that this intensity was "mellowed by a personal approach" (January 25, 1941). The reviewers used words and phrases like "natural enthusiasm," "exultancy of mood," and "gayety" to describe what Upton called the painter's "vigorous and promising account of himself."

Beauford did not sell many paintings at the Vendome, but he did earn a little cash, and Joseph added a bit more, and they sent their mother a gift. The unsold paintings were informally exhibited for several months at the 8th St Cafeteria, where Beauford often went for morning or afternoon coffee.

It was paintings like *Greene Street* that most clearly announced the direction of Beauford's art just before World War II. The flat surface of the painting is divided into three roughly triangular forms and one rectangle. The triangle form is further developed as a leitmotif in a Marin-like jagged framing that separates elements of Beauford's studio—a red-brown carpet and a telephone—from a green area—Greene Street itself—with a darkly enlarged fire hydrant and a whirlpool-like black manhole cover. The third triangle, the sky, is bordered on the left by a rectangle, which is a building viewed from the studio window and is decorated by smaller rectangles as fire escapes and ladders. A small blue rug with red stripes—like the one in the artist's studio—is another rectangle; it brings the studio into the street. More ladders and platforms float in the right side of the triangular sky and out of that light blue-white sky—marked by the artist's heavy Van Gogh brush strokes—fly clearly outlined white birds, which give the painting a joyful and lyrical feeling. The whole work speaks of community, of the connection between the real world, represented by the street, and spiritual questions, represented by the birds, and Beauford's work, represented by the studio. All three elements are brought together by a thin red, white, and blue banner of celebration that drifts into the painting from the top.

One of the paintings in the Vendome show was a somewhat daring portrait of a nude young white woman. Beauford rarely painted nudes. His shyness made the model–painter relationship difficult. In his days at the Art Students' League Beauford had met and become close to a young painter who had earned extra money modeling for League classes. He was relieved to discover the unwritten rule that black painters not attend life classes when the female models were white. But the young woman he did paint, whose name was Jessie, was insistent. She was a dancer and a girlfriend of Emile Capouya, a classmate and close friend of the young James Baldwin. Baldwin met Jessie, who was several years older, at Beauford's, and eventually she became his girlfriend as well. It was perhaps Jessie's posing that led to Baldwin's agreeing to pose for a 1941 painting called *Dark Rapture*, which was also shown at the Vendome (see Color Plate 3).

Beauford did not often write the titles of paintings on the back of the canvas, and this was a strange title for him to give to the portrait of a sixteen-year-old. In fact, Beauford fell in love with Baldwin almost from their first meeting, and it was some time before he could partially accept the lifetime role of surrogate father rather than lover. For the next thirty-eight years the lives of Beauford Delaney and James Baldwin would be deeply intertwined. Baldwin called the painter his "principal witness."

Baldwin, a high school senior who was unhappy at home and in his position as apprentice preacher in a Harlem church, came to Beauford, on the advice of Emile Capouya, because he needed emotional help. As it turned out he could not have chosen a better counselor. Like Baldwin, Beauford was a preacher's son, a homosexual—although Baldwin had by no means accepted that designation for himself yet—and a creative artist. And he was a black man who, although poor, lived downtown and was successful in his work.

Baldwin always associated his first meeting with Beauford with the old song, "Lord, Open the Unusual Door." He remembered knocking on the Greene Street door and being quickly confronted by a "short, round brown man [who] when he had completed his instant X-ray of my brain, lungs, liver, heart, bowels, and spinal column," invited him in for tea.

Once it became apparent that there was no sexual interest on Baldwin's part, Beauford took him on as a protégé. In the boy's agony and guilt over his emerging homosexuality Beauford saw much of his own pain. Because of this identification he was able to help Baldwin accept himself. For Beauford Baldwin was always a "prince" and he never tired of telling him so. During the next few years he took on his new friend as a kind of responsibility. When Baldwin's father died, Beauford helped arrange for the funeral, and when Baldwin needed a job he found him one. Most important, he recognized a real talent in the writing Baldwin showed him, which led him to share with the boy something of his own aesthetic ideas.

Baldwin always said that Beauford taught him to respond to life as an artist—to look for truth and reality where others could not see it. He often told the story of how on one of their frequent walks through Greenwich Village Beauford one day told him to look at the water in a gutter. At first the boy saw nothing, but Beauford—like a Zen master—said "Look again," and this time Baldwin saw a film of oil in the water and noticed the way it distorted and made remarkable the buildings reflected in it. In later years Baldwin said the lesson had to do with complex vision, with learning to be willing to find what the artist has to find in ugliness, even in one's own ugliness. Ultimately Beauford's lesson was that "what one cannot or will not see, says something about you."

A part of what Beauford taught his pupil involved music. He introduced him to classical music and also to the kind of music that the church elders for whom young Baldwin preached associated with sin and degradation. Beauford taught Baldwin that the blues and boogie-woogie and jazz were as "sacred" as the gospel music they both knew and loved in church; he told him about secular music that held the soul together—especially the souls of black folk. After a few months Baldwin and Beauford would sit by the old Victrola, whose cover Beauford had painted, and sing with Ma Rainey, Ethel Waters, Louis Armstrong, Billie Holiday, and even Paul Robeson—Beauford in his deep baritone voice, Baldwin in his soft tenor. Beauford also took Bladwin to galleries and concerts and introduced him to his friends—to Palmer Hayden, Ellis Wilson, his brother Joe, to Theodore Upshure, Teddy Wilson, and many others. These were all successful African Americans, role models for a boy who not many months before had thought himself worthless and without hope of success. One night Beauford took Baldwin to hear Marian Anderson, and after the performance they went backstage to meet the singer. On their way home Beauford could talk of nothing but Anderson's "smoky yellow gown" in relation to her "copper and tan" skin and the red roses scattered about the dressing room. When some time later Beauford painted the portrait he had "fixed in mind" that night, he told Baldwin he had painted it for him.

Over the years Beauford would paint some ten or twelve portraits of his friend—the first *Dark Rapture*, the last in the mid-1970s. From 1941 until Baldwin's departure for Paris in 1948, the painter and his protégé could often be seen "holding court" after hours with a black poet friend, Smith Oliver, at a corner table in Connie William's Calypso Cafe, where Beauford had found Baldwin a job as a dishwasher and waiter.

The Calypso Cafe, on McDougal Street across from the Provincetown Playhouse, was a remarkable establishment. Beauford liked it because it was a place where people of all races met, engaged in discussions, and had fun. There were pre-Beat generation runaways who served as waiters and waitresses, left-wing seamen, would-be artists and writers, as well as already well-known intellectuals such as C. L. R. James and his "Pan Africanists," and Claude McKay, Alain Locke, and Paul Robeson. Malcolm X came by once or twice and so did Eartha Kitt, Burt Lancaster, and the young Marlon Brando. One particularly close friend of Beauford's who ate there was Henry Miller. Joe Delaney sometimes ate there, too. Connie Williams, the Trinidadian owner of the Calypso, said that when either of the Delaney brothers came into the restaurant and noticed the other he would simply nod, say, "Good Evening, Beauford" or "Good Evening, Joe," and move quickly to a table on the other side of the room. Connie had a loft nearby where she would sometimes put Baldwin up and where she held wonderful costume parties to which Beauford loved to come, not as a costumed participant but as an observer. Late in the evening he would sing and play his guitar, with the young James Baldwin—sometimes costumed in the robes of a preacher—curled up at his feet.

five

New York: The War Years

D uring World War II and the years immediately following, Beauford Delaney continued to struggle with his psychological problems and the stark realities facing him as an African American. His primary weapon was still his painting. Through it he could move into a sphere where such problems either had no place or could be transformed into art. Beauford was taunted as a "nigger queer" one night in Washington Square early in 1942 and badly beaten. Later that year a friend of his was the victim in a homophobic murder. Yet Beauford remained at Greene Street, doing patriotic wartime voluntary work as a plane spotter and air raid warden, and in his painting resisting any easy or angry reply to the prejudices that plagued his life and that of most blacks and homosexuals. He also continued to resist the temptation to create the kind of work that would call attention to the very real poverty that, despite the emergence of a wartime boom economy, still undermined his art and the lives of most black Americans. Instead Beauford took further leaps into the modernist mode that had long fascinated him and in which he was a pioneer among African-American artists.

As noted earlier, it was not that Beauford had no interest in social issues or denied the significance of his ethnicity. And it was not that he avoided "Negro" subjects or showing in all black exhibitions. It was simply that he felt less pressure than ever to be a "Negro painter," to allow ethnicity to determine the way he used the materials of his art. In this sense he was not alone among black artists. In the 1940s, it was events rather than theory that most influenced a general change among African-American painters and sculptors.

With the coming of World War II the excitement generated in the black artistic community by the WPA projects, the Artists Union, the Harlem Artists Guild, and more informal organizations of such leaders as Augusta Savage and Charles Alston gave way to new frustrations having to do with the demise of many of those projects because of conservative interference and the lack of equal opportunity in the military and in war-related defense jobs. Reacting publicly to their situation, blacks increasingly came under suspicion for their "radicalism" in pursuit of equality. The conservative Congress reacted with fear and prejudice to such remarks as an anonymous one that made the rounds of Capitol Hill in the early days of the war: "Just carve on my tombstone, 'Here lies a black man killed fighting a yellow man for the protection of a white man'" and slogans such as the *Pittsburgh Courier*'s Double V—for victory at home on the racial front as well as abroad in the war. In the years leading up to America's involvement in the war Martin Dies and his House Un-American Activities Committee had succeeded in gutting many of the WPA projects, closing such supposedly "Communist-inspired" organizations as the Harlem Community Art Center, at whose opening Eleanor Roosevelt had spoken and which had nourished so many black artists during the depression in the interest of bringing "art by the people to the people."

Under pressure from A. Philip Randolph, the head of the Brotherhood of Sleeping Car Porters, who threatened a march on Washington of 100,000 unemployed blacks as early as 1941, President Roosevelt issued an executive order banning discrimination in war industries and set up the Fair Employment Practices Committee. However, in order not to offend southern Democrats, the administration allowed segregation to continue in the military. The antagonism between black and white soldiers often exploded into open fights, and big-city black neighborhoods such as Harlem that were centers of nightlife were increasingly isolated and sometimes destroyed economically by being declared off bounds to white soldiers on leave. There were angry riots in ghettoes throughout the war years—including the great riot of August 1–2, 1943, in Harlem.

The reaction of the black art world to the new situation was mixed. In 1939 Augusta Savage had responded to the destruction of many of the depression projects by opening the Salon of Contemporary Negro Art on 125th Street. Black painters, including Beauford Delaney, showed their works there (it was still difficult for them to find gallery space in the white-dominated art world), but a lack of money and the absence of an audience that could afford to pay for paintings led to the gallery's closing. Many young artists gave up their painting and sculpting in favor of industrial jobs as soon as the war plants opened to black employees. Some, such as William Johnson, remained on scantily funded WPA mural projects for several years before taking factory jobs. For a while Johnson portrayed black soldiers on war posters. Others used their art to comment on the tensions inherent in the situation of black soldiers in the war effort. Jacob Lawrence did this in his paintings of life in the Coast Guard.

In general, it can be said that one effect of World War II was to delete the idea of "Negro art" as envisioned in earlier days by Alain Locke and others. In keeping with the drive for equality in other fields, the feeling among many African-American artists was that it was important to become part of the mainstream art world rather than depend on black solidarity in the face of prejudice.

Furthermore, increased American contact with Europe during the war and immediately after, when study abroad became possible under the GI Bill, led to greater contact between African Americans and European art. The effect of that contact was evident in the work of many important black painters. After the war Romare Bearden's work reveals the influence of cubism in its emphasis on planes and geometric forms. The same can be said of some of Jacob Lawrence's work and the postwar work of Charles Alston. In Lawrence, like Norman Lewis, Bob Thompson, and Hale Woodruff we find a movement into abstract expressionism as well. And the style of Joseph Delaney's street scenes is a cross between Daumier-like caricature and a form of expressionism. One feels the presence of Cézanne, Picasso, Braque, Matisse, Munch, Kandinsky, and other European modernists in much of the African-American painting during and after the war.

When the war began Beauford Delaney was already very much a modernist himself. Although he maintained his friendships with black artists and continued to take advantage of any chance he had to show paintings, which often meant all-black shows, since the late 1930s he had been moving along on his own course toward a style deeply influenced by European painting.

The connection between the European art that interested Beauford and the portraits and cityscapes of the World War II period are clear from journal entries and conversations the painter had with friends. Beauford was an avid reader of books on art and he went to An American Place and other museums and galleries whenever possible. It is important to note that he never worked in a vacuum.

Beauford was an ardent and deliberate student of modernism who began his study with the impressionists with their emphasis on the effect of light on color and forms, moved on to the structural, architectural concerns he found in Cézanne, the painterliness of the large free masses of color in Gauguin and Van Gogh, and eventually to the more abstract but still color-dominated paintings of the Fauves—Dufy, Vlaminck, Derain, and especially Matisse. There was also a theoretical interest in cubism as represented primarily by Braque and Picasso. But although we find cubist elements in the structural aspects of paintings of the Greene Street period, Beauford never let the early cubist interest in form—in geometry—overcome his primary interest in light and color.

It is perhaps surprising that a man so plagued with psychological difficulties would have had little apparent interest—at least in the 1940s—in the works of the more overtly psychological expressionists such as Munch and Nolde. Among the expressionists it was primarily Kandinsky with his Fauve-like violent colors and less morbid subjects who interested Beauford. It can be said as well that, despite his problems, Beauford's nature was optimistic. His personality was much more attuned to the work of painters like Dufy, Matisse, and the early Kandinsky than to the more pessimistic visions of Munch and Nolde.

By the time Beauford was telling the young James Baldwin to explore the effect of light in that gutter in Greenwich Village, he was well into his study of Matisse and the Fauves. The portraits and cityscapes of the 1940s and early 1950s are, like the works of the Europeans in question, devoid of classical perspective and chiaroscuro. Forms emerge by way of simple line and masses of color. Objects are brought up to the flat two dimensional surface of the canvas and placed according to the painter's sense of the inner structure of the subject; in this way the paintings reveal the interest in Picasso and the cubists. Distortion of conventional forms is always present in the Beauford Delaney paintings. We are forced to look at reality through new, unconventional eyes so that objects take on a new importance, as in the poetic vision of the modernist poet William Carlos Williams, whose work—especially "The Red Wheelbarrow"—Beauford particularly admired:

> so much depends
> upon
> a red wheel
> barrow
> glazed with rain
> water
> beside the white
> chickens.

In Williams's vision—as indicated by the way the lines of the poem are broken down—and Beauford's, the red wheel juxtaposed with the glazing light and the whiteness of the chickens was what mattered more than the conventional reality of wheelbarrows, rain water, and white chickens. Beauford continued all his life to paint portraits and cityscapes that expressed these interests, and by 1941 he was already experimenting with pure abstractions concerned with light and color without reference to objective forms.

Early in December 1941, attempting to build on the all-black Baltimore exhibit of 1939 and the all-black McMillen show in November 1941, Edith Halpert assembled at her Downtown Gallery the largest number of African-American paintings yet shown in one place. Halpert was assisted in her selections by Alain Locke and the Harmon Foundation's Mary Beattie Brady. She had arranged with certain New York dealers to show in their own galleries two painters from the exhibition. The idea was to give black artists a jump start in the mainstream gallery scene and help them overcome the deterioration of the WPA projects. There was also a plan to establish a Negro Art Fund with which works by black artists would be bought and donated to museums. The show was much hailed in the art press, but the bombing of Pearl Harbor during its first week and the consequent economic confusion seriously diluted the effectiveness of Halpert's agreement with other dealers. Only Halpert herself honored the arrangement by showing Horace Pippin and Jacob Lawrence, from then on two of the most successful black American painters.

The Downtown Gallery show highlighted the dilemma of Beauford and most other black artists. The show provided a much needed chance to exhibit, but the fact that blacks were "collected" in one show tended to perpetuate the separation of African-American art from the rest of the American art world or, for that matter, from the European art world. Beauford's friend Hale Woodruff would articulate the situation years later:

Everything the Negro does has to do with his image of himself and his aspirations. It involves human as well as racial, fulfillment. The Negro artist faces all the "artistic," hence, economic and cultural problems all artists face. But for the Negro artist these problems are aggravated by the fact that the "power structure" of the art world is not altogether prepared to accept him as "just another artist," particularly in the visual arts. They still desire, seemingly, a non-white quality which presents the Negro artist as being unique and therefore different from other artists. (*Arts and Society* V, 1968, pp. 219–237)

The reviewers, who universally praised the Downtown Gallery show, only added to the stereotypes outlined by Woodruff. They spoke of the homogeneity of the paintings displayed and of "Negro art" in general. The *Art Digest* reviewer said that

> in spite of the difference in style and subject, there is a strong racial tie-up. A distinctly homogeneous quality is felt in the color arrangements (reds and purples predominating) and in a certain characteristic treatment of rhythm and form which distinguishes the Negro race and has added much to our native culture. (XVI, 6, December 15, 1941, p. 5)

The *New Yorker* reviewer, Robert Coates, began his review by suggesting that there must be some truth to the "ancient gag about Negroes loving bright colors" (December 27, 1941, p. 52).

These comments alone indicate the passive racism inherent in the white world's view of African-American art: "We've been right all along; they've got rhythm and they go in for bright colors" was the clear message to the white readers. Yet, despite themselves, the reviewers, having established what they saw as the homogeneity of black art, went on to reveal the immense diversity of the paintings at the Downtown show. Coates, especially, saw the "imaginative vigor, combined with maturity of expression" and the fact that "practically all styles are represented, from the naive paintings of Horace Pippin and Felton Coleman, through the Expressionism of Beauford Delaney." It is of interest that the *New Yorker* review made note of Beauford's modernistic approach and referred specifically to his highly abstract "swirling red-and-yellow 'Still Life'" rather than to the more figurative paintings he showed. Red and yellow abstractions would become a Delaney trademark in later years.

A look into Beauford's sketchbook journal of the early 1940s gives some sense of what the painter was thinking during that period. There are sketches of street people—a woman feeding her baby, a man drinking coffee at an outdoor cafe, two men playing chess in Washington Square Park—a sketch from memory of his mother in the hat he had bought her in New York, realistic sketches of friends—Alfred Stieglitz, Al Hirschfeld, Dante reclining on a couch, for example—a woman's face done in the heavy post cubist "classical" style of Picasso. And there are sketches for now well-known Greene Street and Washington Square paintings of the 1940s and 1950s. But some of the sketches are highly abstract, with only a few indications of representational objects. He writes in the margins of a page, "The ideal of abstraction seems to underlie the whole modern art movement."

And there are notations about technical experiments: he speaks of painting a design in oil, waterproofing it, placing it in a sink of water, adding watercolors and allowing them to drip onto the design "melting into [a] whole." He reminds himself to "take great care with background" and always to "apply the personal note" to his paintings. On many of the sketches are indications as to which colors should be used in various areas of the given work. "Color functions everywhere: body, mass, vibration," he writes. In this connection he jots down several significant names: Cézanne, Renoir, Modigliani, and Rouault, all of whom use color "architecturally" to create form rather than merely to decorate. Some sketches are of particular objects that would become characteristic of Delaney cityscapes from 1940 on: fire hydrants, lampposts with one-way street signs, manhole covers. The sketchbooks he kept throughout his career indicate a painter who planned his work carefully.

The sketches are mingled with the usual Delaney philosophical comments on art and life and quotations from books he had read and notes on lectures on modernism he had attended. "The worries and woes that man makes cannot extinguish the divine fire," he writes. And "recollect that trifles make perfection and perfection is no trifle." He refers to his belief that there is a "central power" to which all the "smaller factors" are related and suggests that it is this understanding out of which important art evolves. In reacting to the war he complains of the "paucity of whole grained affection" in the world, wonders at its cause, and is "keenly aware that it is the basic cause of the great pathological dilemma of our times." He considers "the problem of maturing, which takes so much time" and worries about being followed by evil people.

Among the sketches and recorded thoughts are lists to remind himself to consider or do certain things: take out the laundry, call the plumber to fix the "flush box," call Brooks Atkinson, go look at the archaic marble statue he had seen once in front of a house in Bronxville, read André Gide. He goes to see *Fantasia* and marvels at "Walt Disney's use of art forms"—including music—"in color with the camera," and speaks of the importance of the camera in the hands of an Edward Steichen as a capturer of fleeting instants that are so important to the "modern artist."

Alfred Stieglitz continued to be his primary theoretical teacher. Never seeming to complain that his own work was apparently not considered good enough for An American Place, Beauford continues in the 1940s to speak admiringly of Stieglitz and his circle—particularly Georgia O'Keeffe, John Marin, Arthur Dove, and Steichen: "An American place is white and gray, serene with the spirits of indomitable spirits" who "live by sheer awareness" and who have "extended the dignity of the American spirit into the consciousness of our times." In a sense this was the almost religious goal Beauford set for himself in his own paintings. He would remain a lifelong admirer of the Stieglitz group. In a letter to Henry Miller in February 1946 he would speak of a "magnificent" Marin show, saying that the painter "grows into greater splendor of heights and depths—the unusual spirit pervades his color." About O'Keeffe's paintings he noted how they were "alive and quite amazing." When Stieglitz died in 1946 he wrote to Miller that he "has left us his mantle and we who are here somehow become more precious to each other" (June 26, 1946).

Beauford was particularly intrigued by Stieglitz's idea of simplicity. Stieglitz believed that, like music, the painting must have a theme simple enough on which to build significant variations. The trick, he said, was "to include all that is necessary and eliminate all that is unessential." Of course, simplicity alone was not enough; there must be inherent taste and a willingness to study great art—old and new. Then "that which is personal and original within you will develop into what is called style." Finally, said Stieglitz, there is the all-important element of any great composition: without balance "no picture can ever be satisfying." Any slight error in balance and the painting falls apart. Beauford agreed with his mentor that the serious painting must capture the "drama" of the struggle between balance and imbalance—between holding together and falling apart—that is inherent in life itself, inherent in painting, as it was inherent in the precarious world of his own psyche.

Beginning at the end of the year in 1941 Beauford suffered one of his prolonged periods of depression, aggravated by an increasing dependence on alcohol. There were the usual financial problems as well, and the more intimate personal problems. The non-erotic love relationship with Dante continued, but was often marred by frustrations and jealousies. Beauford fell in love with a young black man who was taken away from him by the army and the war before he was able to break through the old difficulty of bringing sex and love together. Next to the young man's name in the journal are plaintive remarks such as "Please write, baby, please write."

He was also secretly enamored of the actor and sometimes companion of Anais Nin, Canada Lee, whose portrait he painted in 1942 in a style that one critic has compared to Picasso's portrait of Gertrude Stein (see page 66). A strong, stern, and very dark face stares out of a yellow background—yellow, which he called the "color of light," was always Beauford's favorite color. The face is carried by a seated body with an exaggerated set of shoulders, arms, and legs. The colors, like those in many of Van Gogh's portraits and some of Matisse's, are divided into a few large outlined and deeply contrasted segments. The painting expresses anger and tension, the threat of imbalance, not only because of the

subject's facial expression but as a result of the possibility of compositional dis-
ruption conveyed by the diagonal movement of Lee's tight belt in the direction of
the harsh right angle formed by his enlarged left upper arm and forearm. The
angled arm dominates the work, and the downward movement of the left hand
over the right forearm adds still further to the feeling of tension.

James Baldwin was often in the Greene Street loft and although Beauford had
fallen in love with him, too, Baldwin was a teenager intent on living to the fullest
the new intellectual and sensual life he was discovering in Greenwich Village. His
interests did not encompass a love affair with a much older man who stared into
space for long minutes and sometimes cried for no apparent reason. He would sit
occasionally for paintings because he admired Beauford and enjoyed watching
him work.

Perhaps the most important portrait of this difficult period for Beauford was
the one he did of Baldwin at the very end of 1941. This is the nude figure mentioned earlier entitled *Dark Rapture* (see Color Plate 3). It is like nothing else
Beauford ever painted. The figure, whose body structure identifies him almost
certainly as the young Baldwin (although the face is highly distorted), sits upright,
one leg crossed under the other, on a multicolored daybed. His dark skin collects
within it the many colors that surround it and is, like those surroundings, marked
by the heavy pallet and evident brush strokes that Beauford so admired in Van
Gogh. Since everything is brought, in modernist style, up to the surface of the
canvas, the plants behind the bed seem to grow out of it. The vegetation itself
resembles trees rather than houseplants, and there is a large earth-colored pot
textured with red that sits at the painting's bottom left corner. The effect is exotic
and emotional. The work exudes the lushness of a jungle and the possibility of
passion. *Dark Rapture* is an apt title.

Beauford continued in the Van Gogh-influenced style of portraiture. He was
particularly interested in the Dutch painter at this time, feeling, in his depression,
a true comrade in art. The Van Gogh style is evident in the well-known heavily
textured painting of Henry Miller surrounded by an almost religious light done
in 1944 and in the portrait of the broad-browed Dante Pavone in a hat done in
Maine in 1943, a painting reminiscent of Van Gogh's 1888 portrait of Armand
Roulin.

The halo-like light effect around the head is also found in a 1944 pastel of
James Baldwin, done as a present for John Arvonio, a mutual photographer
friend. The pastel presents a very handsome Baldwin with clearly outlined, somewhat heavy features that suggest the Picasso classic style rather than Van Gogh's.
As an idealization the drawing is in keeping with Beauford's supportive insistence

James Baldwin, 1944.
Pastel on paper, 24 x 18¾
in. Photograph by Maria
Sassoonian. Courtesy
of Ernden.

over the years that Baldwin was handsome despite his friend's equally constant
insistence that he was ugly.

During Beauford's depression and the years immediately following, the artist
faced particularly difficult financial problems. He continued giving art classes in
several progressive schools in the Village, but was not paid well and sometimes
could not meet his rent. More often than not he had to resort to wealthy acquaintances to hold off disaster. In a letter to Henry Miller Beauford reports that he has
received a suit, a shirt, two pairs of socks, a change of underwear, and a check for
$20 from the painter Mary Callery (late 1945). In another letter, from Vinalhaven,
he tells Miller that "my good friend" Kenneth Lash has made the trip to Maine—
"God's and John Marin's land"—possible (June 26, 1946). He notes, too, that
Alfred Stieglitz had provided some of his reading for the summer—primarily a
monograph on John Marin. Many of these patrons were friends of Don Freeman
and/or Al Hirschfeld, and several became ardent Delaney collectors. Some continued to send Beauford small amounts of money on a regular basis even after he
moved to Paris.

Joanne Sitwell, a cousin of Dame Edith Sitwell, was an example of such a friend. Hirschfeld introduced her to Beauford in the Greene Street loft and she became a frequent visitor. She bought several paintings—especially the Greene Street and Washington Square cityscapes that dominated the painter's work during the New York years (see Color Plate 5). And with Hirschfeld she introduced him to Albert Hackett, who would later adapt *The Diary of Anne Frank* for the theater, and several other writer friends, including Augustus and Ruth Goetz (*The Heiress*) and William Saroyan; many of these new acquaintances bought paintings. Miss Sitwell would remain a friend through the 1950s and later in the 1960s when she and Beauford were both living in Europe. She was perhaps the first of the Delaney collectors to take him seriously as a bona fide and important modernist painter rather than an eccentric black "primitive." Beauford recognized the unpatronizing attitude and, given the humiliation that had to be an adjunct of his acceptance of help from wealthy white acquaintances, was always grateful for it.

Partly through Hirschfeld, Freeman, and other friends, Beauford continued to have a cultural life outside that of his studio and the cafe society of his painter friends. This helped him through his period of depression. He was given tickets to several plays—Hirschfeld's *Hello Out There*, *Porgy and Bess*, William Saroyan's *Love's Old Sweet Song*, and *Othello*, starring Paul Robeson, to mention a few that he particularly liked.

Beauford also pursued his interest in black culture per se. In his journal he urges himself to pay attention to "primitive art of America" and "folk art of black Africa"(partly because the cubists were interested in it). Black music was still a major interest—especially jazz—and he kept any clipping available on the career of Marian Anderson. He also preserved clippings on the subject of lynchings that plagued the nation, particularly in the South, during and immediately after the war, when white racists were intent on keeping the returning black troops "in their place." In W. C. Handy's *Unsung American's Sung*—a book on black America—published in 1944, the illustrations—of congressmen of the Reconstruction days and other little known black martyrs and leaders, as well as such famous figures as John Brown, Paul Lawrence Dunbar, George Washington Carver, Frederick Douglas, Toussaint L'Ouverture, Harriet Tubman, Phillis Wheatley, Arthur Schomburg, Monroe Trotter, and Booker T. Washington—were pencil sketches in the realistic style by Beauford Delaney.

African-American writers were particularly important to a painter who always wished he could be a writer as well. He read all of Richard Wright and Zora Neale Hurston, for example, and whatever was published in journals by Langston

Hughes and Countee Cullen. And he read manuscript versions of the young James Baldwin's *Go Tell it on the Mountain* before anyone else.

But Beauford's reading was by no means limited only to books written by African Americans. He liked to keep up on literature that, whoever wrote it, reflected his modernist interests. Some books were recommended by Miss Steloff at the Gotham BookMart, which he visited regularly, and by his friend Larry Wallrich, who worked at the 8th Street Bookstore and later ran his own shop on Cornelia Street in the Village. Both Wallrich and Steloff recommended Proust and Gide. Later, Henry Miller would give him copies of *Tropic of Cancer, Tropic of Capricorn, The Colossus of Maroussi, The Wisdom of the Heart,* and the privately published *The World of Sex.* In addition to their modernistic approaches, Miller, Proust, and Gide provided Beauford with insights into homosexuality on the one hand and sexuality in general on the other that both fascinated and relieved him somewhat. The escapades of the Baron Charlus, especially, became an important theme in Beauford's conversations with gay friends.

But it was the reading of Miller that particularly attracted him. Beauford's confrontation with sex had always been secretive and guilt-ridden. He was astounded by what he found in Miller—the explicit sexual descriptions, the defiance of conventional morality. In a journal letter to Miller—never sent—he says, "You exude the [human] race" and speaks of "plastic peoples of the earth" and the "conditioned behavior of humankind" against which he sees Miller struggling. In a letter he did send (February 27, 1944) he spoke of the effect Miller's books had on him: "I am sure you understand me when I say that my way is clearer [now]—vision more serene." Miller's work opened up the possibility that sexuality could be liberating and "good," and if Beauford still had difficulty channeling his own sexual desires into viable relationships, he could accept the sexual activity he did have with greater ease and could counsel younger friends, like James Baldwin, to accept their sexuality, whatever form it took.

The Miller–Delaney friendship began in the fall of 1943 when Harry Herschkow-itch, a merchant marine friend of both men, introduced Miller to Beauford. Carl Van Vechten, who knew Beauford well, had also recommended him as a "good man" whom he would probably like (Miller note, March 7, 1944). The story of the first meeting is told in the Alicat Bookstore's publication of a 1945 essay by Miller, *The Amazing and Invariable Beauford DeLaney.* Miller was well acquainted with other Delaney friends—especially Al Hirschfeld, Alfred Stieglitz, and the black critic and novelist Albert Murray. Hirschfeld took Murray to visit Beauford one afternoon and they enjoyed talking about jazz, an interest they all shared with Henry Miller. Murray compares Beauford to Joe Gould, a character made famous by Joseph Mitchell in the *New Yorker* and in *Up in the Old Hotel*. Gould was an Ivy Leaguer who became a bohemian. Presumably Murray's point is that Beauford, partly because of Miller's article, had established a reputation as a Village bohemian "character." It was a reputation that would provide him with a dangerous means of hiding the demons that increasingly plagued him. At age forty-two, Beauford Delaney was not the serene man that Henry Miller saw; he was a man still only recognized as an eccentric "Negro painter," and he was a man wracked by poverty and an inner pain that was taking its toll.

Romare Bearden and Harry Henderson are right in pointing to Miller's romanticizing and sentimentalizing of Delaney in his essay. The portrait he paints is a patronizing one; we read such phrases as "the mysterious stamina of his race" or "doxology of the blood." We are told that "Beauford is no different from his ancestors; he can bide his time." The portrait is of an eccentric primitive—a natural Buddha—who almost loved his poverty. And although a painter himself, Miller fails to treat his subject as a serious painter.

However, the essay gives us some valuable details about Beauford's life at the time, and the friendship between Miller and Delaney—as subsequent correspondence makes clear—was genuine and lifelong. Miller sent Beauford money at Herschkowitch's urging even before he met him and would help him on several occasions in later years. And the letters between the two were especially warm and supportive through difficult times that both experienced. Miller came to know Beauford's friends well and Beauford came to know Miller's family and friends, including Anaïs Nin, who somewhat terrified him but with whom he enjoyed a drink in her West 13th Street apartment and, at Miller's suggestion, sketched. Beauford had little to say about the meeting beyond an enigmatic smile.

Oddly enough, Beauford did not seem to object to Miller's depiction of him any more than he had objected to Don Freeman's equally sentimental story in *Newsstand*. In February 1945 when in a letter accompanying an advance copy of the chapbook article, Miller asked Beauford whether he had "laid it on too thick about the Negro" (February 2, 1945), Beauford's answer was positive, to say the least:

> Received your amazing story or article on me this a.m. and believe me when I say I have really no words for how pleased I was with it in toto. I have no desire to have you change it in any way unless you wish to make some changes. It is fearlessly written and it's about the negro race of which I am only a humble symbol. Henry, please accept my handshake on your wonderful encouraging and youthful spirit. . . .What you have written is overwhelming but I love it. . . . it released a great throb which I hope you feel out on your mountainside.

It seems likely that the letter was genuine, though Beauford was nothing if not mannerly, and in the 1940s he could not afford to be disdainful of the publicity the Miller work gave him. And as a black man Beauford could not have failed to appreciate Miller's comments on the difficulties that faced a black artist in racist America. Perhaps he was a bit embarrassed by some of Miller's hyperbole. In later years when the article was mentioned he would sometimes roll his eyes and smile—a characteristic reaction to something he did not quite approve of.

Harry Herschkowitch, the man responsible for the Miller–Delaney meeting and his friend Larry King had met Beauford in the 10 Downing Street days. Harry would sometimes stay with Beauford when his ship was in. Often he would be sick and Beauford would nurse him. King often stayed there, too. On one occasion in 1940 when Herschkowitch's ship docked in San Francisco he visited with Miller and told him all about Beauford, urging him to visit the painter on his next trip to New York. Miller describes how he first met Beauford on Macdougal Street during the Washington Square outdoor show one spring in the early 1940s. He says that he stood by the painter, who suddenly interrupted a conversation he was having with someone else and turned around to say, "Why, Henry Miller! You here? How are you?" The story could well be apocryphal, but it does capture something of Beauford's way. In any case, a proper meeting took place during the fall of 1943 when Herschkowitz took Miller to 181 Greene Street, giving him the opportunity to write his now famous description of Beauford's studio. The painter's room was a "heavenly abode" of a loft heated badly by a potbelly stove that could do little against the "chill of the grave which emanates from the dripping walls, floors, and ceilings." The streets outside were "infested with the sinister shadows of crime."

Possibly it was Beauford's meeting with Henry Miller and the enthusiasm with which Miller brought to their friendship that lifted him out of his depression in the spring of 1944. He wrote to Miller saying, "Every time I think of you and read your books or touch your letters or talk with those who know you my spirit gladdens and expands to wider orbits." (undated c. spring 1944). Miller promised to help publicize the painter and sent a stream of his friends to visit and aid him.

There were other positive notes in 1944 as well. A few of Beauford's paintings were shown at the Institute of Modern Art in Boston, the Newark Museum, and the Baltimore Museum of Art as part of a traveling show called "The Negro in Contemporary Art"—an exhibit that grew out of the Downtown Gallery show. The *Art News* reviewer A. D. Emmart especially liked his modernistic *Othello* with its "lyric note, heavily worked paint, and striking scaling of the figures" (May 21, 1944, A,10). The painting had been inspired by Paul Robeson's performance in the Shakespeare play. And after having missed two Washington Square outdoor art shows, Beauford returned to the fall show. He set up in Macdougal Alley. On the corner of the alley and Macdougal Street itself was the elegant little Jumble Shop, Washington Square Park, subject of so many of his paintings, was visible down the alley. It cost $15 to set up a booth, up $5 from the last time he had shown there. His booth was next to his old friend Palmer Hayden's, and brother Joe was nearby. The sun and the crisp air and the crowds of people—the street boys and street girls, the middle class weekend villagers—were exhilarating. Beauford did not sell many already completed paintings; people smiled at the strange new style of the Greene Street and Washington Square paintings. But they liked the few realistic pastels, and once again Beauford found himself doing what he had done during his first months in New York almost fifteen years before: instant sketches of his viewers, which they bought or did not buy according to the degree of likeness he achieved. For Beauford it did not matter; he was back in a world of artists—there were artists all up and down the alley, all along Macdougal and Sullivan Streets, all around the Square. They were a community dedicated to what mattered most—art. If there was a paradise, this must be it.

That summer Beauford went with Dante to Vinalhaven and did sketches for several portraits of his friend. He returned feeling more confident than he had in some time, and a highly productive period began. There was the great portrait of Henry Miller done in 1944 (see page 183), the Dante portraits, a portrait of Jimmy Baldwin, which hung for a long time in the window of Larry Wallrich's bookstore, and, most important, a continuation of the Washington Square and Greene Street cityscape series.

The winter of 1944–45, despite the cold in his loft, was a relatively happy one. He kept warm part of each day by eating at Connie's Calypso Cafe and then joining the eccentric "arty" crowd that spent time at the Waldorf Cafe. Larry King, whose stage name at the New Jewish Folk Theater was Leib Konigsberg, was always at the Waldorf speaking Yiddish with Gene Benton. James Baldwin, who at that time wore a brown stocking cap to keep his stylish "conk" in place, often came by with his East 15th Street roommates, Marty Weissman and Shirley Suttles, both students. Jimmy, Marty, and Shirley would sometimes go back to Beauford's loft to sit around the stove, share his fatherly wisdom, and listen to music. Shirley remembers getting there by walking through unlighted streets and up an equally unlighted narrow stairway. Beauford would sit "on a couch in the middle of this huge, wonderful room, looking like a monarch holding court—but a sweet monarch, a veritable angel of a man." One "lunatic evening sticks in [Shirley's] mind, Jimmy holding a protesting Marty down while I cut his hair, then Beauford cutting Jimmy's hair, and finally Jimmy and I cutting Beauford's."

Beauford in his Greene Street studio, 1944. Courtesy of the Delaney Estate.

In 1945 the Miller article on Beauford appeared and made him even more of a "character." People actually stood outside 181 Greene Street trying to get a glimpse of him. In April he contributed to a show of both black and white painters at Powell House on East 70th Street. Beauford exhibited the Henry Miller portrait and the Jimmy Baldwin pastel, what one reviewer (*Villager*, June 7, 1945) called "psychological portrait studies." He also showed a new cityscape—a scene under the elevated railway on Third Avenue in which "in his characteristic fashion, the paint is thick and the color is so sharp that the picture seems illuminated by neon lights, which he says impressed him when painting the scene." In May there were the VE Day celebrations and in September those of VJ Day. Some of the best paintings by Beauford's brother Joe are of these celebrations.

Beauford continued to concern himself with the simpler excitement of ordinary human activity. In a June journal entry he describes walking one Saturday morning at 6 P.M. by Washington Square into Macdougal Street, "the scene of much strange and complex drama." He describes himself as strolling along slowly, reading some notes he had taken on the life of Tchaikowsky, "Musing on his sad [homosexual] experiences and comparing the sadness and frustrations existing in our emotional and everyday life." He goes on to make a direct comparison to his own life, speaking of "the analogy of the sentiments and emotional need resident in my own consciousness resolving itself to accepting the inevitable responsibilities . . . and the acceptance of one's destiny, seeing clearly the direction thru all the complexities occasioned by struggle, sorrow, enigma, or whatever."

six

New York: The Postwar Years

The summer and fall of 1945 were spent working on several large cityscapes, among the most important of which are an oil on canvas of the Greene Street scene he had painted so often before and the now well-known *Can Fire in the Park* that belongs to the Smithsonian Institution.

In the Greene Street painting we find, as we do in all the cityscapes of the 1940s and 1950s, a continuing movement toward abstraction (see Color Plate 5). There are, however, recognizable and familiar Delaney objects—the lamppost with the one-way arrow, the manhole cover, the fire hydrant, the free-floating fire escape, the banner, which in this case is multicolored smoke from a street vendor's wagon. The lamppost contains a yellow light and is the primary structure at the painting's left. A building of sorts stands at the top of what is a flat-surfaced two-dimensional canvas and the fire escape is on the right, separated from the center by the smoke banner. At the lower center of the painting is an upside-down triangle of circles made up of two wagon wheels and the manhole cover. Attached to the wheels are two vendor wagons. Clear outlining divides the painting into

Can Fire in the Park, 1946. Oil on canvas, 24 x 30 in. Courtesy of the Smithsonian Institution.

architectural angled building blocks and the color is Fauve-like in its brightness. There is something of the style of Vlaminck or Derain's *Hyde Park*. It is a painting in which, as one critic has suggested, Delaney "made it clear that he did not view representation and abstraction as antithetical modes" (Heartney, p. 119).

The *Can Fire* painting also has the familiar objects—the circles—in this case as a manhole cover to the bottom right, balanced by the sun at the upper left—the lamppost with the arrow at the upper right, and an upside-down arrow sitting on its base at the lower left. The central focus is a trashcan emitting the light and heat of a fire lit for warmth by the street people standing around it. In this painting there is the usual free Fauve coloration, but the brush strokes are thick and more Van Gogh-like than ever and the faces of the people are altogether distorted in an impersonal expressionist manner. The design of the painting, in which the trashcan and the people are contained and somehow protected by the ordinary city objects and the sun, expresses, like so many Delaney cityscapes, community rather than despair.

Delaney's idea was to find, as his friend Henry Miller did, the beauty of the human condition in whatever form it took. At about the time he was working on the *Can Fire* painting he wrote to Miller, "The world situation has been terrific to integrate, and to keep on painting has been a major size job, however . . . there are more canvases and some of them I feel articulate some of the things we feel" (undated letter c, fall 1946). When Beauford used terms like "things we feel" or "our approach" with Miller he usually brought up or implicitly included their mutual friend Alfred Stieglitz.

Beauford saw Alfred Stieglitz at the John Marin show in the winter of 1946 and wrote to Miller to tell him about the show and report that Stieglitz continued to read and enjoy Miller's work (February 4, 1946). Miller wrote back praising both Stieglitz and Marin, but mainly praising Beauford as a "royal personage" whose "soul shines through." He suggested that Beauford borrow money in his name from Miss Steloff at the Gotham BookMart for sending the portrait of Miller to Big Sur (February 14, 1946). Beauford wrote back agreeing with these arrangements and announcing that he was involved in "some very vital and intense work both in painting and in other less pleasing efforts such as wall painting, stove repairing, frame making, and washing clothes" (March 1945). With Miss Steloff's help, he did send the painting on—as a gift—and Miller suggested that they might have prints made of it for publicity postcards.

In June Beauford went to Vinalhaven for his annual trip. He wrote to Miller— now his primary correspondent—describing the scene:

> We are away out in the wilderness of Maine on this island twelve miles from the mainland. Its beauty and primeval splendor awake in me wonders and memories covered over with many neon lights and so forth of the city. We use lamplight and fetch in wood to cook with, the smell of pine and sea air perfume the house and the stars at night lead us into mystical reveries which leave me silent and humble and mute with no way of otherwise expressing things. Sometimes I find myself singing old songs long since unremembered. (June 26, 1946)

Beauford reveled in his Maine stay, worked on paintings, and returned to New York, much revived in July.

But in New York he found himself once again in financial difficulty. He still had a teaching job at the Downtown Community School that paid only $30 a month, and he was able to hold on until the winter, when his failure to pay the rent led to an eviction threat and a humiliating solution. In desperation he wrote to a patroness, Marion Rosenwald Ascoli, wife of the founder and editor of the *Reporter* and daughter of philanthropist Julius Rosenwald, who had always been involved in black causes. His foundation would support James Baldwin in the writing of his first novel. He asked Mrs. Ascoli for $100, saying he was painting well but that "there always seems to be the shadow which follows the light" (journal draft). The loft was full of air leaks, he said, and besides needing to fix that problem he thought he might make the apartment "more comfortable" so as to be able to give private classes there twice a week. Mrs. Ascoli gave him the money and continued to buy paintings and to send Beauford money for many years.

In his journal he notes to himself, "One knows so few who are unafraid to assist if such they could." Yet Beauford found time to aid another painter whose difficulties resembled his own, suggesting in a note that she get in touch with anyone who had bought her paintings in the past and giving her a list of friends whom he thought might indeed help. The list included Brooks Atkinson, the drama critic, the art critic Robert Coates, Georgia O'Keeffe, Dorothy Norman, and Al Hirschfeld. Apparently these were friends he felt too embarrassed to ask for help himself.

During this period of tension, Beauford became disoriented. He imagined one night that a group of young people broke into his apartment and raped him. To avoid a repetition of the event he wandered the streets for several nights until he could get someone to stay in the apartment with him.

When a friend and patron arranged a lucrative portrait painting in Lebanon, Pennsylvania, it was necessary for Beauford to write out preparatory instructions for himself before going on the trip: "Repair scuffs. Clean pallet. Look over receipt for flesh tones. Wash a pull over and sport shirt. Be clean and most plain. Get ticket . . . to Lebanon Penn. . . . Carry no luggage to speak of save paintbox."

The year 1947 brought better times financially and several new friendships. At the suggestion of the Philadelphia painter Humbert Howard, Dox Thrash, the inventor of the Carborundum print process, and Dorothy Gates, a prominent supporter of the arts, the Pyramid Club of Philadelphia, made up of elite African-American professional people, invited Beauford to be the featured painter at their seventh annual art exhibition in February. Gates had been a friend since the 1930s. She was a Stieglitz, Dorothy Norman, and O'Keeffe connection and was one of the regulars at The Waldorf Cafeteria. Beauford often went to her home on West 4th Street for dinner and talk, and when he left for Paris in 1953 he deposited many of his paintings in her care. She remained a constant and intimate correspondent until her death.

As Beauford's mental health was still somewhat precarious, Joe Delaney went with him to Philadelphia at their mother's urging. This was the beginning of a kind of reconciliation between the brothers. Joe stayed with friends of his and Beauford was put up by friends of Dorothy Gates, Billy and Irene Rose who lived in the center of the old city. Irene, who was white, was active in the Schackmanite movement, a breakaway group from the Trotskyist wing of Communism. Billy was in "industry" (only a few knew the Henry Jamesian secret that he made "foundation garments"). The Roses, like Dorothy Gates, maintained a close relationship with Beauford throughout their lives, and often visited him in New York; Irene would even visit him in Paris.

Beauford was very well received at the Pyramid Club and one of its prominent members, Dorothy Warrick Taylor, a niece of the sculptor, Meta Vaux Warrick (Fuller), bought several of his Greene Street style paintings. Miss Warrick and her sister had Beauford for dinner at their Germantown house and later visited him at Greene Street. Alain Locke was a close friend of the Warricks and was reintroduced to Beauford's paintings at their home. He, too, visited the Greene Street loft with some regularity after that. The Pyramid catalogue included an introduction by Romare Bearden.

While in Philadelphia Beauford made a visit to a young man with whom he had begun to correspond. Richard Gibson, who would later become a writer, had first written to him after the publication of the Henry Miller essay, and Beauford had been impressed by his maturity and intelligence. He was surprised to discover, however, that his correspondent was a fifteen year old. Gibson remained a close friend for the rest of Beauford's life, visiting him in New York when he was on vacation from school and from Kenyon College and still later when he worked in Paris and Rome. Beauford told Gibson about Proust and talked a great deal about musicians—especially Roland Hayes and Marian Anderson. He took his young friend to Larry Wallrich's bookstore and to the Gotham. He took him to supper with Dorothy Gates, and introduced him to such celebrities as W. E. B. Du Bois and Willem de Kooning. Gibson remembered de Kooning trying to explain to Beauford how to better "market" his work and obtain grants. De Kooning gave up in despair when a smiling Beauford, clearly choosing not to comprehend the schemes, rolled his eyes, patted de Kooning on the arm, and said "Bless you, child."

Another new friend was Wilmer Francis Lucas, a student at New York University who introduced himself to Beauford one evening on a bench in Washington Square near the statue of Garibaldi. Lucas would later become a successful writer and teacher of African-American literature and culture. It soon was apparent to the painter and the young man that they had lots to talk about, and Lucas became almost immediately a member—with James Baldwin, Smith Oliver, and Richard Gibson—of the circle of young black men involved in arts and letters who treated the older painter as a guide as well as a drinking and eating companion.

Lucas spent many days and evenings with Beauford listening to records on his Victrola, learning about jazz and gospel and classical music. Sometimes he and Beauford would have beers in the evening at Ed Winston's, a favorite Delaney watering hole on 8th Street at University Place, or at Bickford's Restaurant, a block away on 6th Avenue. In both places all night conversations were common-place. Henry Miller frequented these restaurants as did Canada Lee, James Baldwin, and many other literary and theater people, all of whom knew Beauford well; to all of them he introduced the young Lucas.

By 1948 Beauford was finally recognized as a member of the expressionist movement in New York. He was given a solo exhibit at the Artists Gallery on 57th Street in May. He wrote to Billy Rose in May that the 57th street show meant something special to him because it justified the support by his friends of his "ter-ribly painful efforts to try to be articulate." The paintings he exhibited the *Art News* reviewer described as "shrill, asymmetrically patterned compositions" that "straddle a fence of modern painting dividing the pictorial hedonism of Matisse and the compulsive emotion of Van Gogh." Delaney's work, said the reviewer, was nevertheless very much his own, and it had "an exotic pulse" (May 1948).

The *New York Times* reviewer, however, still saw a "Negro artist" whose "can-vases are strictly patterned, almost primitive in fashion, exuberantly gay in mood and color, and represent[ing] metropolitan hurly-burly and Southern folk genre" (May 16, 1948, 2:8).One of the finest paintings of this group was one he had worked on and talked about for more than two years and finally completed in 1946. It is a thickly layered and complex work, an energetic, highly colored depic-tion of a black jazz quartet dominated by a candy-striped piano played by a woman in an elaborate hat. Although relatively figurative, the painting, like the Greene Street and Washington Square paintings of the period, is divided into geometric blocks all brought to the surface of the canvas. More than any other, this work reflects Beauford's love of jazz and his attempt to bring jazz rhythms and an African-American spirit into his art (see Color Plate 6).

Beauford sold a painting at the Artists Gallery. It was the first real money he had had in some time, and with it he and his friend Wilmer Lucas bought a huge block of ice and a large bottle of gin on Bleeker Street. They struggled up the narrow stairs at 181 Greene Street with their happy burden, put the ice in the bathtub, and, with James Baldwin and others, celebrated success and the coming of spring with music and drink.

Also in 1948 and in 1949 Beauford showed with other painters—black and white—at the Village Art Center's annual competition. In 1948 he won second prize for a portrait of James Baldwin. The *Art News* reviewer of the 1949 show,

Elaine de Kooning, liked his "thickly painted" *Vagrant* (February 1949). Another *Art News* reviewer liked his portraits "in the style of Van Gogh" and his "African still-lifes, using Arabic motifs" (January 1949).

In the summer of 1948 Dante left New York with the idea of living year round in Maine, and in November James Baldwin departed for Paris. In both cases the good-byes were difficult. Baldwin's trip was made possible by a Julius Rosewald Fund fellowship, officially recommended by Richard Wright and privately recommended via Mrs. Ascoli by Beauford. Ironically, Beauford had applied unsuccessfully for a Rosenwald Fellowship at the same time, with Henry Miller's support. He had hoped to go to Paris, too. At the emotional farewell party for Baldwin at the Calypso Cafe, it was agreed that Beauford should follow as soon as possible.

It was not long after the Pyramid Club show in Philadelphia that Beauford was approached by Michael Leon Freilich at the Roko Gallery on Madison Avenue. Beginning in 1949 he would exhibit regularly there and Freilich became his de facto agent. Freilich lived in the same building as Marcel Duchamp, the one-time Dadaist who had painted the famous *Nude Descending a Staircase*. With some amusement, Beauford would tell his friends that he, with Wilmer Lucas, had met Duchamp "descending the staircase" on a visit to Freilich. Freilich's Roko was one of the first midtown galleries to show black artists on a regular basis. In addition to Delaney, the Roko showed Rose Piper, Walter Williams, Charles White, Charles Alston, Charles Sebree, Norman Lewis, and Beauford's great friend Ellis Wilson.

Freilich was immensely popular; he was sometimes called "Baron Roko" by his friends because of his elegant appearance. Among these friends, who visited the gallery and whom Beauford met, were e.e. cummings, Lotte Lenya, and Marianne Moore. Beauford liked Freilich personally as well as professionally, and he also became close to Michael Leon's sister, Ann Freilich Schutz, and their brother, Lewis ("Happy"). Happy had learned spirituals when he was in the army in the South and loved to sing them with Beauford, whom he would take for drives in his broken down car. Their favorite "number" was "Swing Low Sweet Chariot." Whenever Beauford visited Ann at her mother's house in the Bronx or her own apartment on Hudson Street he would greet her by saying, "Come to the window, come to the window Sister Ann" and would recite all or part of a poem by James Peale Bishop (1892–1944) called "Perspectives Are Precipices." The poem's refrain is "Sister Anne, Sister Anne,/Do you see anybody coming?" It ends, "I saw a man but he is gone/His shadow gone into the sun." Sometimes Beauford would earn extra money by baby-sitting for Ann's daughter Erica. Beauford always said Erica was the best interviewer he ever had; she spent their time together bombarding him with questions about his early life with his brothers and sisters in Knoxville. Erica remembers him as a "big Buddha," who was warm, benign, and loving.

The Freilichs were at the center of a group of friends and colleagues—primarily artists who painted in various forms of the modernist mode—with whom Beauford became close in the late 1940s and early 1950s. These included Sam Spanier, Dorothy Block, Sidney Wasserman, Paul England, Eli Freedensohn, and Theodore Cox. The Roko association gave Beauford not only a midtown place to show his work but a whole community of young modernist painters who met and discussed each other's work.

Beauford's first exhibition at the Roko was in February 1949. It was a group show of black artists to honor Negro History Week. The paintings were for the most part expressionistic. The *Art Digest* reviewer took note of the "violently impasto *Snow Scene* of Beauford Delaney" (February 15 1949). Elaine de Kooning, in *Art News*, also admired the "abstractly conceived" *Snow Scene* for its "style, mood . . . boldness of [impasto] technique" and for its "startling colors," and she particularly noticed the "even more violent impasto" of his *Still-Life with Fruit* (February 1949). A painting of a specifically African-American subject was *Harlem Blue*, in which a nighttime Harlem setting is treated essentially in the Greene Street manner.

Beauford exhibited a second time in 1949 at a Roko group show (in which he was the only black artist). Among the "freshest in tone and most inventively composed" of the paintings in the June show, according to Elaine de Kooning in *Art News*, was Delaney's "violently painted street-scene" (Summer 1949) (see Color Plate 5).

Back in Greenwich Village, Beauford was now more of a character and celebrity than ever, so much so that he was able to act on the art class plans he had outlined earlier to Mrs. Ascoli. For several months the painter held "Philosophy of Art" seminars on Tuesday nights in his candle-lit studio. In the first session, Beauford, dressed in a silk smoking jacket, surrounded by portraits of famous African Americans, lectured on "The Enigma of Art." After the talk a model was presented, and the guests were instructed on how to do charcoal sketches. Later there was singing by Mrs. Carrie Yates and a talk by Mrs. Bessy Embry on the life of the Negro when abroad. Finally, hostess members of the group served tea and caviar. The "hostesses" included Mrs. Gertrude Robinson, Alberta Persons, Clara Long, Ann McVey, Ollie DeLoach, Nell Occomy Becker, and Dorothy Gates. At one of the Tuesdays Dorothy Gates, the "registrar" of the group, lectured on contemporary African-American art. The lecture was followed by a "studio recital" and a "bohemian party," including dinner.

PLATE 1 *Tennessee Landscape,*
1922. Watercolor on paper,
20 x 13 in. Courtesy of the Beck
Cultural Center, Knoxville, Tenn.

PLATE 2 *Joseph Delaney,* 1933.
Pastel on paper, 17 x 15 ½ in.
Courtesy of the Michael Rosenfeld
Gallery.

PLATE 3 *Dark Rapture,* 1941.
Oil on board, 34 x 28 in. *Photo-
graph by Manu Sassoonian.
Courtesy of Ernie Bynum and
Dennis Costin (Ernden).*

PLATE 4   *Greenwich Village,* 1945.
Oil on canvas, 26¼ x 38 ¼ in.
Photograph by Manu Sassoonian.
Courtesy of Ernden.

PLATE 7 *Washington Square,*
1952. Oil on canvas, 40 x 60 in.
Courtesy of the Michael Rosenfeld
Gallery.

PLATE 5 *(top left)* *Greene Street,*
1946. Oil on canvas, 20 x 26 in.
Photograph by Manu Sassoonian.
Courtesy of Ernden.

PLATE 6 *(bottom left)* *Jazz Quartet,*
1946. Oil on canvas, 28 x 36 in.
Courtesy of the Michael Rosenfeld
Gallery and the owner.

PLATE 8 *Marian Anderson*
Poster in Greenwich Village, 1951.
Oil on canvas, 45 ½ x 35 in.
Courtesy of the Michael Rosenfeld
Gallery.

PLATE 9 *Elwood Peterson,*
1967. Oil on canvas, 21 x
25 ½ in. *Courtesy of Elwood
Peterson.*

PLATE 10 *Nativity Scene,*
1961. Oil on canvas, 19 ½ x
23 ½ in. *Courtesy of Solange
du Closel.*

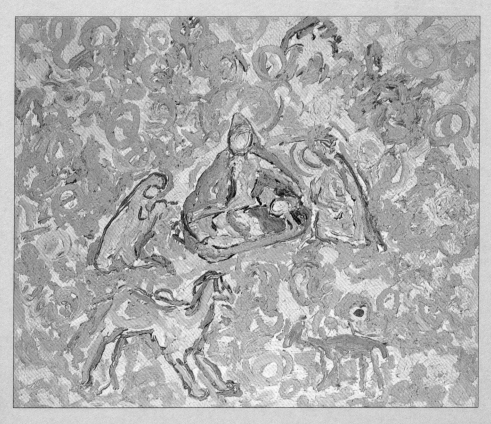

PLATE 11 *Abstraction,* 1962. Oil on canvas, 57 x 45 in. *Courtesy of the Michael Rosenfeld Gallery.*

PLATE 12 *(top right)* *Rosa Parks,* 1970. Oil on canvas, 21 ¼ x 25 ½ in. *Courtesy of the Michael Rosenfeld Gallery.*

PLATE 13 *(bottom right)* *Nurse and Baby Carriage,* 1940. Oil on canvas, 19 x 23 in. *Courtesy of the Michael Rosenfeld Gallery.*

PLATE 18 *Jean Genet,* 1972. Oil on canvas, 36 x 24 in. *Courtesy of the Darthea Speyer Gallery.*

PLATE 19 **Sun and Moon,** 1970. Watercolor and charcoal on paper, 19 ¾ x 25 ½ in. *Photograph by Manu Sassoonian. Courtesy of the owners.*

PLATE 20 **Saint Paul de Vence,** 1972 Oil on canvas, 25 x 21 in. *Courtesy of the Clark-Atlanta University Art Galler*

PLATE 21 *Self-portrait,*
1972. Gouache on paper,
12 ½ x 9 ½ in. *Collection*
of the author.

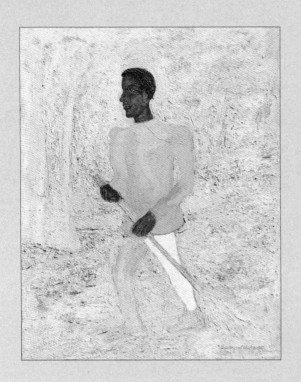

PLATE 22   *Street Sweeper,* 1968.
Oil on canvas, 25 ½ x 32 ½ in.
Photograph by James LeGros.
Courtesy of James and Bunny
Legros.

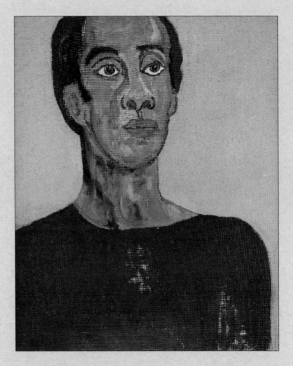

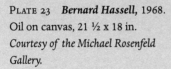

PLATE 23   *Bernard Hassell,* 1968.
Oil on canvas, 21 ½ x 18 in.
Courtesy of the Michael Rosenfeld
Gallery.

An amusing offshoot of Beauford's fame is the inclusion of his recipe for Southern Gumbo in a collection called *Greenwich Village Gourmet*, issued by Bryan Publications in 1949. The book included 100 recipes by Village people in the arts, including such notables as Stuart Davis, Kenneth Fearing, Dorothy van Doren, and Eleanor Roosevelt. Beauford's recipe comes under the category "Studio Supper: Sea Food and Meat." At the end of the recipe, which he had learned from his mother, the painter notes with evident racial pride that "Gumbo was brought to America by Negroes, from Dahomey, W. Africa, where it originated" and from where, according to Delaney tradition, his maternal grandfather had come. The editors note that the recipe is "A good one" (p. 38). It was served at Dorothy Gates's bohemian party at Beauford's studio.

In December the Village Art Center celebrated three favorite sons—Beauford, his good friend Paul England, and Alfred Van Loen—with a show of their watercolors. And in January and February 1950, Beauford was given a solo exhibit at the Roko Gallery. The paintings he showed were his most expressionistic yet, and the critics responded favorably. Ruthven Todd in *Art News* spoke of the "bright and personal expressionistic view of the great big wonderful world he lives in" (February 1950). There were Washington Square and Greene Street paintings, portraits of Dante, including one of a strangely disembodied and ethereal head and folded hands that emerge from a dominant multicolored coat full of lively shapes and one in which the subject is depicted in something of a parody of the early American "ancestor" paintings of the seventeenth and eighteenth centuries. There is a particularly expressionistic still life—a bowl of fruit brought up vertically to the canvas surface and enclosed by angled shapes. Ben Wolf comments in *Pictures on Exhibit* (No. 12, February 1950, p. 24) on "the artist's predilection for impasto technique" in the still life and admires the sense of composition in all the work. Marynell Sharp in *The Art Digest* (January 15, 1950, p. 16) is enthusiastic in her appraisal, finding in the paintings a "fertile imagination" that has "never relaxed in the search for new devices to express the solitude, chaos, all the discordant elements found in contemporary living" and to make them "harmonious" and beautiful. Sharp sees in the Greene Street paintings with their "vitally explosive color and rhythmic, singing design" something of the painter's "ancient African heritage." There is, she says, a "mystical African flavor" in the paintings.

In May one of Beauford's Greene Street paintings was seen by Henry McBride in *Art News* as one of the few "bright spots" in a show at the Whitney Museum (May 1950, p. 58). Only John Marin's *Sea Movement in Grey* rivaled it.

In March 1950 Beauford made a trip to Knoxville to visit his mother; he had not been back in ten years. After Washington, on the Jim Crow car, he wrote in

Dante, 1950. Oil on canvas,
21 ½ x 25 ½ in. Courtesy of
the owner.

his journal. He noticed the "first fly of the season" in Lynchburg at 4 A.M. and
mused on the gentleness of the people in the car and at how "amazingly knowing
the women are and vibrant." He watched the people eating and trying to sleep.
And he remembered a Mahalia Jackson song: "I'm glad salvation is free—free for
you and me." He noted that he had stayed awake all night. Nearing home he "saw
the Morning Star over Hog Back Mountain looking primeval and looming, as a
harbinger of hope to humble people who need an everlasting symbol."

The family was there in Knoxville at the station to meet him, Delia looking
surprisingly well for her eighty-five years and Emery and Gertrude full of love
and welcome. Their children were delighted, as always, to see "Uncle Beauf."
The few days were full of visits to and from family friends, and there was the Sunday morning at church and the obligatory words to the congregation about his
work and the kindness of people he knew in the North.

Back in New York Beauford prepared for a new adventure. A group of friends,
at the instigation of Michael Freilich, had convinced him to apply for a two-

month fellowship at Yaddo, a writer's and artist's colony near Saratoga Springs, New York. The idea was to get him away from the everyday cares of supporting himself so that he could concentrate on moving his painting toward the more abstract form of expressionism that now interested him. The application succeeded and, after a stay with Dante in Maine, Irene Rose and Dorothy Gates drove him to Saratoga on September 5 and settled him in his East House quarters, where there were two studios, the other one occupied by the poet Elizabeth Bishop. Others at Yaddo at the time included poet May Swenson, critic Alfred Kazin, and composer Alexi Haieff.

At first Beauford was miserably homesick, but the bucolic setting, the free time, and the good and ample food pleased him greatly and he found himself working with a new energy on paintings that, although still containing figurative elements, were much more abstract than anything he had done before. He read a great deal—especially Henry Miller's essay on Rimbaud and a book on Appollonaire. He also quickly made good friends of Kazin, Swenson, and especially Elizabeth Bishop.

Bishop and Beauford shared an interest in the blues, classical music, conversation, and drinks. Pauline (Polly) Hanson, the Assistant Director at Yaddo, remembered Beauford and his friendship with Bishop. When Beauford arrived "his feet hurt and he didn't have the right shoes. He emanated warmth and love." With Bishop he was somehow "maternal" (Fountain, p. 120). The two friends would sit in rocking chairs in the area between their studios each afternoon and have a number of drinks before joining the other guests for dinner. Both had symptoms of manic depression—Bishop more acutely so at the time—and they did a great deal of soul sharing. It is very likely that his time with Bishop led Beauford to write to Henry Miller that the Yaddo stay was "enlightening and has released several sides of my own being to me by close contact with various factors of the psyche and perspectives of some of my friends here who are guests" (October 21, 1950).

Elizabeth and Beauford would sit together at dinner, and after dinner Beauford was often asked to sing. Hanson remembered Alfred Kazin saying "Oh, Beauford, if there were only something in the world I could do for you. You don't know what your singing does for me" (Fountain 120). Beauford suggested that Kazin might sing, too, and he did—chants from the *Torah*. One evening one of the Yaddo guests, Matti Haim, was wondering aloud in a somewhat philosophical manner why lions ate smaller animals, when Beauford suddenly cast his eyes upward and said very gently—as to a child—"Matti, maybe the lion is just *hungry*." On another occasion as Polly Hanson was sitting for a portrait Beauford stopped drawing and began gently lecturing her on "living too much to [her]self . . . in too New England a way" (Hanson to BD, December 4, 1963).

In a September letter to Dorothy Gates, Beauford describes an evening with Malcolm Cowley, who was visiting Yaddo as a member of the board of judges:

> . . . the party began very formally. One of the lady guests sang Schubert lieder very affectively and we were very attentive and proper. Finally, when the music was over we served Tom Collinses mixed by yours truly to all and sundry and then Mr. Cowley held forth for a great while—his is a big shaggy man and the ladies tittilate and baby him right much. Finally, however, that great gentleman, augmented by much gin, receded to being more personal and of course all of us were allowing our drinks to sooth our weary beings when one bright genius located the phonograph and lo and behold Count Basie with Generous James Rushing singing "The Good Morning Blues." Well, at that the lid flew off and youth and age were served alike . . . skipping the light fantastic.

It was during his stay at Yaddo that Beauford started talking seriously of following Baldwin and other friends to Paris. He wrote to Miller that after he got back to New York he hoped to "get rid of all my junk and go over to Paris for a while and look around and grow and feel and contemplate some of the things which have been accumulating in myself" (September 29, 1950). He had also told various people that he hoped to go to Rome, where Richard Gibson was.

The first Yaddo period ended on a tragi-comic note. A group of the fellows decided to go to the trotting races in Saratoga and asked Beauford to join them. He had almost no money and was surprised to find he had to pay for an admission ticket. As he wrote to Larry Wallrich, he thought that "being possessed of broom sticks and divining rods" he could recoup his loss by betting on the races and so "come to the great city loaded up with Whitney [the Whitney family owned the track] money" (October 26, 1950). Unfortunately, he "picked dogs and nags each time" and lost the little money he had that was intended to get him back to New York. Once again he had to ask friends to advance him funds.

Beauford's last years in New York were hectic. He painted at a furious pace trying to sell enough work to stave off the always threatening landlord. Meanwhile his reputation as an expressionist grew among the avant-garde. But as Brooks Atkinson wrote in his 1951 book *Once Around the Sun*, "No one knows exactly how Beauford lives. Pegging away at a style of painting that few people understand or appreciate, he has disciplined himself, not only physically but spiritually, to live with a kind of personal magnetism in a barren world" (p. 67). Atkinson's description of Beauford is of a man who "has the authority of a Prophet. Everyone feels relaxed and secure when he is around . . . when he speaks, his words rise out of many long, pinched years of lonely meditation" (p. 67).

Beauford with a new Greene Street painting, 1951.

Beauford continued showing at the Roko Gallery. In March he participated in a show called *Contemporary Americans* with other members of the regular Freilich group. His highly abstract *Yaddo*, a landscape, was noticed by Larry Campbell in *Art News* (March 1951). There was a June show as well in which he showed canvases that Belle Krasne in *Art Digest* referred to as "violently colored" (June 1, 1951).

Beauford returned to Yaddo for November 1951 after a long summer stay with Dante in Maine and prepared for a major show at the Roko in January 1952. During the Vinalhaven summer, Yaddo fall, and the following winter, he created some of his greatest work. Paul Branch, writing in *The Art Digest* (January 15, 1952, p. 18) about the Roko show, praised the "spirited canvases, bouncing with an unrepressed enthusiasm for life." He particularly admired the heavy outlining of figures that "gives extra focus and vibrancy to widely scattered images." Branch did not much like the first totally nonobjective work that the artist had exhibited, a painting called *Cosmos*, but it marked an important departure for the painter and pointed to the Paris years to come.

Earth Mother, 1950. Oil on canvas,
36 x 21 in. Courtesy of the
Delaney Estate.

Among the most significant works in the show were the new Washington
Square paintings with their free and imaginative use of geometric forms that contain individualized activities—lovers in each other's arms, a man playing a guitar,
a white chicken, people around the fountain (see Color Plate 7). Each block of
activity seems oblivious of any other—the way things, in fact, often seem in large
cities—but the disunity is overcome, the Delaney sense of community and joy
articulated by the architecture of the painting, a structure that depends as much
as anything on a tight interweaving of dominant colors, especially the characteristic Delaney yellows and reds. In this sense these are blues paintings that turn
chaos into joy, or paintings that, like the beat poetry of the time, point back to the
optimistic American inclusiveness of Walt Whitman.

    Several paintings of black subjects, most of them done in 1950–1952, are among
the best works of the early 1950s. The paintings have in common a bringing

together of black subject matter with the expressionist Delaney style, now more fully developed. A heavily outlined African *Earth Mother*—a subject seemingly reinterpreted by way of Picasso's paintings based on African sculpture—kneels between exotic but abstractly represented vegetation and holds up a dark object as an act of worship. A painting called *Rehearsal* is also representational—a depiction of what appears to be a church choir rehearsal— but the dynamic relationships between the shapes of the heads of the figures and the shapes on the windows behind them and the angles and curves of their robes are as important a subject here as any event depicted. The same kinds of relationships can be seen in a painting of a jazz club, in which we see an audience, the band, and dancers, but are most aware of the mood of exhilaration created by the architectural composition from left to right and from top to bottom on a flat surface.

An earlier 1951 painting had placed Marian Anderson in a poster overlooking a geometrical cubist-like but vibrantly colored street scene (see Color Plate 8). It tells us of the singer's importance, the dominance of the beauty and power she represented over life itself in the painter's mind. All these paintings bring to mind, as Eleanor Heartney has suggested, elements of jazz with their "visual rhythms and improvisational quality" (p. 119). But despite their sense of joy, they also contain the melancholy aspect of the blues, an aspect that Beauford would naturally have associated with the position of his people in American society. This was a position made particularly articulate to Beauford in James Baldwin's "Many Thousands Gone," the essay on Richard Wright's *Native Son*. He read the essay in the *Partisan Review* (November–December 1951) and admired it.

This melancholy note was increasingly personal as well. It is clear from Beauford's most personal correspondence at the time, which was with his friend Larry Wallrich who, plagued by depression himself, had gone off to live on the Navajo reservation in Arizona. Beauford wrote to Larry sympathizing "with the great unrest of which you speak." He attributed the feeling to the artist's "need to see, move, and live all at once" and confessed that "recently I have had a real need for thinking within myself and deeply trying to understand my true needs." (April 7, 1952). In a later letter he complains of an inability to be articulate (May 20, 1952), And still later he speaks of being "so burdened down with charm and good things" that he is in danger of having "psychological indigestion" (July 14, 1952).

In June Beauford showed still again at the Roko, this time in a group show. Larry Campbell, the *Art News* reviewer, noticed the painter's use of pie-like triangles to create "allotted stations" for a community of "carnival people" in a painting entitled *Guitar Player* (Summer 1952, p. 103). This combination of the architecture, masses of violent color, and playfulness—really the essential Delaney style in all

Jazz Club, 1951. Oil on canvas, 28 x 36 in. Photograph by Joe O'Reilly. Courtesy of the owner.

the Greene Street–Washington Square paintings of the 1940s and early 1950s—is interesting in light of a 1952 journal scribble: "Braque and Dufy are about the best." Beauford also saw and was inspired by a "great exhibition of Cézanne" at the Metropolitan Museum of Art in April.

The painter Paul Jenkins was among the last reporter-visitors to the Greene Street studio. He climbed the dark stairs in late August 1952. By now the studio was a landmark in the art world. It had been visited, after all, by Henry Miller, Alain Locke, Stuart Davis, Alfred Stieglitz, Georgia O'Keeffe, Al Hirschfeld, W. C. Handy, Teddy Wilson, and James Baldwin to mention only a few of Beauford's celebrity admirers. When Baldwin had opened the Greene Street door and seen Beauford for the first time he had thought of the old song "Lord, Open the Unusual Door." When Jenkins opened the door he "walked into the life of a man or the imprint of the man himself which effects us." Jenkins saw the "monastic order about everything," the walls covered by clean white paper, the furniture and paintings draped in white sheets. Then he saw the rich array of paintings brought out one by one—each given the full attention made possible by the noninterfering whiteness of the room. He saw the "screaming fire" of the yellows, the "peacock blue," the "peppermint green," and the "Pomegranate Heart's Blood." He saw the war between "two heroes"—Matisse and Van Gogh.

What Jenkins could not have known was that this was the end of an era, that in a few days the 181 Greene Street studio would be empty, the building sold and turned into a plastics factory, the painter desperately trying to bring order to a loft at 713 Broadway.

The move cost money and Beauford accepted with appreciation gifts from friends, including an overcoat and some shirts and trousers from Henry Miller. In his thank you note Beauford told Miller, "My painting continues and I am aware that it becomes more itself, which pleases me" (November 15, 1952). But he felt a certain emptiness in his life. A quick trip to visit Dante in Maine helped, as did long conversations with Dorothy Gates, "a wonderful comfort in my confusion" (September 21 to Irene Rose). In his journal Beauford considered change and the need to live a life that met his personal as well as his aesthetic needs. In one list of things to do—laundry, letters, buy bookshelves— he adds, poignantly, "some attention to romance."

In January there was a final solo show at the Roko. Beauford exhibited some of the new Washington Square paintings, a version of his Harlem church *Rehearsal*, and one of the interior of McSorley's Bar. Again the critics noted the impasto technique, the unbridled coloration, and the tendency to break the paintings into fragments (e.g., Chris Ritter in *The Art Digest*, January 1, 1953, p. 21). Betty Holliday wrote in *Art News* of the painter's continued use of "Fauvish colors" but noticed that "joyous tapestries" of the immediate past had given way to a new, more "solemn" mood in paintings like *McSorleys* and *Rehearsal* (January 1953, p. 65). Stuart Preston in the *New York Times* was more aware of the "hedonist" aspect of the paintings and called Delaney a "visual mythologist."

After an April group show at the Roko at which he exhibited, among other things, his African *Earth Mother*,and several new mostly abstract paintings, Beauford was ready to leave (see *57th Street Review*, April 1, 1953, p. 25).

Jim Gaston, a wealthy young medical student he had met through Dante, had given him money for his ticket and other friends—Al Hirschfeld and Ben Wasserman—had also. Gaston sent him a copy of the April issue of *Holiday*, which had an article on Paris. If he was ever going to travel to the home of so many of the modernist painters he admired he would have to go now. Not knowing what to do with his paintings, he left some at the Roko and some in the Broadway loft. Many of the latter were never seen again. Some were taken as collateral by the landlord when Beauford failed to pay his rent after he left, some were recovered

Dante and Beauford
in Vinalhaven, 1953.

by his friends Dorothy Gates and Larry Wallrich, who closed down the apartment for him. Some were simply stolen. Beauford took twenty-two paintings to Dante in Vinalhaven—including a series of five Dante portraits. It is not clear whether the intention was to give them away or store them. In any case, when Dante eventually vacated his house in Vinalhaven he sent some of the paintings to Dorothy Gates and some—including the portraits—Gates apparently sent to Beauford in Paris. It seems likely that Beauford was simply overwhelmed by the amount of material he needed to dispose of and that he hoped to sort things out on his return. It is clear from his correspondence that he intended to return after what he saw as a summer vacation in Paris (and perhaps Rome).

Yet part of him must have wondered if he ever would come back. It seems possible that he sensed the need for a new scene altogether rather than a move down the street. After sixteen years in Greene Street, 713 Broadway did not seem right. The loss of the Greene Street loft and its particular view was something like the loss of Mont Saint Victoire would have been for Cézanne. And he was perhaps already tired of being a Village legend. The journal *Our World* had interviewed him for still one more article on the quaintness of his existence and that of a few other black painters in the bohemian Village (VIII, February 1953, p. 2).

Delia Delaney, 1953. Mixed
media on paper, 23½ x 18¼ in.
Courtesy of the Delaney
Estate and the Ewing Gallery,
University of Tennessee.

Furthermore, he was on the verge of developing a new style of painting that new
surroundings might stimulate.

There was certainly a sense of finality in his hasty visit to Knoxville in August.
A mere vacation abroad would not normally have required such a visit. While he
was there he asked many questions about family history and went through family
papers, as if this would be a last chance to do so. Beauford wrote to Larry Wallrich on August 9 that the trip was "filled with important implication," that is, he
sensed it was very possibly a final visit with his mother. While he was in Knoxville
he did a pastel portrait of her.

Finally, before leaving for Europe he jotted some notes in his journal that
seem to suggest the end of a major segment of his life:

The innumerable varieties of adventures we are compelled to make, and the
initiations we are obliged to go through . . . begin to make sense and add up

Beauford leaving on the *Liberté*, 1953.

so long as we can keep working and accepting the various elements of living which make up the great wide canvas of our life. A long and very arduous experience has been covered by me and none of it could have been eliminated. . . .Therefore I would urge continued application of ones deepest and most personal and sincere powers to the completion of work.

On August 22 he went to the penthouse of his patroness Mrs. Ascoli to make final arrangements about payments to be made to him for work done and work commissioned. He arrived early and was left alone for a while with a cigarette and a glass of Dubonnet. His mind wandered "reflecting on many things—feelings of nostalgia and apprehension, of love and sorrow, of joy and regret, of things known and unknown, of a rededication of faith hope and love, of willingness to accept the challenge and do the best I can with it" (Journal August 22, 1953).

On August 28 a large number of friends saw Beauford off on the *Liberté*. He would never see New York again. A new variety of adventure had begun, and there was no turning back. He was completing the last long step of what James Baldwin called his "deliberate walk from Knoxville to Paris."

seven —

Paris: The First Years

The passage from New York to Le Havre was one of the happiest inter-
ludes of Beauford's life. On the French ship he was treated with respect,
and had the rare luxury of comfortable quarters, three full meals a day,
and a midnight snack. Life had never been so easy for him. Drinks at the bar were
cheap, too, and, in any case, for once there was no shortage of money. There
were no immediate worries about the future either as Gaston and another patron
had promised to send him money every month that he was away, and Al
Hirschfeld had arranged for introductions by way of Richard de Rochemont to
Yvonne Oberlin and Pierre-Andre Weill in the Paris gallery world. Furthermore,
he had good company on board. Herbert Gentry, a young African-American
painter had been introduced to him by Joe Delaney at the Waldorf Cafe. Gentry
was interested in the kinds of aesthetic questions that concerned Beauford. There
was a genuine community of interest between the two and they enjoyed each
other's company immensely.

Beauford wrote to Henry Miller full of happiness over the trip; even the
sea, which he had dreaded, remained "calm and variable the whole way over"

(September 7, 1953). He told Larry Wallrich that "the sea cradled and soothed me" (September 6, 1953).

To Dorothy Gates he described a particularly exciting night on the ship:

> Two nights before landing in France the purser came to my cabin and asked me to appear on the impromptu program they were giving., Naturally I was nervously concerned as to why this honor, whereupon he very casually stated that on my passport my profession was "artiste" and that in France that meant performing. . . . So with much bourbon and beer I raised my drunken voice and sang to a drunken audience with much success" (September 1953).

In fact, Beauford was so successful that people asked him what club he would be singing in in Paris. The songs he performed were "Old Man River," "The Saint Louis Blues," and "Stormy Weather." This was the second public performance of a man who had once wanted to be a singer. An undated clipping from the 1940s announces that "Beauford Delaney . . . heretofore known for his luminous paintings, appeared last Friday night in another branch of the arts—singing . . . Negro spirituals at Times Hall."

When the ship docked, Beauford had difficulty gathering his luggage and somehow lost his friends. Settled in the train, however, he took note of the new scenery—first through slightly homesick eyes, then through those of a painter: "Passing through Normandy farm country watching the rural scene with farmers plowing and the rustic landscape with the peasant life free and slow in its rhythm reminded me very much of something in like manner in the deep south at home in the U.S.A." (1963 autobiographical notes). He admired the "natural splendor," and centered his attention on the light and a potential painting: "One of the first deep impressions of France on me was its light . . . the clear sort of strained light of Normandy . . . as we rolled along slowly through the farm land where occasionally one saw several horses being led away from the fields by a young man or woman amid the light, which included everything, the train as well; it all became one picture. . . ." He knew somewhere in the back of his mind that the validity of his journey—"the abstract comfort" of it—"was the light inscrutable, eternal, serene, wordless, yet sovereign, moving yet still including all things . . . silencing all things." Beauford had found his "higher power" in the light of France and although he did not know it then, he would never forsake it.

Yet by the time the train arrived at the Gare St. Lazare, Beauford was frightened. The voices that were always anxious to threaten his painter's confidence began to take over. They warned him that he knew no French, probably did not have enough money after all, that he had no place to stay, and too much luggage to carry. He found himself wondering "what would be the outcome of my being here in a foreign country so far away from home, not . . . finding any valid reason why somehow all this had come about." He felt "all of a sudden a large lump in my throat, realized I'm alone, know no one in Paris." Change of any sort was always difficult for Beauford and led him to fear the worst. He knew, in fact, several people in Paris: not only his shipboard companions, but several other New York friends, including Wilmer Lucas, who was there on a brief leave from the army, and James Baldwin, whom he had neglected to inform of his arrival date.

He looked for his friend Herb Gentry, but in the crowds could not see him. Gentry had told him about a hotel that he sometimes used near the Café de Tournon, a favorite spot of Richard Wright on the Left Bank. Beauford thought if he could find his way there he might also find Wright and then Baldwin and Lucas. But getting anywhere seemed impossible. Standing by his luggage, confused by the crowds, he began to feel a sense of panic, when suddenly staring at him from two feet away were two amazed "Negro friends from New York." These were the cartoonist Ollie Harrington and the printmaker Bob Blackburn who had come to the station to meet Gentry. "What on earth are *you* doing here?" one of them asked. "And where will you stay?" At about that time Gentry came up, and the friends took Beauford to a hotel on the boulevard Raspail in Montparnasse since the Hôtel de Tournon was full. Beauford would say in later years that the chance meeting saved him and that he had "never looked upon [it] as an accident" (notes).

Feeling restless and unable to sleep, he decided at about 11 P.M. to take a walk and buy a sandwich. He entered the first cafe he saw, the Dôme on the rue Delambre—from then on his favorite Paris cafe—and came face to face with a New York painter friend, Earl Kirkham "with a table full of Americans carrying on about painting and living." That first night at the Dôme was spent in talk and "amazement." At three or four in the morning Beauford stumbled "dazed and half drunk to bed."

The next morning he got up and wandered the streets after moving his things to another hotel suggested by his companions of the night before—the Hôtel Odessa on the rue d'Odessa near the Gare Montparnasse. The Paris in which he found himself that morning and the night before and the months and years that followed matched his painter's expectations:

Montparnasse had the appearance at that time of a painting by Renoir or any impressionist painter. There was about it something enduring and rustic—a tree lined avenue or boulevard with sidewalk cafes on either side. There was an atmosphere alive and vital day and night. . . . Some of the cafes never closed. I had never seen such life and could not suppress an eagerness to join into this rhythm and [soon] found myself there day and night. . . . Nights and days we would come together at mealtimes and swap our various experiences or relate how this activity in life and art were fused, what this group or that group thought of this or that school of painting, writing, music.

Beauford was finding in Paris what he needed—intellectual stimulus and a whole new scene for his painter's eye. In the unfamiliar light of Paris there was a new subject for painting on every street corner, in every puddle. With Gentry, Blackburn, Harrington, Kirkham, and a whole circle of young Americans, including painters Ed Clark, Bill Rivers, Sal Romano, sculptor George Sugarman, and later his good friend Larry Potter, and the sculptor Harold Cousins, and still later painters Bob Thompson, Bill Rivers, Bill Hutson, and Sam Middleton—many African American, many studying on the GI Bill, all working in the abstract mode—he could relax and explore the issues that concerned him most. He could discuss Cézanne, and Renoir, and Picasso, and Matisse in the very streets where they had been and in some cases still could be seen. Beauford was introduced to Picasso in a gallery, and for him it was like stumbling into a myth. Finally, there was little of the overt racism that as a black man he had inevitably experienced in New York. "Paris," he told Larry Wallrich, was "a dream and had handed me a jewel"(September 6, 1953):

> Time became different—not just an hour by the clock but a mysterious alive-ness from the tips of your toes to the top of your head, touching everything and everyone. This began to be Paris for me. The dilemma of the human experience never lost its sorrow or joy; it simply had a way of existing for long periods immune to both, and all as if one was moving along a musical score to the orchestration of a complete poem of the emotions, hearing and living the music of the place called Paris. (notes)

Beauford would explain to a reporter many years later that he had never intended to stay in Paris: "I came here for a peep, and there's an awful lot to peep at" (*International Herald Tribune* March 14, 1972). In that fall of 1953 he began by seeing as many exhibitions as he could to make the most of what he then thought of as his limited time. He especially enjoyed the memorial show to Raoul Dufy at the Musée d'Art Moderne and the paintings by Daumier, Goya, Van Gogh, and Cézanne that he saw at the Orangerie several times during his first week. He wrote to friends at home that he was sure he would be back within a matter of weeks. "I believe this will be a brief visit," he wrote to Henry Miller (September 7, 1953), and to many others he spoke of missing them and of the homesickness for New York that sometimes marred his enjoyment of Paris. To Larry Wallrich he confided that there was "a spirit of gravity which almost approaches grimness among the average Frenchman," and he assured his friend that he was "trying to prepare myself already for a return home" (September 23, 1953). He told Dorothy Gates that he would be "home" in two months (September 16, 1953). He would continue in this vein well into the mid-1950s when he would begin talking in letters of a "visit" to New York rather than a "return home."

Late on the afternoon of his first full day in Paris Beauford had made his way down to St. Germain des Près and was crossing the street between the Café Flore and the Brasserie Lipp when he heard a voice urgently shouting his name. In an instant, with horns honking all around him, he was wrapped in the arms of James Baldwin. Baldwin, who had been in Paris since 1948, recently had achieved success with the publication of *Go Tell it on the Mountain*. This was no longer the depressed little boy Beauford had found on his doorstep in 1940 but a young man well on his way to becoming a celebrity. Baldwin had been in the Flore having a drink with his friend Mary Painter when he spotted the familiar shape of the man who more than any other had been his boyhood mentor. Beauford immediately liked Mary Painter. She worked as an economist for the American embassy and was the woman Baldwin always said he would have married if he could have married anyone. Mary quickly became one of Beauford's closest friends and supporters, buying him gifts from the PX and white sheets, which he promptly unwrapped and used to drape over paintings and to cover his walls.

Beauford and Baldwin, sometimes joined by Baldwin's lover, the young Swiss, Lucien Happersburger, and by Bernard Hassell, an African American who danced with the Folies-Bergère, often spent long evenings at Mary Painter's apartment on the rue Bonaparte, drinking PX whiskey and listening to Marian Anderson, Mahalia Jackson, Bessie Smith, and Beethoven on the record player. Mary was an excellent cook and would prepare meals that particularly pleased Beauford, and the conversation at the table was lively. Baldwin would shout down the others with prophetic outcries against racism while Lucien urged him to be calm. Mary would bring food into the conversation; she and Beauford would discuss drinks with an almost mystical appreciation, and Bernard would entertain the group by playing the outrageous temperamental *tapette*.

Often Beauford would be called upon to sing, and he would talk. With his hands folded before him and eyes closed, he would dole out complex if not always comprehensible philosophy. He had a tendency to use particular words—

"ostensibly," "paradoxically," "yakity-yak," and "enigmatic" were favorites—without any specific concern for meaning, rather the way many people use "uh" or "um." He also liked telling stories of his Knoxville past, and he especially amused his listeners with imitations, like the one of a directive woman in his father's church whose self-appointed mission was to keep the "sisters" in line. Beauford would stand up toward the end of the "take" with eyes wide, hands flapping in the air, and in a high-pitched voice would screech the woman's eternal words: "We've got to get BUSY, BUSY; Lord, we've got to get BUSY!!" And usually at this point he would do just that by returning to his garret to write in his journal or sketch.

From his arrival in Paris until the end of his life Beauford became increasingly dependent on Baldwin in an emotional sense, suffering bouts of depression whenever his friend left Paris or forgot—as he often did—to keep an appointment with him. Given a choice as to whom he would spend an evening with Beauford would always have chosen James Baldwin. In fact, the evening of the meeting with Baldwin in front of the Flore marked the beginning of a tradition of nights on the town with "the brothers" that was a side to Beauford's Paris experience in many ways separate from his cafe life with his painter friends, although the two lives did sometimes coincide.

Baldwin had met up with Wilmer Lucas in Paris the day before Beauford arrived and for three days and nights Baldwin, Lucas, and Delaney "did the town" after Lucas and Baldwin and Sal Romano moved the painter from the Odessa to what was, in effect, his first real Parisian home, the Hôtel des Écoles at 15 rue Delambre. The top floors of this hotel were rented as one-room studios by artists as poor as Beauford; the price was the equivalent of about $1 per day for a garret studio. Lucas had to return to the army after a few days, and Beauford did not see him again for many years. But the nights out continued on a fairly regular basis. The group usually included, in addition to Baldwin and Beauford, Bernard Hassell, and the composer Howard Swanson, with whom Beauford had a lifelong close friendship. Sometimes Chester Himes, the young West Indian writer Ernest Charles "Dixie" Nimmo, and various other African American and, more often than not, gay friends would join the circle.

These were nightclub rather than cafe outings and they were always led and, when he had money, paid for by Baldwin, who now, in a reversal of his New York role vis à vis Beauford, became his old mentor's guide. The places of choice were jazz clubs: the Montana at St-Germain, Gordon Heath's Echelle de Jacob on the rue d'Abbaye, where Beauford and Baldwin both liked to take the microphone to sing—sometimes together—and Inez Cavanaugh's Chez Inez. Other spots—

more to Baldwin's liking than those of the heterosexuals in the party and the always sexually shy Beauford—were two gay bars, also in St-Germain—the Reine Blanche and the Fiacre. A favorite eating place for the Baldwin group and most African Americans in Paris was Haynes's, a soul food restaurant in Pigalle run by Leroy Haynes and his French wife Gaby. Beauford painted a portrait of Haynes, which still hangs in the restaurant on rue Clauzel.

Occasionally the group would drop in on Richard Wright and his friends at the garishly decorated Café de Tournon run by the eccentric Madame Alazard across from the Luxembourg Gardens. Beauford knew all the people he was apt to meet there—a Nigerian poet called Slim Sunday who always dressed in black leather, writer William Gardner Smith, Ollie Harrington, Larry Potter, Herb Gentry, Gordon Heath, and Wright himself. Wright had helped James Baldwin in his last years in New York, and they had a mutual friend in Chester Himes, who was a connecting link between the Baldwin and Wright circles. The discussions at the Tournon usually returned to the question of expatriation, with Potter, Harrington, Himes, and Wright standing for a permanent break with racist America and Baldwin, with support from Beauford, arguing for the inevitable importance for African Americans of American roots. The meetings with Wright were infrequent, however. Wright felt uncomfortable with homosexuals and he resented Baldwin's published criticism of his work, so there was always a stiffness in the Tournon encounters. Although he did sometimes drop in at the Tournon—even alone—because he loved any kind of philosophical discussion as long as it was in English, Beauford never became particularly close to Wright.

Meanwhile, his own circle grew quickly. The painter Don Fink became a friend and so did Robert Graves's close associate and "muse" Judith Bledsoe, the writer Leslie Schenk, and artists Shirley Jaffe, John Franklin Koenig, and Gregory Masurovsky. Masurovsky was married to Shirley Goldfarb, whom Beauford had met in his New York days at the Art Students' League and with whom he maintained a close friendship in Paris. He also saw painters Sam Francis and Sam Spanier with some frequency. Beauford would later tell friends that Francis most influenced his early French experiments in abstraction. In Francis's paintings with their swirls of muticolored energy there is evidence of such influence. Still another artist friend was Costa Alex, who managed to get a reluctant Beauford onto a motorcycle for a ride around town, an experience both loved describing but never repeated.

Beauford particularly liked Joe Downing, an abstract expressionist from Kentucky with whom he loved to share southern memories, southern talk, and gay innuendoes. Downing had famous parties at his apartment on the rue Torigny—

complete with jazz bands and suckling pig—and sometimes when the evenings got wild the two men would dance together. And they loved entertaining their friends by reciting the words on the sign that stood outside Joe's hometown: "Horse Cave, City of Progress and Opportunity, where love brings joy in the heart of the tobacco land. Population 1200." But most of their time together was spent alone listening to jazz or sitting in semi-silence, in what Joe Downing called an "atmosphere of benediction." Beauford would drop in for a visit for no particular reason. The two men—one black, one white, both southerners—just liked being together.

Three relationships were the most important of the new Paris associations with American painters. These were the friendships begun in 1953 with Charley and Gita Boggs, Larry Calcagno, and Jim and Bunny LeGros.

Charley Boggs was a painter from West Virginia who, when Beauford arrived in Paris, lived with his wife Gita and their infant son Gordon in a large artist's studio apartment on the boulevard Montparnasse and later in an apartment on rue Procession. Still later Boggs moved to his much smaller studio in Cité Falguiere near the boulevard Pascal. Charley met Beauford casually in the company of many other painters in a Montparnasse cafe early in the fall of 1953.

But it was the first one-to-one encounter between the two men that set the protective and nurturing tone of a relationship that would continue until Beauford's death. When Beauford was sick with flu during his first October in Paris, Charley's wife Gita cooked a chicken broth that Charley delivered to him in the Hôtel des Écoles. From that time on Beauford visited the Boggs often—at unpredictable hours—and became an uncle figure and sometimes baby sitter to their child. Beauford was always happy to be fed, and at the Boggs apartment there were always good meals followed by music on the hi-fi—Mahalia Jackson, Mozart, and a particular favorite of Charley, Gita, and their guest: Albinoni's "Adagio in G-Minor for Strings and Organ." They always called the Albinoni piece "The Doom Music." But Charley associated it in his mind with "the slow progressive march of the human spirit" that he later saw represented also by Beauford's life. After his separation from his wife, Charley remained Beauford's close friend and the two men shared something of the secrets of their intimate lives and the difficulties of succeeding in the Paris art world.

Beauford met Larry Calcagno early on in his stay in Paris through Charley Boggs, who had met him in Florence in 1951. In Calcagno Beauford immediately recognized someone he could open up to. Also a homosexual, Larry was a handsome, gentle, highly sympathetic and loving man of forty who shared Beauford's dedication to art and particularly to abstract art. He was able to appreciate his friend's philosophical bent as well and recognize the depression that always lurked beneath his good nature.

Calcagno had a studio on the rue Vercingétorix near the avenue du Maine. After their introduction Beauford spent a great deal of time there. It is fair to say that he was in love with Larry Calcagno; the relationship was intellectually intense but for the most part physically platonic. The correspondence between the two after Larry left Paris for the United States early in 1954 was direct and intimate but not romantic. In Calcagno Beauford found a replacement for Dante Pavone, but without the emotional turmoil. It was Calcagno who gave Beauford the copy of Lao tsu that he nearly always carried with him and was fond of quoting. The two painters traveled together to Spain in 1955 and 1956. These trips were major landmarks of happiness in Beauford's life.

Over the years people wondered why in times of difficulty or of happiness Beauford would sometimes stop what he was doing, look somewhat vacant, and scratch one ankle with his other heel. This practice originated in a private joke between Larry and Beauford and developed into a kind of good luck gesture. *Calcagno* means heel in Italian and before he left for America after their trip to Spain in 1956 Larry had suggested to his friend that whenever he wanted to remember him he only needed to scratch his ankle with his heel. Beauford would often tell Larry in letters that he had "remembered" him in the prescribed way. Sometimes, indicating just a bit of something other than a platonic feeling, he admitted that "the scratching foot was a goat's."

It was through Calcagno that Beauford was introduced to James LeGros, who, with his wife Bunny, would become, with Charley and Gita Boggs, James Baldwin, and Bernard Hassell, his closest American Paris friends after Calcagno returned for good to New York. Jim and Bunny had come to Paris in 1952; Jim was studying art under the GI Bill. They lived in a small apartment in the rue du Seine in St-Germain. Calcagno took Jim to meet Beauford at the Hôtel des Écoles during his first month in Paris. LeGros's first impression of Beauford was of a small elegant man, dressed in an elaborate robe, his hair slicked down in the style of Nat King Cole. The studio room was full of paintings, some of which were Washington Square and Greene Street scenes sent from New York.

Much later the LeGros would move to Velizy, a suburb of Paris, and Beauford would refer to them as the "good people" or "dear friends in the country." Sometimes he would take the train to Velizy for fairly long visits. On other occasions he would walk there from Clamart; Beauford's walking feats became famous among his fellow Americans in Paris. The LeGros—perhaps especially Bunny—although they were much younger than Beauford, became almost surrogate parents. One night when Beauford was staying in Velizy the family heard him calling for his mother. Bunny called out that she was there, that everything was all right, that he should go back to sleep, and he did. He went to Velizy when he needed comfort and family intimacy.

The LeGros's child, Michelle, was born in 1955 and over the years that followed became one of Beauford's occasional baby-sitting charges. Michelle thought of him as a grandfather who sometimes picked her up at school. He became close enough to the LeGros that he even revealed the carefully kept secret of his dyed hair to Bunny in the late 1950s. Bernard Hassell had convinced his friend that he should not go gray, and when it was time to have the color renewed Beauford would bring what he called "the package" to Bunny and she would administer it. Bunny would also rub a lotion on Beauford's legs to ease the pain from the varicose veins of which she saw no sign. And she would listen patiently to his talk of persecution.

The LeGros were aware of Beauford's paranoia almost from the beginning. He told them how the people in his hotel and later in his apartments in Clamart and Montparnasse would talk about him and plot against him. The voices of paranoia and depression had followed him from New York. They could be held off temporarily by the society of friends outside in the cafes and sometimes by work. But work could be lonely, and at nighttime especially the voices were able to interrupt him. And his inadequacies in French—a problem he never overcame—led to his feeling sometimes that people on the street and in the cafes must be using that strange language to talk about him. He bought a French grammar and desperately tried to learn some of the language, making lists of words and phrases in his notebook: "Je suis = I am, tu es = you are, vous avez faim, n'est-ce pas? = you are hungry, aren't you?" and so forth. With his friends he seemed fine, but alone in his room he sometimes became desperate, both during the day and at night. For all his new acquaintances, he was "much to myself emotionally; my only outlet is my work" (letter to Wallrich, October 1953).

The fall and winter of 1953 were among the coldest in Paris's history. By the middle of October his room was freezing; he tried to paint but the small alcohol cooking stove could only warm his hands momentarily, and the unsympathetic hotelkeeper pointed out that the heat was never turned on before November 1; it was still fall, after all. By December it was unbearable outside and in: "It's so cold in Paris," he wrote in his journal, "the birds have ceased singing." Beauford would wrap himself in a blanket and talk to himself by way of occasional notes in his journal or on the backs of envelopes: "Best I move this easel to the right; it will be in a better light—just dozing, feeling sleepy" or "must think of a date for departure from Paris [but] weigh staying" and, speaking of his homesickness for New York,

> What's in America is perhaps not so important as I make it out to be. Could it be that I am afraid of the challenge. This must not be so.

About his homosexuality he writes,

> Remember that this is only a recurrence of something that has kept you company for years when you were at loose ends. . . . Now you will find a way to meet and live comfortably with this part of your nature. Naturally it will cost you something because you must do all the ground work, but it is never too late.

As if to keep the critical voices at bay he madly copied into his sketchbook the old songs that had eased the pain of his people in the American South: "Nobody Knows the Trouble I've Seen," "Steal Away to Jesus," "In That Great Getting Up Morning," and finally—over and over—"Oh fix me, oh fix me, fix me Jesus . . . fix me for my journey home." He copied blues songs of love, too, which he would sing when he was alone at night, sometimes with Bessie Smith on the phonograph. The copying of the blues songs in particular coincided with the departure of Larry Calcagno for America at the beginning of winter and with the sexual loneliness that was becoming overwhelming: "I can't keep from worrying cause I'm down in the dumps," "You say you're leaving and that you're going away,/but before you leave, dear, please let me have my say," and "Old empty bed springs hard as lead . . . I can't help what's on my face. What did I do to be so black and blue?"

In one journal scribble he writes in a wavering hand of a longing to be with "my lover" in the country. Did he mean Larry Calcagno? Sometimes he would read and re-read letters from home—especially from Larry Wallrich and Henry Miller, and later Calcagno (these men, with James Baldwin, were his primary correspondents for many years). He also read the letters from his brother Joe. Despite the earlier emotional distance between them, the brothers exchanged warm and loving letters on a regular basis after Beauford's arrival in Paris.

One Saturday night in December the voices were particularly powerful and Beauford left his room after a great deal to drink and wandered aimlessly around his quartier. At 1:30 in the morning he found himself in the Gare Montparnasse and made a vow to himself in writing:

> Do not let me ever forget or be unaware of the obligations to duty and consecration included in the profound and selfless devotion of years of knowing and watching loved ones, which being in Europe has not diminished. I make a

new troth on this eve of Sunday. Henceforward, that no matter what, never will I lose sight of the truth as I perceive it or lack the courage to change as it is revealed to me that change is necessary.

In his scribblings of October Beauford had noted the primary route of escape from the voices: "Begin by doing all that is possible with paint." And when the heat finally came on he began doing what he could do. Because Beauford was low on money, primarily because he could not resist paying for the food and drink of others when he had cash, Larry Calcagno had given him canvases and paints and paper for watercolors before sailing, and Beauford used them to paint during the day whenever there were no visitors. The studio paintings were now totally abstract—dense patterns of color done in celebration of the possibilities of paint itself. In his notebook he reminded himself to "remember the sculpture and structure in color" and its "relation to design and particular personal features."

The personal features were certainly there, but they were represented abstractly in the mood conveyed by the painter's obvious joy in the paint, his experiments with light-producing color, and by the wild emotional swirls of his fingers and brushes. The paintings were not a representation in abstract of the painter's psychological problems; they expressed his ability to ignore those problems when he painted. Of these early Paris works his friend, the painter Paul Jenkins, whom he had met in New York, and who also came to Paris, wrote:

> The *way* he painted, moved into a certain radiant generalization. In the paint he let go of a specific personal identity and moved closer and closer toward the constant, the original light coming from the canvas. The orbs within orbs of light, which seemed to be a kind of metaphysical structure in the painting, cut into vast cosmic zones. These paintings could be churches of no denomination. (Jenkins, p. 32)

Beauford wrote to Larry Calcagno of his painting, "I love the struggle . . . and am up to my neck in work, trying to be ready for the moment; things move slowly, but they do move" (December 23, 1953).

On nearly every weekday Beauford would walk to the American Express Office on the rue Scribe next to the Opéra to pick up his mail. There was almost always something, as he carried on extensive correspondences with New York friends and with his family in Knoxville, although his letters sometimes got lost, as he tended to use ordinary rather than airmail stamps. Often there was a little money in the envelopes. Larry Calcagno in the years after his departure always

Abstraction, 1954. Acrylic
on paper, 18 x 12 in.
Courtesy of the Delaney
Estate and the Ewing
Gallery, University of
Tennessee.

sent money with his letters—sometimes five dollars, sometimes much more.
Mrs. Ascoli's money came regularly and so did Jim Gaston's, and once there was a
letter from Joanne Sitwell containing money for his hotel bill and telling how the
famous Harlem preacher and congressman Adam Clayton Powell had admired
the Delaney paintings in her apartment and wanted to help. A week later a check
for $50 came from Powell. Carl van Vechten also wrote and enclosed a bit of cash.
It was through these donations, essentially, and later the occasional sale of a
painting, that Beauford Delaney survived and entertained his friends in Paris.

During the long difficult winter of 1953–54 Beauford did what he could to
make the kinds of contacts that would make his Paris experience more interesting. He was always a "collector" of the rich and famous in the arts. Making use of
his friendship with Alfred Stieglitz and his acquaintance with Marcel Duchamp,
he visited Man Ray in his studio near St.-Sulpice. The Stieglitz and other New

York connections also made possible his paying a call on a somewhat reluctant and formal Alice B. Toklas, to whom he introduced both Larry Calcagno and George Sugarman later in the year.

Through Toklas and Man Ray and other new acquaintances he met still other well-known figures during that first year, including the sculptors Alberto Giacometti and Contstantin Brancusi. He had seen and admired Brancusi's *The Kiss* in the Montparnasse Cemetery and he visited his studio several times. In both Giacometti and Brancusi he noted with interest the simple lines of African sculpture as an influence, and he agreed with Brancusi's idea that "that which they call abstract is the most realist, because what is real is not the exterior form but the idea, the essence of things." Beauford had made similar statements since the late 1930s.

An important counterbalance to the departure of Larry Calcagno was the development of his friendship with Sergei Radamsky, whom he had met first in New York through Al Hirschfeld. Radamsky, a singer and music teacher, was in Paris from 1952 until 1955, when he moved to Vienna to teach opera. In the summers he and his wife ran a music school on an estate in Elba that Beauford visited in 1954. It was with Sergei that Beauford took his first major outings from Paris—not only to Elba but to Chartres, where he was overwhelmed by the cathedral—"the most wonderful thing I have ever seen created by man"—and would return on several occasions to admire and do paintings based on the windows (June 13, 1954 to Dorothy Gates).

In April 1954 Beauford accompanied Sergei by car on a trip to Austria, Germany, Luxembourg, and the Netherlands. As he said to Jim and Bunny LeGros when he returned, "We motored down to Vienna." The trip was exciting for Beauford. In his journals he writes of the art museums and the opera in Vienna. Breugel's *Christ Carrying the Cross to Calvary* stood out in his memory and hearing *Madame Butterfly* and *Salome* at the Staatsoper. There were evenings with some of Sergei's students, who sang arias from *Don Carlos* and *Butterfly* over many glasses of new wine. There was a young black woman from New York whom Beauford, with great pride, heard sing the lead in an operetta in Luxembourg.

Beauford filled his notebooks with sketches, some of which would become the first of the figurative landscape paintings of his post-New York years. He sketched windmills in Holland, churches on hilltops above little villages in Austria and Germany, cafe scenes in Holland and Belgium. Perhaps the best painting to develop from the trip was a particularly painterly one of a white baroque church, its golden turban-topped steeple giving off halo-like light against the blue green mountain behind it. The glowing church stands above and in contrast to the dark trees and the little white houses with outlined red walls and roofs below it. A

Austrian Landscape, 1954.
Oil on canvas, 25½ x 21¼ in.
Courtesy of the owner.

sense of joy and mystery—something of Beauford's newfound interest in Zen—emanates from the painting.

Beauford wrote to a friend of the romance of the countryside in Germany and Austria, the anemones on the breakfast table in a hotel in Holland, and the American music he heard on the radio everywhere—Jelly Roll Morton, Benny Goodman, Ella Fitzgerald and Billie Holiday. Driving through the villages and countryside of Europe in the spring after a long hard winter "defies my ability to speak." He hoped the trip had helped him to achieve "something of completeness . . . tenderness . . . and the common touch patience which mellows and gets results, not the waiting which entails ennui and defeat." He was trying to accept the vitality of the moment—the moment that was his trip and the "moment" that was his stay in Paris. He was coming to understand that nostalgia for New York was not productive.

At the same time, the trip caused some mental disorientation. Beauford missed his friends back home—especially the Roses and Dorothy Gates. He wrote to Dorothy that he was still wearing the clothes Billy had given him when he left New York and that he was "anxious as I have always been to know more how to be with the larger self, more in the changeless rhythm of being" (May 9, 1954). To Larry Wallrich he confided that doing "so much in so short a time made me extremely nervous and now that I am back in Paris I begin to integrate and gather myself together" (April 23, 1954). This reintegration process was helped somewhat by visits from several friends in the spring and summer. The first was from Jim Gaston, whom Beauford vowed, despite his feelings for him, to treat platonically with "charm and correctness according to the quality of the continuity of a beautiful and human relationship." He knew that Jim did not think of him as a lover and he accepted that fact. May Swenson—his poet friend from Yaddo—visited with her daughter and so did Michael Freilich from the Roko Gallery. Michael helped Beauford to obtain a much needed carte d'identité and resident visa by signing an official document confirming the fact that the Roko Gallery showed Delaney paintings regularly and made monthly payments to him (July 21, 1954).

A shock in June was Baldwin's announcement that he planned to leave Paris almost immediately. His departure gave rise to one of the most intimate of Beauford's correspondences. The theme of Baldwin's letters between July 1954 and October 1955, when he returned to Paris, was the work surrounding the production of *The Amen Corner* at Howard University, his work on *Notes of a Native Son* at the MacDowell Colony and Yaddo, his missing Paris, and, most of all, his difficult relationship with Lucien Happersburger. Lucien had left his wife and child and joined his old lover in New York, and the relationship continued to be an emotional disaster.

Beauford's answers to Baldwin's many plaintive letters contain fatherly advice about his relationship and scolding about Baldwin's tendency not to pay his bills. He also expresses gratitude for money sent by Baldwin to him. But usually the letters begin with the theme of his missing his friend. Sometimes his remarks seem to suggest feelings beyond the platonic and fatherly tone that otherwise prevails in the letters: "Really we found each other here in this wonderful city" he writes (September 29, 1954). And "the nectar and qualitative fullness of autumn is deeply present in France and I think of you and remember some of the splendor of our associations together" (September 13, 1954). Beauford was able to feel close to Baldwin by spending more time than usual with Mary Painter. They were, in effect, two lovers pining for the same lost love, and love is the primary theme of Beauford's letters—love and his own precarious mental state.

In August Beauford writes to Baldwin supporting his attempted reunion with Lucien the way a father might encourage his son's love relationship: "You need the closeness of love and the deep incentive which it alone can induce. . . . Love is a buttress against everything." (August 22, 1954). And later: "Love is everything and releases magic and the marvelous in the face of gravest tragedy . . . the shelter . . . in which the miracle and honesty and the power of visions and continuity are housed" (August 22, 1954). In suggesting that love is necessary to the creative process—necessary for "incentive," for the "visions" of art—Beauford is both encouraging his friend and revealing his own despair over the loss of might-have-been lovers such as Baldwin and Calcagno; he is giving vent to his own pain.

The casual sexual encounters Beauford had from time to time were only a temporary solution and were, to him, frightening: "The knowing of the young male here is a constant comfort and also a menace" (September 17, 1954). Beauford implies that what he longs for and needs for his own psychic well-being and success is a real love—"The privilege and right of choice and following love in all its difficult and painful rhythm, knowing the satisfaction that comes from the power of feeling and stimulation that comes from those we love; it's the essence of our work" (October 1954). And, he writes, "Our gods, the gods of love are very difficult, but lovers can't help being lovers" (December 13, 1954).

As for the state of his inner life, Beauford confessed his pain and disorientation to Baldwin as he did to no one else: "Have been working and living with the many people who make up Beauford," he writes, "and trying to merge them into some sense of composition and a workable form of painting . . . there is a great chamber in my house which has been vacant for a long time; I don't think I have ever spoken of it—pretend you did not hear . . . —this can often account for a great many odd placements of [mental] furniture" (September 17, 1954). And he speaks of needing "light" to overcome his "dimness" (September 29, 1954). Baldwin was to a great extent that light: "Naturally I miss one James Baldwin for we could stomp and fly all at once, . . . weep and laugh in one breath" (November 5, 1954).

As for Baldwin, he missed Beauford, too. He wrote to Mary Painter that Beauford and his mother were examples to him of the fact that "if you don't get stopped" by the barriers placed before one by racism, "you haven't got to die" (undated 1954). Later, still in the States, Baldwin would write to Mary that Beauford "corrects me." Beauford and Mary were the only two people with whom he felt "released from" the "strange power" that was possessing him in his developing role as a spokesperson (undated 1955).

Beauford's first exhibitions in Paris were in the summer of 1954—large group shows at the Salon des Réalités Nouvelles in the Musée d'Art Moderne and the Ninth Salon at the Musée des Beaux Arts. Undoubtedly Beauford's good connections in the American and now French art world led to his invitations to exhibit in these shows. It was a major step for him and somewhat solidified his position as a resident in Paris rather than as a New Yorker on a visit.

The winter of 1954–55 was considerably less harsh than his first winter in Paris, and Beauford continued to make friends and receive visitors. An important event was the arrival in Paris of one of the New York "Saints," Palmer Hayden, and his wife Miriam ("Mimi"). The Haydens and Beauford saw each other regularly in Paris and, although Palmer and Mimi were often away on trips, they were a couple Beauford could and did depend on in times of trouble.

The spring of 1955 brought with it Larry Calcagno, and he and Beauford went together to Madrid in April for three weeks, primarily to attend an exhibition of Larry's work at the Gallery Clan. The show was highly successful and because of it Calcagno was able to convince the gallery to show Beauford's work in June. Beauford's show—his first solo in Europe—was also a success; several abstract paintings in oil and pastel were sold. The reviewers spoke of Delaney's spontaneity, intuitiveness, and the joy that emanated from his "games of color." But back in Paris, with Calcagno's departure at the end of April, Beauford fell into another state of depression and wrote to friends at home of his intentions to return, something that a lack of money made impossible even if he was serious. The depression was somewhat alleviated by a short trip to Italy with Friends in June. He was particularly moved by the Piazza St. Marco in Venice and *The Last Supper* of Leonardo in Milan.

In a series of letters after Calcagno's departure, the two painters attempt to express their affection for each other. Calcagno writes, "Well, dear Beauford, I could write on and on, but somehow the most important things seem to be left unsaid, so I will end this letter with warmest affection for you" (October 21, 1955). Beauford's answers are similar and tend also to be emotional descriptions from one painter to another of the status of his work: "Many things grow inside of me that as yet find release only in very abbreviated moments. You know what I mean. However, they are sacred and intense. Look forward to a time of release and reflection with more work" (November 15, 1955).

In October James Baldwin returned from New York without Lucien but with a new lover, a musician named Arnold. Baldwin immediately saw that Beauford's mental state was unsettled. With Bernard Hassell and Bernard's friend Richard Olney he arranged a move out of Paris into a roomy garden apartment in the house where Bernard and Richard lived in the little suburb of Clamart. Beauford was wary of leaving the city; in his journal he wondered about his living in "the country," and for several months he resisted. The decision was put off further by a happy visit from Irene Rose, which involved outings to Versailles and Chartres and evenings on the town.

Then one night in December he cooked a meal in his room in the Hôtel des Écoles for Baldwin, Bernard, Richard, Howard Swanson, and Mary Painter. There was much drinking—Baldwin had brought along a bottle of cognac—and the group made a great deal of noise, which was their habit, and it attracted the attention of the hotel owners. Baldwin had just finished *Giovanni's Room*, and he read it aloud to the others. The process took all night, and when the owners noted that Baldwin did not leave with the others early in the morning, they accused Beauford of putting up a "guest" without paying. This was all the incentive Beauford needed. In one of his rare rages he announced that he was leaving. He called Bernard and went out to see the Clamart apartment, and after agreeing to rent it called Mary, who helped him pack. By that evening he had moved.

Making the change was difficult, but Beauford knew that cafe life, with its surplus of alcohol, was taking a toll, and, in any case, he had long felt that the people in his hotel bore him malice. And Baldwin had promised that when he was in Paris he would make the Clamart apartment his home as well. It seemed that the return to New York was not to be, especially as he had now definitely lost his apartment there, so he agreed to a change of direction in Paris. In August he had written to Dorothy Gates in answer to her question as to whether he intended to remain in Europe "like Ezra Pound and T. S. Eliot" by saying that he had "never entertained the idea of not coming home" and noting that "Mr. Eliot and Mr. Pound . . . have never been in my material position." He would return home when he had accomplished enough to justify the move (August 10, 1955). But such a move did not seem imminent.

In his journals Beauford wrote down a list of things to do in his new life:

Keep the faith and trust in so far as possible. Love humility and don't mind the insinuations that cause sorrow . . . and loneliness and limitations. We learn self-reliance and to hear the voice of God, too . . . and how to . . . not break but bend gently. Learning to love is learning to suffer deeply and with quietness.

—————————————————————————— *eight*

Paris: The Clamart Years

T he apartment in the house at 68 rue Paul Vaillant Couturies in Clamart was on the ground floor. Beauford immediately covered the walls of the studio in white sheets to accentuate the light. There was a window that looked through the branches of a large tree onto a garden in the back. James Baldwin loved sitting with Beauford in front of this window—"a kind of universe, moaning and wailing when it rained, black and bitter when it thundered, hesitant and delicate with the first light of the morning, and as blue as the blues when the last light of the sun departed" (Baldwin, Studio Museum catalogue). Writer and painter would sit there for hours, drinking, sometimes talking, sometimes just meditating on the changing light through the filtering leaves. Baldwin said he began to see that light in his friend's paintings: it was a light that reached back over the years he had known Beauford—back to the light that Beauford had shown him in that Greenwich Village gutter. As represented by Beauford it was a religious light—Beauford's God—a light that "held the power to illuminate, even to redeem and reconcile and heal."

Life in Clamart was not always so tranquil. During the first year Jimmy and Arnold were in an out and so were Bernard Hassell and Richard Olney who lived upstairs. When Baldwin was in town, especially, there were parties—sometimes quite raucous—and there was a great deal of drinking. Dinner was sometimes in one flat, sometimes in the other. On most weekends between January and November 1956 whoever was in residence went to Mary Painter's new and very grand apartment in the rue des Carmes in Paris, an apartment she shared with her Siamese cat Caesar, much loved by Beauford. Beauford, Jimmy, Richard, and Arnold or Lucien would go to Mary's on Friday evening and would be joined by Bernard after he got off work at the Folies-Bergère at midnight. The party would sometimes go on until Sunday. A great deal of PX whiskey was consumed and elaborate meals were prepared by Mary and Richard. Jazz and blues were the music of choice in this period. These parties became known as the "Saturday Night Functions," so named after one of the group's favorite records.

Beauford loved these weekends—looked forward to them and talked about them with a kind of awe—and was much saddened by Mary's departure for Washington after a final celebration on Thanksgiving Day in 1956. He was also upset by Richard and Bernard's leaving for two years in New York beginning early in 1957. That loss was somewhat made up for by Baldwin's renting the Olney–Hassell apartment in their absence and using it from time to time.

The landlady in Clamart had an apartment on the top floor. Mlle. Marty wore exotic hats and a great deal of makeup, and Beauford soon became convinced that she had designs on him. In fact, Mlle. Marty was what one might call a virgin with a vengeance. Beauford's suspicions were a lighter side of the chronic paranoia that would later lead him to believe that Mlle. Marty wanted to kill him. What is true is that Mlle. Marty both loved Beauford—platonically—and took a somewhat sadistic interest in teasing him. She found, for instance, that she could terrify him by sneaking into the garden and scratching on his closed shutters in the middle of the night. People who visited in the house complained that sleep was almost impossible. Mlle. Marty often moved heavy furniture around as late as 3 A.M., Beauford was constantly up and down slamming doors, and Baldwin could be heard banging away at his typewriter at all hours.

For all its confusion, the Clamart situation, because it alleviated—at least before the departure of Bernard and Richard—what had been Beauford's loneliness in his hotel studio, eventually became conducive to good work. The new surroundings were roomier than the old and the light, unimpeded by surrounding buildings, was better. Beauford always referred to his Clamart apartment as his "place in the country." There was a large room and a separate kitchen, the garden, and, above all, the light.

But the adjustment process was, as always for Beauford, difficult. One constant theme in his correspondence was his chronic lack of money. The gifts from friends and patrons were simply not sufficient to pay for food, painting supplies, rent, and the coal he needed to keep the stove in his apartment going. Beauford confided in letters to Larry Wallrich that poverty was getting to him: "I have suffered terribly here from privations of many kinds. I only relate this to give you some small idea of my plight" (February 2, 1956). "At times," he said, "I have . . . barely escaped perishing." Desperate for a canvas one day, he stretched an old raincoat that Billy Rose had given him.

Beauford's belief in himself and his pride were undermined by his poverty. What he wanted to do was sell paintings to people who believed in his work. What he resented was the tendency of patronizing people he called "darling friends," whom he really despised, to give him things such as old shoes and old magazines instead of taking his art seriously. For so many years he had been a "character," a "good Negro"; now he wanted to be recognized as the painter he knew he was. One day when a "darling friend" left after delivering some used clothes, Beauford turned his back to the closed door and leaned over as if lifting skirts to say "kiss my ass." He threw the clothes on the floor, stomped on them, and stuffed them into the stove to burn. On another occasion a wealthy white American came on a mission of "good will" to meet the Beauford Delaney he had read about in the Henry Miller article of years before. When Beauford understood that his guest knew nothing about and cared little for his art he refused to sell a painting and, in fact, politely asked the man to leave. There were other similar instances when, if Beauford did not like his prospective buyer, he would avoid uncovering any paintings, claiming that he had none for sale.

James Baldwin would write to Mary Painter (undated) about the inner world of Beauford Delaney externalized in incidents like these. Baldwin felt that years—from Beauford's earliest childhood in the South—of having to be afraid of, accommodate, and depend on white people and a fear of offending them had made him both hate and in some perverse way to enjoy being "treated like shit" by them. As a strident battler for rights, Baldwin resented Beauford's dressing "like a bum" and his acceptance of his condition. His "dignity" in poverty resembled that of the "house nigger," who was proud of his ability to handle other black folk and "outwit" white folks. Baldwin believed that inside "this despised black man" was a Beauford who judged the world "harshly" and who had a "secret," a "power" that if he chose to "unleash" it would "humble" his enemies. But Beauford was content to let his surrogate son speak for him and consistently encouraged Baldwin even in the harshest of his outcries against white hypocrisy and bias.

If, on the other hand, Beauford liked a person—black or white—who came to see his paintings, the showing would be something of a seance. One day in the winter of 1956 the composer Howard Swanson took his friend Elwood Peterson, then a young student singer in Paris on the GI Bill, to Clamart to meet Beauford. On later occasions Peterson noticed that Beauford would smile radiantly as he "sized up" anyone he happened to meet: "If the smile did not fade, you were 'in.'" Peterson was clearly "in"; the smile did not fade and the singer was ushered "into the space where . . . this wise Merlin . . . wrought his magic" (Peterson to DL, March 22, 1996). When Peterson asked to see his paintings Beauford showed them deliberately, studying each one after he placed it on the easel, his eyes partly closed, his hands folded in front of him. There was a "vibrant" air of "ritual" about the showing. From that first meeting Peterson felt that Beauford did not paint with anyone's pleasure in mind—not even his own. He painted because it was a question of his "fighting with devils," since there was "no way out of it," and he felt compelled to explore the mystery of light through the use of form and color. He had to struggle to stop the colors and forms that swirled about in his head, to control them long enough to arrange them on canvas or paper so that he could see the mysterious light represented.

Beauford recognized that his mind often approached a state of dangerous unbalance and spoke enviously of those who "are able to pay for psychiatry or analysis . . . this therapy [would be] a great blessing" (February 17, 1956). News of the death of his great friend Dorothy Gates in April set him back considerably. He lost interest in painting and neglected his appearance even more than usual. Baldwin tried to console him but he also was prone to frequent depressions. His unexplained absences from the upstairs apartment, and his obsessions with Lucien and Arnold depressed Beauford further. During bad psychological times Beauford took to walking or busing into Paris almost every day on various excuses. He still liked having his mail sent to American Express, for instance, since he was convinced the postmen withheld his letters addressed to Clamart.

Generally, however, he tried to stay at home, partly to avoid what he recognized were the harmful effects to his mind and body of the cafe existence. There were visits to a little restaurant in Petit Clamart run by an eccentric woman named Pierrette and occasional trips into town, but, for the most part, he spent more time in his studio than he had in his Hôtel des Écoles days. In time he began to paint again.

Besides painting, he pursued what he saw as a therapeutic reading of the "wisdom literature" of the Far East. Lao tsu remained a favorite along with various Buddhist writings and a biography of Gandhi. He also enjoyed the poetry of

William Blake. He hoped that his reading would help to overcome the inner coldness that he felt—a coldness in keeping with another harsh winter in 1955–56, which he suspected was "emanating from the fear and great unhappiness in the hearts of most people." What was needed, he felt, was "a great reevaluation." (February 26, 1956).

Beauford always had a religious streak. He loved visiting the great cathedrals—Chartres and Notre Dame especially—not only for aesthetic purposes but because he envied the order and constancy he saw them as representing: "A view of people doing something together for hundreds of years and remaining faithful to the ideal and vision" (letter to Wallrich, October 4, 1957). With perhaps only a little bit of mockery he would always genuflect (it appeared more like a curtsey) when he entered a Catholic church, and often he would cross himself. He was a genuine admirer of Pope John the XXIII, always referring to him simply as "Twenty-three."

In February 1956 he sent some paintings back to New York for the "First Exposition of Negro Progress" show at the Wanamaker Building on lower Broadway in April. Ellis Wilson, Eldzier Cortor, Ernest Crichlow, and Jacob Lawrence were other artists whose works were shown. He also began, with the help of Larry Wallrich, Michael Freilich, and the heirs of Dorothy Gates, an attempt to retrieve the paintings he had left behind in New York, with the idea that Wallrich could arrange a show and raise money by selling the paintings. For various reasons the New York show never took place. Eventually some of the paintings arrived in France, but many were lost, destroyed, or stolen. Their whereabouts remain a mystery.

In March Delaney joined Sam Francis, Shirley Goldfarb, Joe Downing, Don Fink, Shirley Jaffe, Paul Jenkins, John Koenig, and others for a group exhibition of "Abstract American" artists at the Galerie Arnaud. Essentially the same show had been presented earlier in the year at Iserholn, Germany. And in May, Beauford had his first solo show at the Galerie Prisme. The exhibition was well attended and well reviewed, but only one painting was sold. The works he showed were very much in the style of those he had displayed at the Galerie Arnaud earlier in the year. These were abstractions marked by large areas of paint applied thickly in swirls and various colors—blues, pinks, softer colors than those of the Greene Street period. In a sense these were transitional paintings between those characterized by the more Fauve-like coloration of the New York period and those with the tightly textured, less varied coloration of the later Paris years—the red dominated paintings of the late Clamart years and the yellow ones of the Vercingetorix period.

In 1956 Beauford returned seriously to portrait painting. As Richard Long has rightly suggested, this continuation of figurative art was no conflict of interest as far as Beauford's approach to painting was concerned. "The abstraction," Beauford said to Long,

> ostensibly, is simply for me a penetration of something that is more profound in many ways than the rigidity of form. A form if it breathes some, if it has some enigma to it, it is also the enigma that is the abstract, I would think. (Long interview, Sept 5, 1970 in Studio Museum Catalogue)

In any case, Beauford's portraiture had long been more about masses of color and the "enigma" of form than about likeness and, as Beauford always claimed, about "inner light." From his point of view the abstractions and portraits were extensions of each other. The first of the new portraits was one of an American expatriate writer and friend of Baldwin, Leslie Schenk. When it was finished Schenk was surprised that, although figurative, it did not look more like him and even more astonished when Beauford asked him for $100 for the painting, a price then considered extravagant in the Paris bohemian circle. Writing about a portrait of this period to his old friend Mary Callery, who was visiting in Europe and had come to the Galerie Prisme show, Beauford mentioned that it seemed to be independent of "my expressionistic way so far" (December 10, 1956). Yet if the portrait was hardly abstract, it was, nevertheless, a natural aspect of his art at this time.

Several years later, Elwood Peterson, a fellow African American, for whom, as for Beauford, life in the arts had been a struggle, also would be surprised by *his* portrait, especially given its radical change from the "classic" charcoal drawing that preceded it. When, like so many others, Peterson made his surprise known, pointing out that the portrait made him look eighteen, the painter answered, "If you wanted an exact likeness you could have gone to a photographer . . . when you sing you become eighteen again, and that's what I wanted to capture." Again, "inner light" was the painter's goal. But Peterson was not displeased; he conveyed the pleasure he took in "the splendor of the portrait's colors" and form and asked to buy it (see Color Plate 9). Beauford gave him the painting, refusing to take money: "You're one of the blessed," he said, "and you've paid your dues . . . so just get along with yourself and keep the faith" (Peterson to DL, March 22, 1996).

Beauford received early summer visits in 1956 from a New York friend, Lynn Stone. He was saddened by the departure for New York of his friend George Sugarman and later in the year of Sam Spanier. The old group was diminishing. But Richard Gibson had moved to Paris from Rome with his wife and young child, and this was some comfort.

Left to Right, Arnold, James Baldwin, Larry Calcagno, and Beauford at Ibiza, 1956. Photograph by Leslie Schenk.

The real bright spot of the summer of 1956, however, was the return of Larry Calcagno, who took Beauford to Spain for the month of August. They were joined at the LeGros retreat in Ibiza by James Baldwin, Leslie Schenk, and Baldwin's friend Arnold, and later went to Majorca. From Ibiza Beauford wrote to Henry Miller of the beauty and power of the Mediterranean and its surroundings, of the watercolors he was doing, and how he was "trying to say with my life the unsayable." He took immense pleasure in the colors of the sea, the countryside, and the ancient towns, and loved the warmth and the brightness of the light. Emotionally the time with Larry was soothing. Baldwin wrote to Mary Painter from Ibiza commenting on how well Beauford looked and noting the importance of the Calcagno relationship to him (undated 1956). It was clear that the two men talked of Beauford's problems, the poverty, and the voices that plagued him. In a series of letters after Larry's return to the States, Larry encouraged his friend to try to "hold on" and sent money, and Beauford promised to try his best. In October Beauford wrote to Henry Miller's wife Eve of his hope to remain working in Paris "until some of the inner and outer lights fuse into that which I seem to hear them saying "(October 25, 1956).

In the fall Beauford began his association with two important art entrepreneurs, Paul Facchetti and Darthea Speyer. Facchetti promised to include him in a

Christmas party, 1956.

group show at his Paris gallery and in a gallery in Bordighera, Italy, in the following year, and Speyer bought one of the Ibiza watercolors for 7,000 francs.

In Clamart Beauford's work progressed. And there were the fall exhibitions in
the city and a thrilling concert by Marian Anderson, whom Beauford had not
seen since the New York years. And there was a happy Christmas visit with
Charley and Gita Boggs.

But the winter was cold again—and cold was something that depressed him.
Furthermore, the old money problems began to resurface along with the inner
voices of despair. These voices were particularly present when James Baldwin
came from Corsica at the end of the year. Baldwin was obsessed with the problem
of his relationship with Arnold and for once Beauford's inner feelings for Baldwin
were expressed in jealousy when he spoke of the "ill effects of fame on some people." When Baldwin used the term "old aunties" in reference to them both Beauford became enraged and disappeared for several days. Baldwin was concerned
and one afternoon began calling hospitals. On that evening a message came from
Beauford to Baldwin by way of a phone call from a friend: "I love you" it said, but
he stayed away. A few nights later Baldwin, who was sleeping in Beauford's bed,

woke up to find his friend staring at him, but when he tried to say something Beauford mumbled a few words and left the house. Eventually the crisis passed, and Baldwin, in describing it to Mary Painter, spoke of his relief. Beauford had been good to him when no one else had, he said: "I owe him, really, more than I can ever pay"; Beauford was both "lovable" and "heroic" (undated 1957).

Beauford's only hope in the face of this renewed bout of depression was his painting, and he turned to it with new energy and tried to live a much quieter life. He wrote to Larry Wallrich in January 1957 that he had been "withdrawn and working and thinking these past several months and plan somehow to even withdraw more, as deep introspection and [the] search for me is vitally necessary. . . . Painting is tremendously physical and vital and naturally calls for all your mental and spiritual strength and devotion" (January 8, 1957). The next month he wrote to Wallrich of his nostalgia for Greene Street ("really the only home I ever had") and noted that in Clamart "I work and live an inner life and learn" (February 2, 1957).

In March he celebrated his new solitary lifestyle and the coming of spring by reading the sonnets of Shakespearefor the first time. He was moved by their depiction of passionate love, something of which he had little. To Larry Calcagno he wrote of this lack and said that throughout the winter he "had of necessity to hold on to myself and things with very firm control . . . everything has been a challenge to continuity." He "had to sit alone and weigh and look within myself for answers—the only reply has been work and duty" (March 13, 1957).

May brought some good luck. Calcagno sent money and Beauford sold another painting. He also announced that he had a "little friend" who came around from time to time (Calcagno letter, May 5, 1957). As for the money, he had spent most of it on a dinner party for "dear ones."

In June Beauford was included in a group show called 'L'insurrection Contre La Forme." Other painters in it included Larry Calcagno's friend René Laubiès and Frederic Benrath, a French painter Beauford had come to know well. The exhibition traveled from the Galerie Prisme in Paris to several galleries in Germany. The introduction in the catalogue was written by the French art critic Julien Alvard. The group show at the Galerie Facchetti would take place in October and then travel to Italy and the University of Wisconsin.

The summer of 1957 was quiet. Baldwin was away in the States. Beauford wrote to him praising *Giovanni's Room* for its art and honesty and "Sonny's Blues" for its sensitivity and structural wholeness (July 31, 1957, August 26, 1957). Summer visitors included the Hirschfelds and the Freilichs from New York and Richard Long, a new friend brought one Sunday by Howard Swanson. Long would remain one of Beauford's most faithful friends and supporters and would become a principal scholar of his works.

After the Facchetti group show, Beauford went still further into seclusion than usual, struggling against the nagging inner voices by reading and painting. His favorite book that winter was Rilke's *Letter to a Young Poet*. During the winter he had a dangerous bout with Asian flu and, because Baldwin, Hassell, and Olney were away, was nursed by the terrifying Mlle. Marty. He wrote to Baldwin of "many difficulties"—primarily financial and psychological—but affirmed his belief that "[in] time . . . some kind of true reward will be mine" (February 7, 1958).

In March a great service was done for Beauford when Jim Gaston paid for the release of two cases of paintings stored in New York. These would include many of the important paintings of the Greene Street period. Beauford had been struggling since his arrival in Paris to have these paintings released and was elated at the prospect of their coming to Paris. The good news, however, was overshadowed by a death that was more disturbing even than that of Dorothy Gates. He received a cable from Knoxville on March 1 that his mother had died on February 28. He had, of course, expected this death as his mother was ninty-three, but the reality of it was shattering. It was something, as he wrote to James Baldwin, that he had "presumed and hoped . . . would never happen"; and because of it the first weeks in March had been "one of the most dramatic and difficult times" of his life (March 20, 1958). To Henry Miller he wrote of the "enigmatic beginnings and endings" and of his frustration at not having been able to do anything for his mother at the end (March 31, 1958). To Larry Wallrich he commented that he hoped to "gather [himself] together" so as to "use some of the heritage of endurance left me by her" (April 8, 1958).

Beauford's unhappiness continued well into May. One Sunday he wandered into Notre Dame and was moved by the music he heard, the Fauré *Requiem*. It was music he had also experienced with Larry Calcagno in Ibiza as they listened to it sung by the choir of the boys' school across the street from where they were staying. He thought of it now as a requiem for his mother. In answer to a letter of sympathy from James Baldwin he wrote of his depression and ended with a hope: "May all darkness fall into light."

It was fortunate that Mary Painter arrived back in Paris at about the time Beauford heard the news of Delia Delaney's death. Mary recognized her friend's pain and insisted that he spend as much time in her apartment as possible, and she encouraged him to meet friends in cafes and visit galleries. In one gallery they visited in March he was thrilled to meet and talk with Max Ernst, whom he found "wonderful and most kind" (letter to Miller, (March 31, 1958). Mary would leave soon on government business in Africa, and Beauford suggested to Baldwin that it was "wonderful having our Mary going before us to our ancestral roots" (April 20, 1958).

The Facchettis bought two abstract paintings in May and Beauford began to think of using the money for a trip south to visit René Laubiès. Laubies had also recently lost *his* mother. The trip was short, as Beauford was anxious to be back in Paris for a June 3 concert at the Alhambra of American jazz greats—including his friend Dizzy Gillespie. Other friends, Duke Ellington and Billie Holiday, would come for a concert later in the year.

By June Beauford was back at work with renewed energy and confidence. Aesthetically he was changing directions slightly, attempting to solve a new problem, which involved the use of color to convey his own inner life. Before this period Delaney's paintings had been an attempt to hold off his inner tormentors with celebrations of light. He seemed now to be moving toward a more expressionist use of painting to represent the inner turmoil itself. "Am today still trying to bring together color compositions from the strange and many-faceted thing that is my life," he wrote to Larry Wallrich (June 2, 1958). Later he would point out that it was "difficult to capture the shock of life—it's a thing of magic and not technique, you know" (August 22, 1958). To Henry and Eve Miller he suggested that his work was "growing"—that it "becomes more personal or impersonal; they are both about the same it seems to me." And he added that the "constant gray here creates a marvelous setting in the mind for color" (June 24, 1958). Beauford was on a search for the "inner light" that might defeat the dark forces that constantly attacked his mind.

In the fall he sent six large abstract canvases to a group show at the Museum in Leverkusen, Germany. And with support from James Baldwin, Henry Miller, and Larry Calcagno, he applied—unsuccessfully, as it turned out—for a Guggenheim grant.

In the summer of 1958 author James Jones and his wife Gloria moved to Paris and settled on the Ile St. Louis. They had become friendly with James Baldwin in New York, and when Baldwin returned to Paris for a stay in Clamart beginning in July, he introduced Beauford to them. Before long the Jones's liked the painter so much that they gave him a key to their apartment and invited him frequently for meals. In time they also commissioned several paintings—including one of their baby in a crib and the now famous portrait of Jones himself—and in so doing greatly relieved Beauford's financial pain.

The summer of 1958 with Baldwin in Clamart was one of the most peaceful periods Beauford had experienced in years. Richard and Bernard were away, and for once Baldwin was not occupied with a lover. Both men were content to remain for the most part in Clamart, and they settled into a routine that suited them. They worked all day, Baldwin cooked the meals, and they spent hours at night sitting in the window talking. Beauford was noticeably older and "madder," yet sometimes he talked "profound good sense." Baldwin was in France primarily for Beauford that summer and wrote to Mary Painter that he had never listened to anyone so closely, never tried so hard to "put myself in someone else's skin" (undated 1958).

Baldwin knew how much Beauford had suffered and how much he was still suffering, and also realized how much he owed to his old friend, how much his own success could be traced to the painter. Beauford represented the "endurance" of the artist and the black man, and he represented the price of that endurance. Perhaps one day when Baldwin was old and "half mad from labor and disappointment" he would need the kind of love and support he hoped he was now giving his friend. Somehow Beauford made Baldwin think, too, of what he himself cost his own friends as a difficult and famous man. And Beauford made him face the fact that when an artist realizes that life has passed by and that life has become art, there is a danger of madness. Most of all, Beauford taught him to believe, despite madness, despite the understandable paranoia that threatens those who are the victims of racism, homophobia, or other prejudices, that there were "infinite possibilities" in the miracle of life (undated letter JB to Mary Painter, 1958).

Baldwin realized that to Beauford he represented the black man and the homosexual speaking out for him and others against white and sexual tyranny while he—Beauford— depended on white patronage to survive. Baldwin was Beauford's hope—"the spiritual heir, the son, the lover, the friend" who did what he wished he could have done. All that was important now was to make him less "miserable" (JB undated to Mary Painter, summer 1958).

When Baldwin left in the fall the chronic depression returned: "I work and search after the all which we both know is fleeting and difficult . . . going along somehow finding solace somewhere somehow," Beauford wrote to him (November 7, 1958). Still, he managed, with the help of Charley Boggs, whose apartment he stayed in for several weeks that winter, to survive another serious case of flu and prepare for two group shows in 1959—one in February with Boggs on the rue Marbeuf under the sponsorship of the Special Services Division of the U.S. Army, and one later in the year at the Galerie Breteau. But he sold almost nothing and drifted into what his friends saw as a peculiarly quiet mood. To Larry Calcagno he confided his depression, but also reaffirmed his "love of life, people and painting . . . my heart and mind remain dedicated and my faith steadfast."

Beauford's state of mind was improved by another long stay with the Boggses in June 1959—time with little Gordon seemed particularly to soothe him—and by the return of Jim and Bunny LeGros from New York. Henry Miller visited as well and so did Anaïs Nin, and there was a series of letters from Dante Pavone, the first in some six years. Baldwin came back, too, but, as Richard Olney and Bernard Hassell had reoccupied their apartment at Mlle. Marty's, he moved into a small apartment in Petite Clamart over Pierrette's restaurant. But Baldwin was preoccupied with various projects and disastrous love affairs that took him away a great deal. The result was that he was unable to give Beauford the time and support he needed. By September Charley Boggs noted a continued quietness in Beauford, who more often than not came into Paris and stayed overnight rather than return to Clamart. He was discouraged by the failure of the Guggenheim application, worried by what he saw as Baldwin's own depressed state, and he seemed to be falling back into the cafe life and drinking too much.

When he returned from a trip to Sweden in October, Baldwin paid more attention to Beauford's condition. He spent as much time with him as possible, but his own state of mind made him more a patient than a doctor, and the most helpful thing he could do, finally, was to throw an elaborate Thanksgiving dinner in his friend's honor at Pierrette's. The party was, in fact, memorable, and Beauford demonstrated his happiness by for the first time in years singing some of the old songs with Baldwin. Just before Christmas there were some of the old-style nights on the town, including a Christmas Eve around West Indian writer friend Dixie Nimmo's Coleman stove in his tiny unheated apartment on the Seine. Dixie somehow cooked a whole chicken on the single burner while Baldwin, Beauford, and he drank quantities of red wine. Beauford pronounced the meal the best he had ever eaten and the evening the happiest he could remember.

But Baldwin was about to leave Paris with no plans to return soon; he would begin assuming an almost full-time role as a civil rights spokesman. His old friend's deep unhappiness returned with Baldwin's departure for New York on January 27. Baldwin wrote to Mary Painter of Beauford's "clinging" to him and how, on the other hand, Beauford urged him on in his activist role, as if Baldwin were "his connection" with the "great world"—his "presence in it" (undated 1959).

February and March were cold, difficult months and light was scarce, but in February Beauford participated in a group exhibition called "Antagonismes" at the Musée des Arts Décoratifs. The show was organized by Julien Alvard and François Mathey. In the catalogue, Herbert Read spoke of Beauford's extraordinary use of light and color in the paintings.

Later in the month Beauford drove with a friend to Cannes, where he stayed for two days before visiting Aix en Provence, which he "adored," and painting his version of Mont Saint Victoire as an homage not only to the southern light but to one of his primary heroes, Cézanne. He came back to Paris by train via Avignon, where he also made a brief stop. The elation brought about by this trip was undermined, however, by mocking inner voices on the ride back. And to his friends—primarily Baldwin, Larry Wallrich, Larry Calcagno, and Henry Miller— he wrote of his essential loneliness. The painting was progressing but, "however work comes along one does finally have to make peace with aloneness" (letter to Miller, March 14, 1960). There was, he recognized, a need to "meet the challenge with the courage to begin again" (to Wallrich, March 18, 1960).

The chance to begin again came from Paul Facchetti, who had bought several of his paintings and now offered him a solo exhibition in May. Facchetti's invitation and the immense amount of work it involved distracted the painter's mind somewhat from his loneliness and his depression. By working eight or nine hours a day he could keep the voices at bay or, more accurately, make them work for him in his paintings.

The exhibition was postponed because of problems with the catalogue, and Beauford began in late May to suspect that evil people were preventing his show, undercutting his one chance to expand his orbit as a painter. Perhaps Facchetti had been lying, perhaps he only wanted to steal the paintings, perhaps he would give them all away. But on June 21—a month late—the *"vernissage de l'exposition des oeuvres de* BEAUFORD DELANEY*"* took place from 6 to 9 p.m at the Galerie Paul Facchetti in the rue de Lille in Paris.

The party was a celebration of Beauford. His Paris friends were there, and a particularly warm joint letter arrived from James Baldwin, Mary Painter, Ellis Wilson, and Palmer Hayden, who were all in New York at the time. Henry Miller wrote an encouraging letter, too, as did Brother Joe and many old New York friends. The catalogue included a long excerpt from the Henry Miller article and a short introduction by Julien Alvard, who noted the uniqueness of Delaney's work and admired the ways in which the planes of his paintings appeared in unexpected ways. In the New York days Dante Pavone observed this characteristic and Beauford had reminded him of the old song "Lord, Open the Unusual Door," and suggested that this was what he hoped his paintings could do.

The paintings, mostly large oils on canvas, were all abstract. As Richard Long noted, they were marked by a "richness of impasto" and "a frequent tone of melancholy, imposed either by a somber palette or by the sheer power of clashing color-masses" (Long, Studio Museum catalogue). The tone of melancholy was in

Beauford dressed for his
opening, 1960.

keeping with the painter's attempt during this period to confront his demons by
integrating them into his painting.

The exhibition was well received, but only two small paintings were sold.
Elwood Peterson, who was there, wondered "How many of those who came to
it were aware that what they were looking at was not only the sum total of
your own existence up till now, but the manifestation of a whole rich past and
an even richer future for all of us—what you call 'continued continuity'" (July
18, 1960).

Because the expenses of the show exceeded its costs, the Facchettis eventually
arranged a deal by which they "bought" several paintings and paid Beauford a
monthly allowance. Beauford never liked this arrangement but was in no position
to bargain. Exhausted by the work leading up to the show and by the excitement
of the occasion itself, and once again tortured by the voices—"my forces," as he
sometimes called them—he used money sent by Larry Calcagno to buy a train
ticket to Florence. He had not been outside France since his trip to Spain with
Larry and the brief trip to Italy in 1956. Florence had always been what he called a
"painter's goal." While there he walked the streets and visited the galleries in a
state of "ecstasy," reveling in the light and warmth of Italy, and he painted twelve

watercolors in the more figurative style that tended to characterize his outdoor as opposed to his studio paintings.

Back in Paris Beauford placed paintings in two group shows—at the Facchetti Gallery and the Salon des Réalités Nouvelles in the Musée d'Art Moderne—and was shown on a Télévision Française show working in his Clamart studio. He also began experimenting with silk screen work. But sales were minimal and his chronic loneliness still present. He saw the Boggses often, and the LeGros and the Joneses, and sometimes the Haydens, now back in Paris, of whom he was especially fond. But he wrote to Larry Calcagno agreeing that "my life could use some of the sweet reason of passion." (August 25, 1960). Once again he began to spend more time in the cafes of Montparnasse, finding the occasional lover, drinking too much, and depending on the Boggses for meals.

In 1961 there were more group shows. One early in the year with Caroline Lee and old friend Joe Downing at the Centre Culturel Américain was arranged by Darthea Speyer, who would begin to displace Paul Facchetti as the principal agent for his paintings. And again the catalogue introduction was by Julien Alvard. In the journal *Témoinage Chrétien* (February 3, 1961), critic Guichard-Meili wrote of the "celestial clarity" of Beauford's works and arranged to visit the painter in his Clamart studio for a comprehensive private showing. There were group shows with Benrath, Laubiès, and others later in the year at the Lincoln Gallery in London, and again at the Galerie Breteau in Paris.

On March 1 Beauford commented in a letter to Lynn Stone, his old New York friend and supporter, that he had failed to find a "solution" to the problem of existing "in this jungle of a world." And on March 10 Beauford wrote two letters, both indicating something of the state of his mind in the months leading to the greatest of his misfortunes. To Larry Calcagno he mentioned that his life has become "mostly introspective . . . movement for me is inside rather than without." And to brother Joe he wrote: "However sad at times we might be we have come through great trials and tribulations but must never lose sight of our sainted parents and God's great gifts . . . it's difficult to bear but God understands us all and has love for us and mercy."

On July 22 Beauford left Paris by train to begin a long-talked of trip to Greece. Through her position as Cultural Attaché at the American Embassy in Paris Darthea Speyer had arranged some financial support for him to paint for two weeks in Hydra, where she would be on vacation, and in Rhodes. At the Gare de Lyon Beauford was sure he saw a letter being given to the police. It was clear that it was signed by thrity-six people who denounced his character and called him a "black bastard." The trip went relatively well, however, until just outside Lausanne, Switzerland, when he began to hear people around him threatening to "cut off

Beauford in thought, 1961.

his balls" so that he would "become the woman he really was." They called him a "nigger" and a "pederast" and a "Communist." The people were staring at him, so he showed them his money and said they could have it if they wanted it so badly. They laughed at him, but began whispering about how they would kill him and rob him when the right time came. He was not surprised by the presence of these people. They were the criminals or friends of the criminals who had long followed him on the streets of Paris and even New York—perhaps they were Mafia people. They always spoke English unless they did not want him to hear— then they spoke French—and he could never understand why his friends and companions seemed to ignore what they said. He knew that one day he would have to fight back against the criminals, even though they had powers—could perhaps see him through the walls of his apartment. The criminals wanted his money, of course, but they seemed to want him, too.

Beauford got off the train at Brindisi to find the ship to Patras. The criminals from the train followed and threatened him. Suddenly they were joined by a shouting mob that surrounded him; to escape he picked up a cobblestone and began hitting himself over the head. The police "rescued" him and, finding the ticket to Patras in his pocket, carried him to the ship, promising all the way to protect him. On the ship things were fine as long as he stayed with the "kind people" in the bar, who bought him drinks. Only in the pre-dawn darkness in the harbor at Patras on July 25 did the trouble begin again—this time with the old voices within, who told him he was about to be murdered. To "fool" the murderers he threw his overcoat—containing money, passport, and tickets—overboard on one side of the ship and then ran to the other side and "stepped off" himself. Beauford could not swim, but a fisherman saw him fall and pulled him into his boat.

After a brief hospital stay he was released to the police, who interrogated him and read aloud letters found in his retrieved bag, letters from Henry Miller and friends in Paris and a copy of one from Darthea Speyer to the American Consulate in Athens announcing his arrival.

The American Consul in Patras was called in and an arrangement was made for Beauford to be met in Athens by a representative of the Embassy. The voices on the bus nagged him but did nothing more than that, and in Athens he was met as promised. Unshaven, rumpled, and unwashed, wearing a pair of old shoes given to him in Patras—shoes with holes he had to cut in them to make room for his toes—Beauford had the appearance of a derelict. The Embassy man found him a room in a cheap hotel, gave him 6 drachmas for spending money, and set up an Embassy appointment for the next morning. Because he had not eaten since breakfast, Beauford was hungry. The hotel porter directed him to a small taverna, where he had no sooner ordered his meal "when a mob descended outside calling my name in English and threatening me." He rushed out of the restaurant without eating, retreated to his hotel, and put a dresser in front of his door to keep the mob, which "heckled" him all night, from breaking into the room. Somehow, despite his precautions, the mob managed to get close to him, and he "spent the night dodging as best I could some kind of pellet they shot into my head, legs, and feet." In desperation he rushed into a corner, took a penknife he still had in his trousers and cut his wrists, but not sufficiently to do major damage. He moved the dresser, stumbled down the stairs, and placed himself in the hands of the porter, who bandaged the cuts and took Beauford to the Embassy. There he applied for "sanctuary" and was immediately placed in a hospital for the insane. His panic became even more acute because he could not understand the Greek he heard and could not make himself understood.

The Embassy contacted Charles and Gita Boggs, whose names Beauford had volunteered, but the only information transmitted was that the painter had had "an

The artist's self-portrait, 1961. Acrylic on paper, 26 x 19¼ in. Courtesy of the Delaney Estate and the Ewing Gallery, University of Tennessee.

accident." The Boggses reached Darthea Speyer, who was about to leave for Athens and Hydra, and she had Beauford moved to a private clinic on the outskirts of the city, where he remained for several weeks.

During his stay Beauford wrote a will leaving his paintings to his brother Joe, his "personal effects" to Richard and Bernard, and "my body to the potter's field." His passport and money were found and returned, and through the haze of heavy medication, he kept hearing the voice of a friend. This friend was Darthea Speyer, who not only had arranged for his move to the clinic but also, with some difficulty, managed to reserve a place for him on a flight to Paris on El Al, the only airline willing to carry a man in Beauford's mental state.

The trip from Athens to Paris was Beauford's first flight, and the trip was terrifying for him for that reason and because the "criminals" somehow got onto the plane with him. He was met by Gita Boggs at Orly airport on August 21, and before even saying hello, he told her, "You go on ahead or these two men will kill you."

In answer to a plea from the Boggses for help in paying for Beauford's hospitalization and care, $1,600 came in from Henry Miller, Larry Calcagno, Al Hirschfeld,
James Baldwin, Michael Freilich, Darthea Speyer, and many other friends. Beauford was anxious not to go back to Clamart since he feared Mlle. Marty; he also
felt the voices were particularly powerful there. The Boggses agreed to take
responsibility for him until some solution could be found. They thought it might
be best for him to travel with them to San Telmo in Majorca for their annual vacation, and so he did. Their friends Joe and Bernice O'Reilly, who also knew Beauford well, joined the party.

The O'Reillys and Boggses hoped that being in a small village in Spain would
settle Beauford's mind. But the plotters who had tried to kill him in Italy and
Greece followed their prey even into the little hotels the travelers stayed in on
their way to Spain. At first they lurked in the garden at San Telmo and prevented
Beauford from leaving his room. In San Telmo he did eat well and rest, and, with
the help of soothing talks with Bernice and Gita especially, managed to maintain
a surface calm and even began to do some watercolors. As always, time with little
Gordon seemed to help as well. But he began to talk of the need of a gun to
defend himself against his enemies. The most difficult chore for the Boggses was
to keep alcohol away from their guest since the hospital in Athens had diagnosed
severe liver and kidney problems, and drinking clearly accentuated the power of
Beauford's tormentors. The alcohol problem would continue to exist for Beauford and his friends the rest of his life. It involved a constant struggle between
those who would deny him alcohol and those who maintained that a "little bit"
would do him no harm and keep him happy.

Back in Paris in early September, Beauford entered the American Hospital for a
few days of tests. The kidney and liver problems were confirmed. When released
he still preferred to avoid Clamart and remained with the Boggses. At first he
seemed buoyed by letters of encouragement from his many friends, but Charley
and Gita began to lose hope when they found that neither familiar surroundings
nor the lack of alcohol seemed to quiet the voices. They were appalled, too, that
Beauford's Paris friends did not always take his condition seriously. The general
attitude was that Beauford had always been a "character" and that these voices
were somehow a "normal" part of his personality. The Boggses began to be criticized for being overly protective and sometimes Beauford believed their critics,
viewing Charley and Gita at certain moments as enemies. Yet their generosity
toward him was evident, and their household had come under extreme strain with
the presence under one roof of a deeply paranoid man and an eight-year-old child
who could not possibly understand what was happening to someone he had long

thought of as a benevolent part of the family. The situation became acute when delirium tremens occurred as a result of bouts of excessive drinking in the cafes. The Boggses urged Beauford to accept psychological help, but he refused.

Charley and Gita's major moral support came from Jim and Bunny LeGros and from Palmer and Mimi Hayden, who all entertained Beauford to relieve some of their burden. Mimi, especially, tried to do what she could to bring her friend around to his old self and urged him to seek professional help. She remembered that he had once told her a story about how Alice B. Toklas had confronted a robber in priest's clothing who was climbing over the wall into the Toklas–Gertrude Stein garden. She had stood up and left the garden, after ordering the robber to "be gone" by the time she got back. He had done exactly as he was told. Mimi reminded Beauford that he had used this story as an example of the "moral courage" necessary for confronting difficult circumstances, and she begged him to "call on all the moral strength . . . which is yours to exorcise the unreal materializations of hostility which trouble you." Why had he told her the Toklas story, she asked, if he would not now "work with those who can help you?" Later Beauford would confide in the Haydens that he always kept Mimi's Toklas note with him and that he would "try to find the love and faith needed for the simple truth," but that "love and hate are Siamese twins" (December 29, 1961).

Another ardent supporter was Larry Calcagno, who flew to Paris to be with Beauford in October and managed to get him to return to Clamart until an apartment in Paris could be found. Later Beauford would write, "You have been here and gone like a great angel of mercy." He promised to follow "your great good counsel to the limit, am working."(November 19, 1961). For a few weeks after Larry's visit Beauford seemed more cheerful. Palmer Hayden wrote to Joe Delaney that he had "met your big brother" on the boulevard, who had greeted him with words used among the "Saints" in the New York days: "Good morning, Captain," he had said. "Good morning, shine," had been the mock reply, and Beauford's answer had followed the ritual pattern: "There ain't a damn thing the matter; I just ain't gwine" (November 13, 1961).

Henry Miller wrote Beauford somewhat naively in early December saying how happy he was that his friend was working and "that neither outside nor inside voices disturb you. . . . One wouldn't mind if one heard Jesus, let us say, or Ramakrishna, or dear St. Francis, eh?" (December 4, 1961). Beauford wrote back a Christmas greeting saying, "I seek to find within myself the voice of peace and love for all mankind" (December 13, 1961).

By that time Beauford knew he was not improving inside and finally agreed to accept help, allowing Gita to take him to a psychiatrist for consultation. What bothered him most was that his friends, whom he trusted, would not believe in the voices. One night, when everything was perfectly quiet—without even any city sounds—Beauford came into Charley and Gita's room, fully dressed, intent on leaving. "You don't mean to tell me you don't hear them, Charley?" he said. The psychiatrist eventually arrived at a diagnosis of acute paranoid delusions aggravated by alcoholism, and advised that his patient be sent back to the United States for treatment under an American doctor who would be able to communicate more easily with him. He ordered that Beauford drink no alcohol.

Thus began a struggle between those friends, led by his brothers Joe and Emery, who thought he should return home, and his Montparnasse friends who thought he belonged in Paris whatever the circumstances. Close friends like the Boggses and the LeGros were somewhere between these opposite extremes, and could not bring themselves to undertake the appeal to the American Embassy that might have resulted in their friend's being sent home against his will.

The Boggs–LeGros position was essentially Baldwin's as well. He had found out about the suicide attempt after the fact, since he had been in Israel and then Turkey working on a project. Beauford wrote to him in Turkey as soon as he learned his address and the correspondence between the two men is full of apologies—from Beauford for what he had "done" and from Baldwin for not being there to help. Beauford's first letter after the Greek episode begins "My Dear Adorable Jimmy" and speaks in an almost fatherly way of how "Life has so many ways of teaching and preparing us" (October 15, 1961). Baldwin's answer begins "My Dearest Beauford" and ends with a plea for his friend to "be good." He promised to return to Paris for Christmas and did, but by that time Beauford was undergoing a rest cure at La Maison du Santé de Nogent sur Marne outside Paris and was allowed no visitors.

This treatment had been arranged, with Beauford's approval, by Madame Solange du Closel, a French art collector who had known and helped Beauford since 1958 with the moral support of Professor Ahmed Bioud, a North African who was a scholar at the Bibliothèque Nationale. When it became clear that Charley and Gita Boggs had kept Beauford as long as they could and that the return to Clamart was not a solution to his problems, Beauford was taken in at first by M. Bioud and his family and then by Madame du Closel and her husband.

Beauford had met Bioud at the Facchetti exhibition in June and had struck up a friendship even though the two men had little knowledge of each other's language. This friendship was to become one the most valued of Beauford's personal associations. From 1960 on he would take frequent trips with the Biouds and would, more often than not, join them for Sunday lunch. He had met

Madame du Closel at the end of 1958 when she had visited his studio as a representative of "Baralipton I," a group dedicated to the support of talented but insufficiently known artists. She had been horrified by Beauford's living conditions in Clamart, astonished by the mastery of light in his paintings, and immediately taken by the painter's tenderness. She had bought several paintings for her association and for herself, and became a major Delaney supporter.

Beauford was lucid at times during the days at the du Closels; at other times he was oppressed by threats from evil men hidden in various rooms of the house. One evening he interrupted a dinner party of important figures in the Paris art and political world to warn Madame du Closel of her imminent death at the hands of men lurking in the next room. Madame got up from the table, took her friend from room to room, closet to closet, to show him that there were no murderers, and for a while he was satisfied. As Christmas was approaching she suggested the next day that he paint some Christmas scenes. The result was a series of outlined crèches on yellow backgrounds that would mark the beginning of what might be called the late Delaney style. Beauford gave one of these paintings to his hostess, one to her maid, and one to the concierge (see Color Plate 10).

Meanwhile, Madame du Closel made the final arrangements for Beauford's rest cure. To cover expenses there was the money already collected by the Boggses, augmented by some more sent at Beauford's own request by a few friends, and funds contributed by the du Closels themselves. On December 20 Solange du Closel and her husband drove Beauford to the Nogent clinic where he was placed under the care of the well-known psychiatrist Dr. Ferdière, whose specialty was depression. Ferdière quickly confirmed the diagnosis of acute paranoia and gave Beauford anti-depressant medicine that stopped the hallucinations. He warned Beauford that alcohol would negate the benefits of his treatment. Ferdière spoke English and had a good knowledge of painting and the arts—he had treated the mental disorders of the dramatist Antoin Artaud and had written a book critical of the handling of Vincent Van Gogh's depression.

Eventually, in the course of regular appointments during the years immediately after Beauford's hospitalization, Ferdière and his family also became Beauford's social friends. At first, even though Beauford seemed willing to talk freely with him and appeared to welcome treatment, Ferdière felt that it would be best for his patient to return to the United States. Beauford would stay at Nogent, with the exception of a brief visit to Clamart, until January 14. He definitively rejected the idea of returning to the States. What he wanted was an apartment in Paris—in Montparnasse—near the galleries and his painter friends. But for now there was the necessity of the cure.

Beauford's sixtieth birthday on December 30, 1961, was spent a long way from home in a quiet room with no friends and, under doctor's orders, no possibility of communicating with them. James Baldwin made a spirited attempt to see him, but was not admitted. Beauford had never been so alone, yet he loved the whiteness of his room and the hope of light it seemed to signify. In his journal he wrote the words of an old song: "He was called to Bethlehem/Oh tell me where to find Him/They took my Lord away/Oh tell me where to find him."

nine

Paris: The Vercingétorix Years

A few days before delivering him to the clinic in Nogent, Madame du Closel had informed Beauford that she and her husband had found a possible atelier/apartment for him in the rue Vercingétorix in Montparnasse. A visit to the apartment had raised Beauford's hopes for the future and made him more willing to undergo the treatment. He wrote to Henry Miller of his "astonishment" at Madame du Closel's accomplishment. The atelier was a large room with a huge window admitting south light. There was also the luxury of a "shower bath" (December 13, 1961). To Larry Calcagno he wrote that "some dear friends have given me a studio," and that he was particularly thrilled that it was on the very street in which Larry had lived when Beauford first arrived in Paris. He noted that the "light is wonderful" and that the ambiance of Paris was conducive to work although, under medication, he was "much becalmed now" (January 20, 1962). In that atelier at 53 rue Vercingétorix Beauford Delaney produced the works which were arguably the best of his career.

Madame du Closel's original plan, made in consultation with M. Bioud and the Boggses, was that the money collected by Charley and Gita from Beauford's

Beauford in his Vercingétorix studio, 1962.

friends should be used toward leasing the atelier, but it quickly became clear that
these funds would cover only the medical treatment and basic living expenses for a
few months. The du Closels thus decided to purchase the apartment in their name
for Beauford. Unfortunately, this act of generosity led in later years to false accusa-
tions against them—charges that they had used Beauford's money to buy an
apartment for themselves and then collected rent from the painter and demanded
paintings. In fact, the du Closels undertook the expenses of co-owners, paid all
necessary taxes, and asked no rent at all of Beauford from 1962 to 1975. They did
accept the occasional painting that, out of gratitude, he gave them—especially
each year at Christmas time.

     The du Closels also helped Beauford move directly from the clinic to the new
apartment, had his possessions transferred from Clamart, and arranged for painting
the atelier and plumbing and electrical repairs. The next step, for which Madame du
Closel was also wrongly criticized, was to devise, with aid from the Boggses and
Ahmed Bioud, a system for paying Beauford a certain sum each week from the
money collected for him. This money was augmented by having Madame du

Closel, with the artist's approval, sell several Delaney paintings. These funds would be distributed first by Charley Boggs and then by M. Bioud, who invited Beauford to dinner at least once a week to be sure that he had nourishment.

Being back in Montparnasse suited Beauford. He enjoyed the possibility of meeting old friends as he strolled through the quartier. He wrote to Larry Calcagno of the nostalgia he felt when he passed Larry's old place on the street, how he had recently run into Shirley Goldfarb "looking wonderful" sitting with Alberto Giacometti in a cafe, how he could easily walk over for lunch at his friend Arlene Higuily's studio (February 8, 1962 and to Miller February 12, 1962). Henry Miller added to the "ambiance"—a favorite Beauford word—by pointing out that Beauford's new place was "near Gauguin's old studio where he kept a Javanese mistress"(February 25, 1962). M. Bioud brought by the philosopher and art critic Jean Grenier, from then on a faithful friend and supporter. When Henry Miller promised to visit soon Beauford was in a sufficiently playful mood to sign his reply "Beauford Delaney (Negro painter)" (February 27, 1962).

With the coming of spring, however, Beauford's improved health and the urging of his uninformed friends led to his taking at first occasional and then more frequent drinks. He became increasingly listless. On an early April visit to Dr. Ferdière he was sternly warned against drinking. The doctor gave him a note in French and English to show friends who offered him alcohol: "I certify that our friend is currently under treatment: any alcohol, even mild (wine, beer, etc.) can cause serious illness"(April 5, 1962). Beauford never showed the note to anyone, continued drinking, and by early May had relapsed into a psychotic state. On May 5 Dr. Ferdière admitted him to the clinic at Nogent, where he remained until May 25. During his first days there he once again contemplated suicide. On May 6 he wrote a strange entry in his journal:

> Is this the last day of my life? How does one tally the score? Love is all and that I give the world. Painting only now begins to explore all that I have felt and suffered.

He speaks of the "misunderstanding" that has led him to believe that his work would be appreciated by others and of the failure of his friends to inform him of his mistake. He notes that he has "abandoned" most of the correspondence that had once been so important to him. At the top of one page he draws a square with a circle in it. In the circle are the names of his family members, the ultimate loved ones—Emery, Gertrude, Joseph, Ogust, Imogene, and Junior—those to whom the final message was to be addressed. Around the circle he writes: "Mention not remembering some of the things that cannot be done and what a shock not to have known sooner so as to arrange my things. No one told me of this tragedy."

Once again Beauford was isolated in the clinic. Madame du Closel, as the responsible party, was allowed in, but when Henry Miller came with Gita Boggs they were denied admission. Miller did talk with Ferdière, however, and was impressed with his understanding of Beauford's problems. He sent the doctor a copy of his little book *To Paint Is to Love Again* and continued to consult with him on Beauford's condition for the next few years.

While Beauford was in Nogent his friends again attempted to raise money to pay for his hospitalization and day-to-day living when he would return to Vercingétorix. Henry Miller sent money as did various New York and Paris friends. But it became clear to the Boggses, M. Bioud, and Madame du Closel that some more permanent financial system would have to be made in addition to the one they had already worked out. A lack of money and fear of losing his residence permit because of that lack haunted Beauford. For him to have some peace of mind and, as M. Bioud put it, "restore confidence in life and in himself" (to Mme. du Closel, May 10, 1962), the best solution seemed to lie in Beauford's own work since through its sale Beauford would be supporting himself. M. Bioud approached the Facchettis and attempted to make an arrangement whereby they would keep the paintings they already had and show the ones in Beauford's atelier in return for an increased allowance. The Facchettis had paid Beauford nothing under the old arrangement since his crisis in Greece because they had not believed the painter would survive his ordeal. The Facchettis, who first agreed to this new system, seem to have had second thoughts, because by mid-June Beauford was writing to Larry Calcagno that they had "done nothing for me" (June 18, 1962).

For the moment Beauford had to depend on the generosity of friends like Calcagno and Mrs. Ascoli, who continued to send money. Still under the regular care of Dr. Ferdière, who gave him frequent appointments and charged nothing, Beauford was primarily concerned with his inner life and his painting: "I look deeply within myself and include the new adjustments to life and work and change as best I can" (to Calcagno, June 18, 1962).

Beauford's spirits were somewhat raised by his being represented in the Carnegie International Exhibition in Pittsburgh, by Jean Grenier's glowing article about him in the June issue of *Preuves*, and by his friend Paul Jenkins' article, "A Quiet Legend" in the December *Art International*. Grenier also bought a large painting and paid Beauford handsomely.

Dr. Ferdière suggested that Beauford try to write about his early life and his own sense of where his art came from and what it meant to him. This "assignment" gave rise to a series of autobiographical notes about the Knoxville days (see Chapter 1) and to the following passage about his essential anonymity — despite his many friends — and his lonely commitment to art:

> Life in Paris gives me an anonymity and objectivity to release long stored up memories of [the] beauty and sorrows of the difficult work of orchestrating and releasing into a personal form of color and design what seems to me a long apprenticeship to jazz and spiritual songs augmented by the deep hope given to my people in the deep south at home. I gave myself to these experiences devotedly. . . . Somehow painting found me when I was very young — there was no obvious environment for its outlet, which suppressed it. With me it was very private, obscure, and fascinating.

He goes on to speak of the importance of light, which is, "somehow the same everywhere" and the way in which, whatever one paints, "one's voice retains its own unique sound."

> Wherever one is, painting is a continuous flow and includes its own sources. . . . Living here gives one the necessity of reflection through the window of personal intuition — through this window comes sorrow, frustration, and very occasionally cause for joy.

He mentions the "indifference of the Creative Process to the person through whom it must function."

> The artist may perhaps . . . never have any other satisfaction than being a willing worker hoping for revelation and time enough to release what life and experience has brought through his apprenticeship.

The word "apprenticeship" had become a prominent addition to favorite Beauford words.

Early in July Beauford went to a show of Joan Miro's work at the Musée d'Art Moderne and saw in Miro's art "the universal movement of man in search, saying the unsayable." He came home happy, able to write, "It is long since my inner spirit felt like it does now" (to Miller, July 2, 1962). Beauford took advantage of this new enthusiasm to begin painting regularly again — really for the first time since his breakdown in Greece — and showed three abstractions in a group show at the Musée des Arts Décoratifs in July and several others at a group show called "Resurgence" at the Galerie Breteau, also in July. His immediate concern as an artist was to "work with the problem of trying to get color into proper form and texture on canvas" and make it jibe with "the form in our mind and life" (to Miller, undated, summer 1962).

The paintings that emerged were the first of the large, densely painted yellow abstractions that would mark the Vercingétorix years. Henk van Gelre, Henry

Miller's Dutch publisher, to whom Beauford gave one of these paintings, saw in them "a world of loneliness on one side but to the other side full holy admiration, perplexity and silence for the mystery life is" (August 27, 1962) (see Color Plate 11).

The summer brought the usual train of visitors from New York. Michael Freilich came and so did Sam Spanier and Sam's friend Lynn Stone; they all tried to interest Beauford once again in a New York show. Stone's idea, eventually supported by James Baldwin, was to bring as many Delaney paintings as possible to New York and combine them with older paintings to which Larry Wallrich could gain access. The show would be sponsored by the Urban League, and money raised by the sale of the paintings along with private donations would be divided between the League and Beauford.

Beauford took up the idea somewhat reluctantly since he was afraid of the effect on his precarious mental state of the tension involved in a trip to America and a major show. In November 1962 Charley Boggs wrote to Stone of his own misgivings about Beauford's condition and his ability to stand up to the strain. After reassurances from Stone, however, the plans proceeded. Beauford arranged to have paintings sent, and when the Urban League made known its need for considerable donations to support the preparations for the show, Beauford gave Stone a list of possible donors, including, in addition to many others, Palmer Hayden, the Hirschfelds, Henry Miller, and Carl van Vechten, who had photographed Beauford in 1952 during a visit to his New York studio.

James Baldwin wrote a form letter to solicit donations and support his friend's exhibition, noting that the purpose of the proposed show was to raise money for the Urban League and "to bring to wider attention the work of a very great artist." In the letter Baldwin pointed to the influences of Cézanne, Van Gogh, and especially the blues on his friend's art. Delaney, he said, "brings great light out of the darkness of his journey, and makes his journey, and his endeavor, and his triumph ours." He referred to Beauford as his "spiritual father" to whom "I owe a debt that can never be repaid." Baldwin then pledged the first $500 for the campaign. The letter moved Beauford greatly when he saw it some months later.

But the yearlong attempt on the part of Stone and Baldwin to bring about the show would ultimately fail because of a lack of money and the conflicting priorities of the Urban League. Beauford put a great deal of effort into this project and was both disappointed by its failure and relieved that he would not have to undergo the strain its realization would have required.

He threw himself with a great deal of energy into his work during the fall of 1962 and the winter that followed. There was the usual round of fall shows, including ones of the works of his friends Don Fink and Paul Jenkins, and he was represented in September and October in a group show with Bob Thompson and Abe Rattner at the American Artists' Center on the boulevard Raspail. He saw a great deal of Howard Swanson, with whom he shared frequent meals and could talk more freely than with most people. When the cold weather came he spent many nights at the Boggs apartment or the Bioud home. A concert by Elwood Peterson pleased him greatly, as did a performance of "Black Nativity" and visits in December and May from James Baldwin, who sat many hours with him in the new atelier and brought him up to date on the civil rights struggle in America. Later in the year he would write to Henry Miller, who also visited in May, "My spirit is with the struggle for human rights taking place in the south and my prayers are with the Blacks and Whites." (May 16, 1963).

The inefficient heating system at 53 rue Vercingétorix was somewhat overcome by a gift of a blanket and warm clothes from Lynn Stone, and, with the nondrinking regime, he had more time and significant new energy to devote to his painting. Both portraits and abstractions occupied him; there were several 1963 group shows to prepare for, including one at the Salon des Réalités Nouvelles at the Musée d'Art Moderne and one at the Musée Cantonal des Beaux-Arts in Lausanne.

His conversations with Baldwin led to the first sketch of a Rosa Parks series that would take several years and would show a black woman on a bench sometimes alone and sometimes with a white woman. The first sketch depicts Mrs. Parks sitting in the middle of a bus seat next to the words "I will not be moved." On the back of a later Park paintings, in which the woman is alone on a bench, are the words "She ain't getting up, Mrs. Parks" (see Color Plate 12).

When Beauford read Baldwin's "Letter from a Region of My Mind" (later "Down at the Cross" in The Fire Next Time), he wrote to Baldwin that the article revealed "to all of us so much that we feel but cannot put into words." It was "remarkable," he said, perhaps somewhat enviously, "how consistently you flow into your own medium and keep your life moving and of one piece in these difficult times" (January 1963). Beauford tried to express his feelings through his own medium in those Parks paintings in which he returned to a theme he treated only slightly more figuratively in the 1930s and 1940s, as in the poignant depiction of a black woman caring for a white child in a baby carriage (see Color Plate 13).

Psychologically Beauford continued to improve. Occasional "mistakes" occurred—a glass of red wine accepted when urged on him by a friend—but for the most part he followed Dr. Ferdière's orders. In his journals he spoke of "expected periods of depression and negation" that "take over temporarily" and

reveal "inadequacy which prepares us for the . . . humility necessary for . . . elimi-
nating some of the . . . ridiculous outmoded habits." And once again he found
solace in the wisdom literature of the Far East, reading especially in the *Dhamma-
pada*—words of the Buddha—recommended to him by an old New York friend,
Eleanor Olson. This reading helped him "to continue and also to feel a part of the
human family" (to Lynn Stone, December 3, 1962).

With Dr. Ferdière's help Beauford was exploring himself more profoundly than
he had been willing to do in the past. He had "been aware for many years of . . . a
very vigorous infection deep within myself . . . but have had little or no opportunity to talk with anyone at all about it or to delve into myself except only very
lately." He had had good, even intimate conversations with friends such as Baldwin, Ellis Wilson, and Howard Swanson, but had avoided discussion about the
need for "full carnal freedom." Through Dr. Ferdière he was apparently more sys-
tematically confronting an aspect of himself—his sexuality—that had long bothered him and that Henry Miller's work had helped him to begin to face years
earlier. In conversations with his doctor he was "touching on many levels of
courage necessary" for achieving full relationships with "cultivated and
approachable people" instead of dangerous relationships with those who had
only their own needs in mind (notes in journal). It was necessary to change his
old habits, but "the birth pains" involved in emerging into "enlightenment," he
wrote to Henry Miller, "are almost unbearable . . . yet . . . morning comes after
the darkest night" (undated, winter 1963).

The spring brought a new burst of painting and a concentrated attempt to
translate the "long interims of probity into our thoughts" into paintings "which
are never what our inner vision expected" (to Calcagno, undated, spring 1963).
This process was stimulated by a Kandinsky show in May and by Kandinsky's
own words copied into his journal: "The observer must learn to look at a picture
as a graphic representation of a mood and not as a representation of objects."
Beauford remembered John Marin's similar view that works of art are meant as
"constructed expressions of the inner senses, responding to things seen and felt."
He spoke of Kandinsky's working with "mood values" of color—of his primary
concern with the "artist's inner life."

In July the Biouds invited Beauford for a visit to Embrun in the southern Alps
and put him up for two weeks in an eighteenth-century hotel. Beauford loved the
"mystery of the lakes and mountains." The "color of the mountains and valley
look like old Italian paintings from the 14th century" (journal). The scene at dinner with the hotel family was like "just another Van Gogh—the predominant
color was yellow." In his own painting he was "trying to merge color and form

into the essences of things felt and remembered," and yellow was the dominant color (to Miller, July 19, 1963).

Soon after his return to Paris Beauford left for the south again, this time for a month with Bernard Hassell and Richard Olney at their house in Solliès Toucas, near Toulon. Mary Painter accompanied him. Beauford painted a great deal and, as always, enjoyed the sun, but was upset at missing James Baldwin's quick visit to Paris to gather expatriate support for the March on Washington.

In December, after a brief first trip to London with Mary Painter, Beauford wrote to Henry Miller and to his brother Joe expressing his sadness over the assassination of President Kennedy. He thanked Miller for the therapeutic gift of his writing: "Your concepts . . . gather direction and lucidity and arrive at their own conclusions like a great river flowing through the land arranging its bed according to its necessities . . . [your] writing produces a new influence into the meaning of the song of words, the universal flow of music or a mute enigmatic feeling of joy unique beside the presence of woe, all taking on the color of a rainbow in a cube of ice" (December 16, 1963).

He thanked Joe for the "light from your star" on a Christmas card—a star that "illumines and brings warmth"—and advises Joe to "hold on and keep your hand on the plow—it takes time for the light to penetrate, but it's always there" (December 24, 1963).

With the support of letters from Henry Miller, James Jones, and James Baldwin, Beauford received a two-year Fairfield Foundation grant of $3,500 beginning in January 1964. Baldwin's letter to John Thompson, the foundation's director, spoke eloquently of Beauford's predicament:

He has been starving and working all of his life—in Tennessee, in Boston, in New York, and now in Paris. He has been menaced more than any other man I know by his social circumstances and also by all the emotional and psychological stratagems he has been forced to use to survive; and, more than any other man I know, he has transcended both the inner and the outer darkness. (December 4, 1963)

Beauford's response to the grant was to send checks to his brothers, to Dante Pavone, who was sick, and to Ellis Wilson. He also invited his brother Emery to visit him during the summer; when he accepted Beauford made improvements to his studio, even buying a refrigerator, which he used as a storage cabinet. One friend remembers that when Beauford came by her studio one day and saw that she was feeling "blue," he opened his checkbook and began writing a check for her from his fellowship account. She refused but unfortunately others who heard of his grant were not so considerate. Before long Beauford found himself giving out money to "friends" who quite simply took advantage of his generosity.

On the surface 1964 was a good year for Beauford. He participated in spring group show at the Galerie Internationale d'Art Contemporaine for which Julien Alvard wrote the catalogue introduction, praising "Beaufort-Delaney"'s yellow abstraction as "une émanation du soleil" (an emanation of the sun) in which one finds all seasons but winter, and light is filtered through the painter's tone and touch.

In July Beauford showed ten abstract gouaches in a Copenhagen exhibition, "10 American Negro Artists," with Herbert Gentry, Sam Middleton, Larry Potter, Harvey Cropper, and others. He also sold a large oil to the Musée Cantonal des Beaux-Arts in Lausanne, where he had exhibited the year before. The sale was arranged by Ahmed Bioud, who wrote to Beauford of his joy that in the art world there was still "un peu de justice" (a little justice) (August 1, 1964).

But all was not well. M. Bioud had noticed in the early spring that Beauford was drinking again and that he talked a great deal about his "failure" as a painter. To Larry Calcagno Beauford confided, "This has been the most difficult year of my life—loneliness, rheumatism, and *la grippe*, but I have battled with it all and managed to do more painting than ever before in my life"(April 16, 1964).

He was now preparing for a major solo exhibition at the Galerie Lambert scheduled for the end of the year and working both on portraits and abstractions dominated by his favorite yellow. He wrote to Henry Miller, "My work intensifies itself and some of the years of groping begin to take root in color and form—the human situation invades and pours; I am humbly dedicated and try to find orchestration for this deluge. . . . One does not strive after fame but one does desire 'to be'" (May 21, 1964).

Still, Beauford's friends noticed that although his mind seemed clear, he was constantly tired. Dinners and overnights with the Boggses or Biouds helped, and he began making fairly regular weekend visits to Jim and Bunny LeGros in Velizy, "the dear friends in the country." Meanwhile, he looked forward with some trepidation to the visit from his brother Emery, who would be accompanied by his wife Gertrude and their daughter Imogene. He had seen no one from his family in twelve years.

When Emery's arrival was delayed several times by complications with passports, inoculations, and finances, Beauford began to suspect that the visit would not take place. When, by July 18, he had not heard from Emery he began to have a breakdown. In the middle of the night on July 26 he found his way to the Boggs apartment, without his usual gift of a watercolor and a gâteau de Bretagne, but no one answered the bell. On the July 27 he wrote to Larry Calcagno complaining that "life is difficult and I try each day to brighten its darkness—the world is cruel and indifferent" (July 27, 1964). Later that day he went to Dr. Ferdière in a state of panic and the doctor increased the level of his medication. That afternoon he appeared at the door of Madame du Closel, who took him in and calmed him down before he left to spend the night with Charley and Gita.

Word came that the family was to arrive on August 4, but Beauford was terrified at the last minute of going to the airport. He was afraid his family would be shocked by his living conditions. It fell to a new friend, Addie Herder, to take him to the airport in a taxi. Herder, also a painter, had come to Paris the year before and met Beauford through her close friends the Joneses, with whom they both often had dinner on Saturday nights. The meeting at the airport was emotional and Emery was upset by his brother's confusion and apparent ill health. The family at first went to a hotel, but after a day they moved into Beauford's one-room studio and were much happier. Beauford wrote to Joe, "A strange magic has come to pass—as I write I converse with Gertrude, Emery, and Imogene . . . 12 years since seeing any of you—no doubt I have become a bit strange; however, all things seem mysteriously like they have always been" (August 10, 1964).

On the first Sunday Emery and Beauford went alone together to mass at Notre Dame and Emery found it "heart-thrilling" to hear such music, with thousands of worshippers, and to be there with his brother (Emery to Joe, August 9, 1964). Beauford's friends entertained his family "royally" in the evenings; during the day there was time to sightsee, exchange news, and remember childhood, as well as time for Beauford to do sketches for portraits of all three loved ones along with a self-portrait, his greatest of many, that would be finished in 1965 (see Color Plate 14).

The departure of Emery and his family was sad, but Beauford seemed energized by their visit. He began painting with added enthusiasm for the December show at the Lambert. To Miller he wrote, "Have worked terribly hard here in Europe and much has sundered and exploded, but now it coalesces with lava-like smoke and fluid color, sometimes a veritable flame, other times subdued essences . . . yes, I am again painting in my old feeling—tense, difficult, but compulsive, and I *love it*" September 14, 1964).

A visit from Richard Long and a trip to the south with Bernard Hassell and Richard Olney helped keep Beauford settled in the fall. In October the collector Donald Stralem, introduced to Beauford by the Joneses, bought several Delaney paintings at a good price, and in November the painter received $500 as an advance on the first installment of his share of the sale of the old Vine Street house in Knoxville—the house he had grown up in that had been marked for demolition by Knoxville's urban renewal program—called the "urban removal" program by the Delaneys and others. Most of the money was given away to "more needy dear friends."

In October and November paintings by Beauford Delaney were shown at Fairleigh Dickinson University, with works by Romare Bearden and Lorenzo Gilcrist, as part of an exhibition called "Some Negro Artists." And on October 15 there was a press–television preview of artists (with their paintings) and writers who were members of the Artists Abroad for Johnson Committee. Tria French, James Baldwin's agent in France, and a close friend of Beauford, had urged him to participate.

But the big event of the year was the opening of his one-man show at the Galerie Lambert at 14 rue St-Louis-en-L'ile. As with the 1960 Facchetti opening, the occasion was a celebration of Beauford Delaney and his newfound health and productivity. All his Paris friends were in attendance and James Baldwin provided a stirring catalogue introduction calling Delaney a "great painter" whose "work leads the inner and outer eye, directly and inexorably, to a new confrontation with reality." The theme of the article is light: "The light contained in every thing, in every surface, in every face." Beauford, said Baldwin, was a painter who sought the light wherever it could be found and whose work was a primary metaphor for an essential lesson in life. Beauford had taught the young Baldwin to find light even in a brown leaf on black asphalt:

> To stare at the leaf long enough, to try to apprehend the leaf, was to discover many colors in it; and though black had been described to me as the absence of light, it became very clear to me that if this were true, we would never have been able to see the color, black: the light is trapped in it and struggles upward. . . . It was humbling to be forced to realize that the light fell down from heaven, on everything, on everybody, and that the light was always changing.

There was also a tribute from James Jones at the exhibition, and the catalogue cover featured a portrait of Beauford's great friend Ahmed Bioud.

The paintings in the show consisted of the best of the new works done at the Vercingétorix studio, both abstractions and portraits. Reviewers and viewers were surprised at the existence in a single show of two seemingly opposite modes of expression, but once again Beauford explained to friends that both approaches were studies in light revealed—the light that gave meaning to the individuals depicted in the large volumes of color in the portraits and the light considered directly as contained in the juxtaposition of minute and closely packed bits of blue, red, and especially yellow in the abstract paintings.

Professor Bioud, 1964. Oil on canvas, 25½ x 19¼ in. Courtesy of the Delaney Estate and the Ewing Gallery, University of Tennessee.

The reviewer in *Nouvelles Littéraires* (December 31, 1964) spoke of the Janus-like "double visage" of the paintings. It was as if when one color was visible another behind it was hidden, ready to reveal its own understanding of light in turn (see Color Plate 11).

In the journal *Arts* (December 16–32, 1964) Jean Guichard-Meili, a noted art critic who had visited Beauford's studio with M. Bioud, wrote of "the movements of internal convection" in the paintings, "the vibrations of underlying design." The portraits, he said, finally "do not differ from the other works. . . . Background, clothing, hands, faces are the pretext for autonomous harmonies" (Richard Long translation).

In March Beauford traveled by car with friends to Genoa, Monte Carlo, and Nice, where he was thrilled to visit sites important to Picasso, Chagall, and Matisse. In the summer Richard Long, the Hirschfelds, Don and Lydia Freeman, and the Haydens all came to Paris. The summer's highlight was the performance of the Ellis Haizlip–Lloyd Richards production of Baldwin's *The Amen Corner* on June 20 at the Théatre des Nations and the party afterwards, attended by the cast, Baldwin himself, and Langston Hughes. And in August friends drove Beauford to Brittany. He wrote to Irene and Billy Rose of the beauty of the landscape and especially of Mont Saint Michel.

To Larry Calcagno and others, however, Beauford continued to speak of the "difficulty" in his life. The strain of following Dr. Ferdière's orders was increasingly felt and lapses occurred. At one point Ferdière came to Beauford's apartment and left a note asking where he was and why he had not kept his appointments. Without the incentive of a major show, Beauford sometimes became listless. Darthea Speyer tried to help by commissioning portraits of herself and members of her family and paying well for them.

In September Beauford found some more solace in a brief visit to Richard Long, who was in Poitiers. Long would work hard during 1965 and 1966 to arrange a show of Delaney paintings at Morgan State College in 1967, and during that period Beauford painted Long's portrait.

In October an abstract painting entitled *Agonie Solaire* appeared on the cover of the USIS's *Le Mouvement Ouvrier aux États-Unis*, and Beauford made that painting, along with the portrait of Professor Bioud, available for a group show in the same month at the American Cultural Center, now directed by Hélène Baltrusaitis, always a devoted supporter. It was an exhibition of works by fifteen American painters, including old friends Joe Downing, Jim LeGros, and Don Fink. It also included works by Ike Muse and Siv Holme, a couple with whom Beauford had become particularly friendly through the LeGros.

At about the time of the show Beauford wrote to Henry Miller, his stalwart confidant on the subject of art, to say, "Something has happened to my color and the paintings seem to have sunlight and the feeling sometimes of all you wonderful people it has been my privilege to have as friends and architects of the spirit" (November 3, 1965).

In December Beauford received an unexpected early Christmas present, a book from James Baldwin dedicated to him. The book was Baldwin's collection of short stories, *Going to Meet the Man*. Beauford was genuinely moved by the gesture and bought several copies to give to friends.

But the new year began tragically with the death of fellow African-American Parisian painter Larry Potter. His death, of an asthma attack, shocked the expatriate art community and sent Beauford into something of a decline. He confided some of his feelings to the Roses:

> I have not been too well and have had to get myself together. . . . I supported it [the death of Potter] not too well. . . . I work and try to take care of myself . . . and I am not complaining because the miracle is that I am still about and loving life more than ever . . . . Have had to take things easy and begin to look after myself a bit. The miracle is that somehow I have gotten away with more than I was aware of but there comes a time when we must recognize limits. . . . Have

(*Left to right*) Larry Calcagno, Beauford, and Charley Boggs in Venice, 1966.

given more time to getting my health together than ever before in my life (smile). This doesn't mean I'm sacred, it means that I am learning how wonderful the gift of life is and how little I have allowed it to teach me. (February 21, 1966).

The situation was not helped by the failure of still another Guggenheim application. With the coming of spring, however, Beauford felt better. He was included in an article of American painters in France by John Ashbery (*Art News Annual*, 31, 1966, p. 146) in which the writer recognized in his friend Delaney's abstract paintings the attempt "to show off light, to reveal it in as many of its manifestations as possible." One morning Beauford wrote to Baldwin describing how he was attempting to "exploit the light" of "a beautiful spring day" and how "writing to you is also exploiting light, (smile)" (March 16, 1966).

The summer of 1966 would be particularly eventful. Larry Calcagno arrived in June and he and Darthea Speyer and Charley Boggs took Beauford with them to Venice for the Biennale. Beauford loved the painting he saw, and especially Venice itself—the canals, the gondolas, the food, the Piazza. It was a trip, like earlier ones he had taken with Larry to Spain, that became a dominant theme in his memory. A second theme from that summer was the trip to Istanbul, Turkey; it was just before that trip that I met Beauford Delaney.

James Baldwin had been in Istanbul for several months working on a novel. I was working for him as a secretary-assistant and in June he sent me to New York with part of his manuscript. On the way back I planned to stop in Paris to take delivery of a car I had bought. Baldwin asked that I collect a friend named Richard in London on my way to Paris and that in Paris I pick up Beauford Delaney. I knew Richard as an eccentric young poet of Armenian-Russian-English ancestry whom Baldwin had met in London earlier in the year. I had only heard of but not met Beauford and asked Baldwin to describe him: "He's a cross between Brer Rabbit and St. Francis of Asissi," he said and sent me on my way.

On July 1, having deposited Richard with a cousin of his in Paris and picked up my car, I made my way to 53 rue Vercingétorix. I found a Zolaesque courtyard guarded by an ancient female concierge dressed in black. She pointed to the corner entryway when I asked for M. Delaney and I climbed several stories, passing dark, sour smelling corridors before reaching the landing on which there was a door with a note announcing in bold script, "Welcome David." Clearly Jimmy had warned his friend of my coming. I knocked on the door and a soft, musical voice answered, "Come in, David." The vision that greeted me can only be called mysterious. There was whiteness everywhere—the walls and furniture were covered with sheets and the carrier of the voice was dressed in a white shirt and white trousers; in the midst of all that whiteness was a round, dark, quizzical but smiling face illumined by the yellow sunlight that poured through the large window. I thought of Baldwin's description, and of St. Francis in his hermitage. After his greeting, Beauford's first words to me were, "Won't you lie down." Somehow at the time the suggestion, accompanied by a gentle movement of one hand toward a sheet-draped cot along the wall, did not seem strange. I immediately lay down on the cot and Beauford reclined on the one in line with mine along the east wall.

Essentially we stayed head to head on those cots for three days and nights except for visits to the latrine in the outside corridor and brief moments of canned tuna nourishment. Sometimes we slept, but when we did not we talked. Beauford knew why I was there but he had no intention of getting into a car with me to drive anywhere until he knew who I was and I knew who he was. Day and night had little effect on our interview—sometimes Beauford's soft voice came out of the darkness, sometimes out of the light. We talked about everything—our childhoods, our loves, our work, Baldwin, the artist's difficult quest for survival. We talked about life as an "apprenticeship" rather than an end, about the works of

Proust, about Zen. Beauford's was a sad but loving voice—soft, with a slight southern melody to it; it was a voice that probed difficult and even painful places. When the three days were over and Beauford said, "Shall we go to Jimmy now?"—as if he were across the street—I felt at once exhausted and somehow sated, as if we had had three days and nights of energetic intimacy. Before leaving I asked to see the paintings and when the sheets were lifted was given my first showing of the art of Beauford Delaney—an amazing profusion of yellow abstractions intermingled with extraordinary portraits whom the painter identified as Walter Anderson, James Baldwin, Bernard Hassell, and many others.

We picked up Richard and started out. The trip was a terrifying experience. I had been told nothing of Beauford's paranoia, and his "voices" had not been included in our three-day conversation. The first day and night were fine, if a bit bizarre because of Richard's cries of appreciation for odd objects he noticed along the road—old shoes, discarded cans and tires. Beauford smiled at these remarks; if I had read Baldwin's introduction to the Lambert show I would have tried to find the "light" in those objects as well.

The first real trouble came in Yugoslavia after a difficult border crossing—difficult because the customs officials were upset by Richard's voided British passport containing his picture at age six and because we were an unlikely trio, probably importing drugs. As we drove along the road Beauford, sitting next to me in the front seat, asked in his usual quiet voice, "Did you hear what they said?" When I inquired "Who?" Beauford pointed back at the car that had just passed us. Trained in the processes of blind reason by years of schooling, I pointed out that, given the fact of two cars traveling at sixty miles an hour in opposite directions with the windows closed and that the people in the other car were almost certainly speaking Serbo-Croatian if they were speaking anything, Beauford could have heard nothing at all.

"Maybe you didn't hear them, but I did."

"OK, what did they say?"

"They said, 'Look at that old black faggot driving with those two white boys'."

"Those people were Yugoslavian, Beauford."

"I don't care what they were; that's what they said, and I'm getting out."

I managed to grab Beauford by the arm before he could do just that, the car now speeding along with the door unlatched.

That night the three of us fell asleep early on cots lined up side by side in a transit passengers' dormitory containing perhaps twelve cots for several other men. When I awoke later to find Beauford gone I suddenly understood something strange Baldwin had said before I left Istanbul. "Don't lose him," he urged, "just don't lose him."

Outside in the village square I found my charge—now clearly Brer Rabbit—
accusing the confused but somewhat angry Yugoslavian villagers of trying to kill
him. I took Beauford back into the dormitory and did the only thing, short of
tying him up, I could do both to sleep and not "lose" him again. I got into his cot
with him and together, in each other's arms, we held off the voices, which by now
I had begun to hear, too. I wondered what kind of picture we must have made to
the men staring at us the next morning—an elderly black man of 65 and a white
man of 29 (who looked 18) wrapped in each other's arms in bed. No one seemed
to care, however, and we finally arrived in Istanbul on July 7.

For several days Beauford continued to be disoriented and could only sleep if
I lay with him—as a platonic lover, but certainly as a lover; by then I loved him
as I had rarely loved anyone. I had seen him as St. Francis, witnessed him as Brer
Rabbit, and had listened to his voices with him and no longer doubted their reality.
Clearly James Baldwin had sent me to Beauford Delaney hoping that through contact with him I would learn directly a lesson I could not learn in books about the
loneliness and pain brought about by sexual and racial deprivation and bigotry.

During the stay in Istanbul Beauford gradually regained his equilibrium. He
loved living with Jimmy, Richard, and me in the little house on the Bosphorus.
There were nights out eating *meze* with Baldwin's and my circle of friends—
including singer Bertice Redding, who was in town. Beauford sang spirituals and
the blues with Bertice, and he smoked Turkish cigarettes with special pleasure.
He painted portraits of us all (see Color Plate 15 and the portrait of the author on
the jacket), did watercolors of the hills of Asia across the straits, bestowed a
much needed aura of peace on the usually tumultuous Baldwin scene, and
became an object of veneration among our Turkish friends, who would come to
him each afternoon as to a wise guru. Beauford loved everything he saw: "Being
in Turkey is more exciting to me than being in Venice . . . there are ancient
essences . . . the weather and the light are beyond my power to resist" (to Miller,
July 27, 1966).

Baldwin and I, followed by several carloads of Delaney admirers, took Beauford to the plane to fly back to Paris at the end of August. He left sadly, carrying a
kilim and several tiles and copper pots given him by new Turkish friends. I saw
Beauford only one more time after that, at the end of December 1967 when my
wife and I took him, at his request, to one of Josephine Baker's many farewell
concerts at the Olympia in Paris. We corresponded until the early 1970s.

In the late summer and early fall of 1966 a few works by Beauford were being
shown at the Gallery Facchetti with those of nineteen other French and Ameri-

Beauford in Istanbul with Richard (left), Baldwin, and Yanni, 1966.

can painters, including René Laubiès, Henri Michaux, and his old friend and mentor Sam Francis. He also had a painting in a group show at Galerie A in Paris. But the activity surrounding the fall shows and his return to Paris did not prevent another relapse. Beauford had given in to his desire for drink at a birthday party for Baldwin in Istanbul and had taken drinks on several occasions after that, despite attempts on the part of at least some of his friends to prevent him. In Paris the voices were back with a vengeance; only still heavier medication from Dr. Ferdière succeeded in controlling them. But when Charley Boggs attempted to convince him to join AA Beauford went to one or two meetings and then balked. He was embarrassed by the exposure and unwilling to definitively give up alcohol. The pattern of periods of abstinence followed by dangerous bouts of what Beauford called "nipping" established itself during the next three years. In those years Beauford was productive during "dry" periods and even somewhat so when he drank. He continued with his abstractions and did many more portraits.

Occasionally the approach used in the abstractions would be applied in the portraits, as in the final version of the portrait of James Baldwin begun in Istanbul (see Color Plate 15). In this work the face, which is not a likeness so much as a comment on Baldwin's and perhaps the painter's inner agony, is drawn in simple black outline against a rich yellow impasto. This background without the face would be much like the abstractions he was working on at the same time.

Beauford also went back to pastel work, doing drawings of friends and family members from memory. And on trips south with friends he continued to do somewhat representational landscapes in watercolor.

Baldwin came for Thanksgiving and encouraged Beauford to avoid the drinking that was so much his own problem as well. The Boggses, as always, were supportive, inviting Beauford at Christmas to a smorgasbord prepared especially for him and having him stay in their apartment during the cold nights. Larry Calcagno continued to be encouraging as well, and so did the LeGros. But it was often difficult to prevent Beauford from having a drink if he was determined to have one. Few of his friends were willing to embarrass him by absolute refusal when they themselves were drinking.

There were times, too, when Beauford felt that his voices were necessary, that his depression gave rise to the very art that would save him. To Larry Calcagno he wrote, "Some of the mystery of my strange life now and again throws light into great darkness and I kneel before the light and am renewed and encouraged to patience and restarting and rehabilitation . . . the whole palette of life is ours" (December 15, 1966).

Despite his deep problems Beauford continued to be busy. In December 1966 he contributed three abstract gouaches to the American Cultural Center at the request of his friend Hélène Baltrusaitis, the USIS Fine Arts Consultant, for a show of fifteen American artists that would be exhibited for a year in various museums in the French provinces. Beauford would attend its opening in Amiens in March. The cultural attaché admired the paintings so much that after the tour the paintings were hung in the American Embassy in Paris. During the next two years Hélène Baltrusaitis arranged for Beauford's participation in several other shows at the center. In May there were Delaney paintings in a group show at the Facchetti Gallery, and a group show at the Musée Galleria called "L'Age du Jazz" in which Beauford had several works, including some abstractions that were attempts to convey in light and color the dynamics of jazz.

An avid reader of the *International Tribune*, Beauford was concerned at the time with the civil rights struggle continuing in America and was anxious to bring the question of race somehow into his work. He wrote to Henry Miller (January 9, 1967) that he was particularly interested in painting "some portraits of Negroes in my fashion." Elwood Peterson, Richard Long, James Baldwin, Howard Swanson, Walter Anderson, Bernard Hassell, Marian Anderson, and his mother (from memory) were all subjects in this category in the mid-1960s (see Color Plate 9).

Beauford with his portrait of
Marian Anderson, 1965

The Winter of 1966–67 was marked by several minor relapses and spells of
flu. Matters were made worse by the departure of Howard Swanson for the
States. Swanson had long been a source of good counsel and friendship. Brother
Joe wrote urging him to "try and look around those mountains one more time"
(June 2, 1967), and Baldwin came from Istanbul to take him with Bernard Hassell
to Cannes for three weeks in the sun.

The summer and fall were full of important events. Letters from home contained upsetting news about "race riots" and anti-war protests in the cities, and
Beauford wrote back supporting the cause of poor blacks and the anti-war movement. But he spoke always of the need for what he called "universal love."

The fall brought Henry Miller to Paris and an emotional reunion. There was a
show of Miller's watercolors and a small party for him at Beauford's studio, and in
the days that followed the two friends got together frequently. Friends wrote from
New York praising works by Beauford included in a retrospective "Negro Art"
show at City College in October. And Beauford took a course in modern art fea-
turing Braque, Picasso, and Vlaminck at the Musée d'Art Moderne. In November

Through a glass darkly, 1967

the Ministry of Cultural Affairs in France bought a Delaney painting entitled *Jazz* from "L'Age du Jazz" exhibition.

The year 1968 was one of "revolution." Beauford became increasingly concerned with racial questions in America. The assassination of Martin Luther King in on April 4 had a disastrous effect on his mental state. He drank again; later during the street riots in Paris Bernard Hassell found him wandering in a bedraggled, confused state, unable to comprehend what was happening or recognize friends. Hassell took him to the south of France where they remained for six weeks, first in a "castle" belonging to Bernard's friends in Avignon, then a house in the mountains, and then the house near Toulon. The trip had the desired effect, and Beauford returned to Paris in relatively good shape, paid a brief visit to his musician friend Walter Anderson in Geneva, and contributed to several group shows, including one to support the Humphrey–Muskie presidential campaign. There were significant lapses of memory, however; he forgot, for example, to attend the opening of an exhibition of paintings by his friend Charley Boggs.

But in December came the surprising news that after so many failed Guggenheim applications, he had been awarded a $5,000 grant by the National Council of the Arts. Much of the money was spent on "loans" to others, and once again Beauford sent money home to friends and family; the money went quickly, but he was elated by it. Friends were delighted to see him at one party in his honor doing the boogie-woogie.

In January 1969 James Baldwin was in town for a television show. Part of the video was shot in Beauford's studio, in keeping with Baldwin's desire to make his friend better known. Beauford had been deeply depressed by James Jones's assertion that Baldwin had referred to him as an "Uncle Tom." Baldwin denied the accusation, which led to a rift between Jones and him, including a bitter argument in front of Beauford at the Jones apartment. Baldwin apologized to Beauford for the scene and explained that he had referred to Beauford's lack of interest in politics per se, not to any lack of concern with the struggle for equality. He reminded his old mentor that he had dedicated *Going to Meet the Man* to him, a book that contained, in the title story, the most radical of his works.

On March 21, under the direction of Hélène Baltrusaitis, the American Cultural Center on the rue du Dragon, with the help of Beauford's Paris friends, sponsored an evening dedicated to the painter. There was a retrospective exhibition of his works borrowed from various galleries and collectors and a huge colorful sign painted by Joe Downing that said "We love Beauford." There was food and champagne and a jazz band. Speeches were made by Professor Bioud, Henry Miller on tape, and James Baldwin by proxy. James Jones, said live, "Beauford, you are the complete artist, not just in the medium of paint but in the medium of life." When a reporter asked the honored guest, "Do you as a Negro feel that you should go home to America where the action is?" he answered, "I can't go home because I never really left . . . I sailed to France sixteen years ago, but I've never left America. The body goes somewhere, that's all" (*Tribune*, April 28, 1969).

In the spring Beauford often became confused. News of deaths and sicknesses of several friends at home disturbed him, and when old friend Joanne Sitwell visited he told her there were men on the roof of his building who were trying to "get him." He made an appointment to meet Joanne to go to Chartres but never appeared.

In June James Baldwin, hearing that Beauford was once more in a precarious state, came to Paris and brought him briefly to Cannes to pick up another friend and then to Athens before settling with him for a few weeks in the countryside outside Istanbul. Baldwin said he felt like Candide cultivating his garden in Constantinople with his beloved but now rather vague Dr. Pangloss.

Visits from Ellis Wilson in July and Brother Joe in August lifted Beauford's spirits somewhat. With Ellis there was free talk about mutual friends and many evenings out on the town. Joe's visit was less cheerful—the two men had always been closer in their correspondence than in person—but those three weeks gave them an opportunity to be together in a way they had not been since childhood. They explored the bookstores and galleries, talked of the past and of their work, and went to jazz clubs and the opera. Back in New York, Joe wrote, "Our great blessing is that we have walked the streets [of Paris] together; Bless his Name!" (September 12, 1969).

For several months Beauford had complained that he had built up such a large inventory of paintings that his apartment had become too crowded to serve as both a living space and a studio. With some of his grant money, therefore, he arranged in October to rent a studio near Charley Boggs's atelier in the Cité Falguière, not far from rue Vercingétorix. Beauford was never able to use that atelier very much as the effort of moving from one place to the other was beyond his physical and mental capacities at the time. It was also beyond his financial capabilities since he had given away a great deal of his grant money and spent most of the rest on a trip to Knoxville at Christmas.

Beauford had not been in the United States since 1953, and the Knoxville trip was made at the urging of his brother Emery who was not well. Beauford was so disoriented before he left that others had to take responsibility for getting him to the travel agency to pick up his ticket, seeing that he had the proper immunization certificate, and putting him on the plane. Bunny LeGros took him to a store to have a gabardine suit made to order, and to buy gloves, a hat, and a coat. A few days before Christmas Beauford took off from Orly without informing the Knoxville family of any dates of arrival or departure. At Kennedy Airport he was to take a bus to go to Newark, but somehow got lost and his bag, containing all his new clothes, was stolen. He did not remember anything about how he got from JFK to Newark or how he found the plane to Knoxville. He remembered being followed by people who wanted everything he had, and said that people took him up in a small plane when he arrived in Knoxville to show him how changed the city was—how everyone and every place he knew were gone.

At the airport taxi stand he could not remember his brother's address since he only knew the old house on Vine Street. He told a taxi driver who he was, and he happened to know of Beauford's family and where their new home was.

The stay in Knoxville was a happy blur in Beauford's mind. He loved being with the family and painted a little—including sketches for a southern landscape and family portraits (see Color Plates 16 and 17). He ate a great deal, rolling his eyes in pleasure over his favorites, Gertrude's German butter rolls and her boiled custard and pound cake. Most of all he liked going over to the old Vine Street house with his brother, where Emery still had his barber shop and the conversation was good. It took him back to the days when he would accompany his father to the old barber shop in Jefferson City. He went to church with the family and was asked by the minister to say a few words. There was a party on his birthday for family and friends. When word got around that one of the famous Delaney brothers was in town reporters and friends stopped by.

Wilmer Lucas was in Knoxville teaching and had tried by mail to interest his old friend in selling some of his paintings to Knoxville College. When the men met Beauford seemed confused, worried, and tired and was not capable of discussing business. He wrote in his journals of malicious people who even in the sanctuary of the family home would come late at night "and speak unpleasant and vulgar language and threaten malicious treatment . . . interfering with my health and urgent work . . . the constant, continuous creation."

Despite the urging of his family that he stay in Knoxville, he left on January 14. He felt there was little time for work and work meant returning to Paris.

ten

Paris: The Final Years

eauford Delaney's final years were a race against his voices. Periods of lucidity were interrupted by days and sometimes weeks of madness. His friends tried to keep him from drinking but he drank anyway and stopped taking his medication. The voices frequently came to his room at night so that he felt it necessary to go to the cafes and wander the streets in the very late hours. Charley Boggs repeatedly invited him to stay but with the beginning of the breakup of the Boggs marriage in 1971 Beauford felt less comfortable there, and resisted and resented Charley's urging to join him at AA meetings. Furthermore, given his condition, he was embarrassed to have Madame du Closel or Professor Bioud see him as often as they once had. As he moved into his seventies he forgot or purposely missed appointments and neglected the correspondence that had always been so meaningful; he would start letters and leave them unfinished, or finish them and not mail them. People continued to send him checks from New York, but he would fail to cash them. When he did have cash he would give it to "friends" in the cafes or the "evil ones" would steal it; he would often use it to take a taxi from Paris to visit Jim and Bunny LeGros in Velizy. Sometimes he would tell one genuine friend that another genuine friend had taken his money. Not surprisingly, this aroused suspicion and some anger among even those closest to him.

The LeGros, Madame du Closel, Bernard Hassell, Darthea Speyer, and James Baldwin were Beauford's primary sources of moral support in the early 1970s. Although much of the time he was his familiar Buddha-like gentle self, more and more often he was Brer Rabbit leading a frightening chase—the voices behind him, his real friends trying to head them off, his would-be friends unwittingly urging them on. Yet between the return from Knoxville in January 1970 and his commitment to St. Anne's Hospital for the Insane in 1975, Beauford did some fine painting.

The year 1970 began with Beauford readapting to Paris and fighting off the cold of his atelier. He became quite sick with flu and heart palpitations in early February and was treated at the clinic of the American Hospital. Yet during the daylight hours he was working consistently, and desperately trying to hold his life together. To Mrs. Ascoli he wrote, but never sent the letter, explaining that he was forwarding twelve watercolors in return for her continued monthly payments (February 24, 1970). To Joe he wrote that 1969 had been "difficult" and that he was preoccupied with work, that he was trying to "fuse some of the scent of something I found at home" (January 19, 1970, March 24, 1970). In a letter to Richard Long he told of his "tremendous time" working on portraits and abstractions (February 24, 1970). Henry Miller sent him money for painting supplies and scolded him gently for always sending him paintings in return for such help. "Hold on to your work!" Miller wrote. "Someday these paintings will be in great demand" (March 24, 1970).

The paintings were already in demand in Knoxville. During the visit to his family, Beauford had been approached by Elsa Honig Fine at the University of Tennessee about the possibility of a joint exhibition of his paintings and those of his brother Joseph. Beauford had agreed in principle, and on April 4 Ms. Fine wrote to say that the show—in September and October at the university's McClung Gallery—would be sponsored by the Black Student Union, that it would be retrospective, and that the Union would pay for shipping the paintings from Paris and New York or elsewhere. Meanwhile, the Knoxville family members were delighted that their brother/uncle would be coming back so soon, and a stream of encouraging letters came from Imogene, Ogust, Gertrude, and Emery. Ms. Fine wrote asking for biographical information and an opening invitation list. Joe wrote often, too, pressing his brother for information about a date of arrival, the prices of paintings, and the number of works each should show "in order to have a balance." So began a mini saga that the well-intentioned people in Knoxville could not have realized was pure agony for Beauford. He was holding himself together in Paris only with great difficulty. The thought of actually getting everything done, making his way back to Tennessee, and facing the exhibition overwhelmed him.

Beauford's first approach to the problem was to ignore it. He wrote letters home and did not mention the planned show. He did mention that news of the trips of the astronauts to the moon made him realize that Knoxville was not really so far away (April 24, 1970, to Emery et al.). Letters from Joe were understandably pressing. He wrote in June saying that he had heard that Beauford was in the States, but the Knoxville family had assured him this was not the case. He reminded his brother that their mother had once worked as a cleaning woman at the McClung Museum—now they would exhibit their art there as honored guests: "Life is *blessed* and strange" (July 8, 1970).

By late July the family became worried at the lack of response to their exhibition questions. Joe was especially impatient and even angry. The university sent the head of its art department to Paris to attempt to firm things up for the show and Beauford finally told him that he would not be coming to Knoxville. Emery wrote a loving letter pleading with Beauford, even at the last minute, to come, and in October, after what became a Joseph Delaney show had opened, Beauford wrote a letter to Joe trying to explain his position. The letter shows signs of emotional turmoil and great confusion:

Dearest Joe,

. . . My health is middling but my faith is always where the Delaneys are. It was impossible for me to bring paintings to America at this time. . . . Since leaving America my whole energy has been with painting and Mrs. Fine sent a gentle man to visit me but according to my health and constant work and also while being in Knoxville it was wonderful but having returned my life has been one thing Painting. I move slowly but thank "God" constantly. Mrs Fine sent a gentleman visiting in Paris to visit—spoke of the exhibition but according to my committings in Paris made it impossible at the time. My health is good considering all things but I must be careful and many things I would like to do must wait until my condition is more composed.

Beauford goes on to praise his brother's works (Joe had sent photographs of the show) and ends his letter with an expression of love for the family and his "people": "I embrace you and all of those dear ones known and unknown who have born the burden in the heat of the day" (October 10, 1970).

Although Beauford did not get to Knoxville, 1970 and 1971 were years of success of sorts. Georgia O'Keeffe's portrait of him was on display at the Whitney
Museum in New York, the Smithsonian's National Portrait Gallery asked to borrow the Marian Anderson portrait that only a few years earlier they had declined
to buy, *Jet* magazine referred to him as the "Dean" of African-American painters,
his portrait of Henry Miller was in the November 1971 issue of *Playboy*, and he
was included in a 1970 exhibition called "Afro-American Artists Abroad" presented at the Elma Lewis School of Fine Arts at the National Center of Afro-
American Artists in Dorchester, Massachusetts, and at the University of Texas Art
Museum in Texas. Professor James Lewis, Chairman of the Morgan State College
Art Department, who knew Beauford and his work well, wrote the catalogue for
the Austin show. Beauford's art, he said, "Radiates the joy of an artist with one
concern, the challenging joy of painting" (p. 6). But when Romare Bearden, Sam
Middleton, and Herbert Gentry came by to visit one afternoon and commented
on their friend's fame, he answered, "I ain't seen no famous money, and I'm hungry." The trio went off that night to Haynes's for soul food and reminiscing.

During the difficult summer and fall of the agonizing over the Knoxville exhibition, Richard Long was in Paris and did a great deal to help his friend. He also
conducted a taped interview with him that would form the basis for a catalogue
by Long for a 1978 Delaney retrospective in New York. Long visited often in 1971
and 1972. The Haydens also came back to Paris in 1971; they too were a source of
moral support and often drove Beauford out to visit Jim and Bunny LeGros in
Velizy. And there was a brief visit from Al and Dolly Hirschfeld.

A family tragedy dominated 1971, however. On April 17 Emery and Gertrude's
son Sam ("Junior") died in Knoxville of complications from pneumonia. Junior's
life had been unhappy since a World War II injury partially incapacitated him
both physically and mentally, but in recent years, with the determined encouragement of his family—especially his sister Ogust—his condition had improved.
Informed of the death by cable, Beauford was shocked. He wanted to go to the
funeral but knew that his psychological and physical state would make him more
of a burden than a support. He wrote to the family explaining that he was ill and
could not come, and he went into several weeks of steep decline, including a
great deal of drinking.

James Baldwin got word of Beauford's condition and had him brought to his
new home in St. Paul de Vence where Bernard Hassell had settled in the old gate-
house. There Beauford painted and seemed to gain some peace of mind. For this
reason Baldwin invited him to come again for Christmas along with his agent
Tria French and her children.

Henry Miller beside his
portrait by Delaney, 1972.

Henry Miller returned to Paris for his eightieth birthday celebration in January
1972. The American Cultural Center on the rue Dragon invited a small group of
Miller's Paris friends—Michonze, Reichel, the photographer Brassai, and Beauford Delaney—to exhibit paintings under the title "Les Amis Parisiens de Henry
Miller." Beauford showed a portrait of Jean Genet, whom he had met through
Baldwin, and several other portraits and abstractions (see Color Plate 18). The central piece of the show was his great portrait of Miller. Miller had transported the
canvas from California, making the occasion of his birthday also a celebration of
Beauford Delaney—now seventy. Beauford sat on a chair in the middle of the
room where the Miller portrait was and watched the people looking at it. Whenever a young person was introduced to him, he would say in answer to compli-
ments, "You are planting a seed. Give it time. Give it time and that seed will
maturate and flower" (*Herald Tribune*, March 14, 1972).

In honor of Miller Beauford wrote a short but moving tribute, which required
an immense effort at concentration and a notebook of rewrites. It was an act of
love that spoke of Miller as a "transcendental spirit whose vision illumines the cos-
mic heritage of mankind." The piece was in gratitude for Miller's lifelong loyalty

and friendship. It is of interest to note that the final paragraph could have applied as well to Beauford as to his friend:

> What sometimes seems impossible, his faith augments by years of discovery of himself, and with joy accomplishes the almost impossible task of uniting into his art the entire substance of this experience. This source in a work of art has magnetism that engages all mankind, because, like the "sun," it is eternal and benevolent. Miller reveals to all people that life is a miracle to be lived and exploited to release its fullness.

Beauford did a little sketch of his old friend when he came to the Vercingétorix studio. This would be their last meeting and both seemed to know it. The two old men spoke of the strange passage of time since their first meeting in the little Greene Street studio thirty years earlier. Beauford remarked that the two places were remarkably the same and that material progress seemed to have eluded him. Miller spoke of his hatred of the idea of dying.

In the months following Henry Miller's visit, Beauford became particularly vague and depressed and disappeared for long periods. Charley Boggs, Ahmed Bioud, Madame du Closel, Darthea Speyer, Jim LeGros, and many others left notes, asking in vain that he contact them. In February he wrote a disconnected letter to Baldwin announcing both that he had just been to St. Paul de Vence—ever so briefly—and that he longed to come again "for 2 or 3 days to see you and your remarkable genius and love . . . I have been working like a slave . . . only wanting to see our dear Jimmy" (February 18, 1972). In fact, he had recently taken a train to the south with the intention of visiting Baldwin, but had not announced his coming. When no one was at the train in Cagnes sur Mer to meet him he had apparently forgotten why he was there and got on the next train back to Paris.

An article by Harry Stein on Beauford, including a photograph of him, was published in the *International Herald Tribune* on March 14. Beauford seemed hardly to notice it, never mentioning it in a letter home he did not send and in which he spoke about the evil he sensed everywhere (March 27, 1972). This evil was more and more in the atelier itself. To escape the threatening voices he went with some frequency to Jim and Bunny in Velizy, where one of the bedrooms was always called "Beauford's room." Bunny helped him care for his clothes, and took him to the dentist when he needed work done on his teeth, which he often did. On one occasion he wrote that he could not come because the "evil ones" had forced the government to stop the trains when it became known that he planned to go to Velizy. In fact there was a train strike that day.

One week in the summer of 1970 the LeGros planned a short trip to Cannes and invited Beauford along. At the last minute they changed their plans and went to Normandy, but Beauford insisted they were in Cannes; he sent postcards to friends and marked little watercolors and drawings he did there "Cannes." One early morning he commented on the moon coming up. When it was pointed out that it was not the moon but the sun, Beauford painted both in the sky—one red, the other yellow (see Color Plate 19).

One of the most disturbing events of the early 1970s for Beauford was the gradual destruction of his neighborhood. For some time Madame du Closel and Charley Boggs had tried to break the news that he would have to move because the government was tearing down and renewing the part of Montparnasse where he lived. Beauford "knew" that, in fact, the "evil ones" were once again responsible. To get rid of him the government was being made to tear down the rue Vercingétorix and Number 53 in particular. One time when Beauford was staying with the LeGros he appeared in their bedroom in the middle of the night and announced that he must return immediately to Paris. Jim drove him and when they arrived at 53 rue Vercingétorix Beauford said it was not his building. It was as if he had noticed for the first time the changes in the neighborhood and realized that another stage in his life would have to begin.

Beauford had always been an eccentric figure in Montparnasse, but now the stories about him became even more bizarre. People told of how he would inexplicably lose his temper over something someone had said, how he would order large meals at the Dôme or Select and then have no money to pay. He was so well known that cafe owners would ignore the unpaid bill or a friend would simply take care of it. Once when a group of acquaintances invited him for dinner and everyone chipped in at the end to pay, Beauford stood up, took the money, pocketed it, said, "Thank you very much, darling friends" and left. No one said a word or did anything to stop him.

Beauford seemed to enjoy but have difficulty focusing on visits from old friends Larry Calcagno and Michael Freilich in the summer of 1972. And when his musician friend Walter Anderson came to take the portrait he had paid for, Beauford hid it under his bed. He was pleased when for the second time James Baldwin dedicated a book to him—the long essay No Name in the Street, a copy of which Baldwin sent in August. But when Richard Long visited in September he found Beauford in such a bad state that he called Baldwin asking what to do. Baldwin suggested bringing Beauford to St. Paul de Vence, where he stayed for two weeks and, as usual, regained some stability and made a series of sketches of the ancient village, some of which would be turned into oil paintings back in Paris (See Color Plate 20).

In his sketchbook Beauford wrote of the good effect on him of St. Paul, of its "atmosphere of great age," of the many ways he was "comforted" by "the calm and patience . . . the pleasure and history of its unique and remarkable calm." He spoke of the "light" of Vence and the good effect it had on "the work of our Lonely people," the "people" represented by Baldwin and himself.

But the stay in St. Paul and still another visit at Christmas e did not change essential matters. Baldwin had written early in December saying, "Guess who's coming to dinner, at Christmas, at my house?" and had sent his brother David to Paris to bring Beauford back to St. Paul (December 13, 1972). Beauford had again promised his Knoxville family that he would come home for Christmas and then stopped communicating with them. A self-portrait done at this time indicates something of Beauford's mental state (see Color Plate 21). Worried by a lack of news, the Knoxville family considered sending Ogust to Paris but the trip was put off when Beauford finally wrote just before Christmas from St. Paul saying he was well.

In St. Paul Beauford always loved visiting the Galerie Maeght, an easy walk up the hill from the Baldwin house. On one occasion a Francis Bacon exhibition inspired him to make some notes in his sketchbook, notes that began with a commentary on Bacon and suddenly became an exploration of his own work. They provide some insight into Delaney's sense of the artist's role:

> Francis Bacon . . . portrays the deep inner problems and despair of man today—that is to say his probing intellectual and emotional problems. His understanding and portrayal of these phases of mind and behavior stimulates in the beholder compassion and a desire to go toward the deep and intimate sorrow. . . .
>
> The scope of painting is so vast . . . a prayer to point to finding courage to continue the search for beauty amidst the poverty of feeling . . . [it] expresses itself sometimes in naturalistic pictures and at other times variable abstractions of color—mostly of the Sun or some form of light. Or it might be Marian Anderson singing or a black boy laughing or perhaps a child holding a bird on its shoulders—also maybe a woman sitting in the sun as if she were in Heaven. Sometimes it is a jazz orchestra. . . .

Back in Paris after Christmas, Beauford began working hard for a solo exhibition planned for March at Darthea Speyer's new gallery on the rue Jacques Callot. There was no real urgency to create many new works, however, because his atelier was literally filled with unsold paintings. And soon Beauford fell into the habit of inviting homeless people to spend time with him in his apartment, people who became, in effect, permanent squatters. At least they were a buffer against the voices that accompanied his return to excessive drinking. Beauford now also began to lose the fastidiousness that had kept him at least clean and somewhat orderly even in his poorest days. People who visited the atelier were shocked and worried at what they saw as its sordidness. Henry Miller had noticed this tendency even during his 1972 visit.

But Miller had also witnessed the extraordinary beauty of Beauford's late canvases. In the magazine *Informations et Documents* (#326, January 1973) he wrote that his friend had had the luck to have an extraordinary mother and a preacher father and had found in painting (and in letters) a means of expressing himself that was superior to traditional eloquence.

In late January Beauford wandered into Charley Boggs's studio so drunk that he could not remember Larry Calcagno's name and hardly knew Charley's. Matters were becoming desperate and Beauford's friends knew that something had to be done—and soon. Several times Madame du Closel went to the atelier looking for Beauford only to find the squatters, who threatened her. On one visit Jim LeGros found Beauford in bed with two of the squatters giggling. He called Baldwin, who eventually arranged to have Barry Tompkins, a black painter friend, move in with Beauford in place of the squatters.

On February 3, the day of the Speyer Gallery opening, Darthea asked Addie Herder to spend the whole day at 53 rue Vercingétorix and bring Beauford to the gallery; she was afraid he might forget the show and disappear. Beauford did show up, and, although vague in his conversation, managed to charm the many friends who were there. Catalogue tributes were written by Henry Miller, James Baldwin, James Jones, and Georgia O'Keeffe. Jones described Beauford's generosity of heart, which was revealed in the colors, the forms, textures, and energy of his paintings. He noted the meticulous treatment of forms and the sure sense of color combinations. Henry Miller spoke more of Beauford's saintliness and inner beauty than of his paintings. Georgia O'Keeffe, too, wrote of the uniqueness of his character and personality. James Baldwin commented, as he had for the Lambert catalogue in 1964, on Beauford's particular understanding of light: "When we are before a Delaney painting," he said, "we are in the light."

The exhibition included abstractions dominated by the yellows of the late years, and several semi-abstract paintings were based on African themes and African sculpture. Beauford had developed a renewed interest in African art in his many visits with Professor Bioud to the Musée de l'Homme.

There were swirling Van Gogh-like landscapes from the St. Paul de Vence visits, too (see Color Plate 20), a wonderfully playful depiction of dancers, and a particularly fine painting of a black street sweeper against a thickly layered late

Beauford with his African figure and mask, 1970s.

Delaney background (see Color Plate 22). But what stood out were the portraits composed during the years since the 1964 Lambert show. Portraits of Jean Genet (see Color Plate 18), René Laubiès, Bernard Hassell (see Color Plate 23), Mary Painter's cat Caesar, a Moroccan woman, Howard Swanson, Ahmed Bioud, James Baldwin, Marian Anderson, one done from memory of his mother, and many others, including one of Robert Kennedy, the coldness of his blue eyes emphasized by the whiteness of his shirt.

The portraits are not psychological studies, however. They become vehicles for Beauford's concern with color and the production of light. But whereas there are no boundaries, as it were, in the abstract paintings, representational figures are used in the portraits to keep the painter within defining bounds, rather the way a poet consciously chooses the dynamic tension created by a form like the sonnet. Beauford's purpose in the late portraits seems not to have been to reveal the inner James Baldwin or the inner Marian Anderson or Howard Swanson so much as to use their extraordinary faces—not, for the most part, photographically but with a freedom sometimes bordering on the purposely "primitive" or naive, sometimes on caricature—to celebrate the art of painting itself.

Dancers, 1973. Mixed media
on paper, 19½ x 13 in. Courtesy of the Delaney Estate
and the Ewing Gallery,
University of Tennessee.

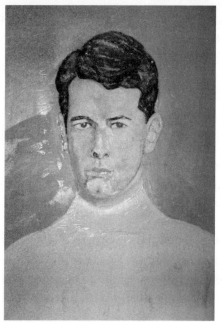

Robert Kennedy, 1968. Oil on
canvas, 24 x 20 in. Courtesy
of the Delaney Estate.

Reviews of the exhibition were positive. Poet Ted Joans in *Black World* admired the painter's ability to create light and suggested that Beauford's work "stimulates the human soul, like a Billie Holiday recording"(January 1974, p. 93). Art critic Edouard Roditi writing in *Jeune Afrique* (March 3, 1973) concentrated on the abstractions, noting their connections with the works of Sam Francis and the late Monet. Roditi seemed puzzled by the representational quality of the portraits in comparison with the abstractions, but pointed to the fact that they were painted with the "same palette and the same colors, at once gay and angelic" (translated by Long, Studio Museum catalogue). Jacques Michel in *Le Monde* (February 25, 1973) said Delaney's "raw paint fills the canvas from end to end like skin quivering and saturated with itself" (translated by Long).

A friend asked Beauford if he would write down his thoughts on his art and what effect Paris had on his work. The painter was not up to such a task, but he did jot down a few words that provide some sense of his own understanding of his work:

> Paris has not changed my desires, however here painting has included designs in color vibrating the rhythm of tunes and sounds that have assisted and arranged a somewhat broader continuation of the same obsession of emotion and love of music for its universal appeal. Together with the designs there are compositions of hot jazz and studies and portraits of Negroes and many types of the varied variety of my friends. Have been stimulated by the reaction of the art world here and in America regarding my present work.

Several paintings were sold during the Gallerie Speyer exhibition, which ran until March 2. Ms. Speyer was regular in her advance payments to Beauford, but much of that money went to the desperate people with whom the painter spent more and more time.

On February 18 Beauford dropped by at Charley Boggs's studio. He was once again confused—unable to remember much of anything, not even the name of Charley's son Gordon of whom he had once been so fond.

News in late February of the death of Palmer Hayden disturbed Beauford, but he could not assimilate it. To make matters worse, Tria French, who had taken over much of the duty of checking on Beauford for James Baldwin, had a cerebral hemorrhage and died leaving two children. James Jones had a wake for Tria attended by Bernard Hassell and Baldwin but Beauford forgot to go. Failing to find their friend, Baldwin and Hassell returned to the south only to be called in May by Gloria Jones, who told them Beauford had fallen in his studio, aggravating an old hernia problem, and mentally and physically was unable to care for himself. Baldwin sent Bernard to bring Beauford to St. Paul.

The situation in St. Paul was grave. Baldwin was having emotional difficulties of his own, and he had also taken on temporary responsibility for Tria French's children who were now in his house. Furthermore, his income had been cut off because it came by way of his agent, and Tria's accounts were all frozen by probate. And now Beauford arrived in a desperate state needing not only emotional care but an expensive operation. The situation was temporarily saved by the arrival of a check from Darthea Speyer for 1,500 francs. This was one of the agreed payments to Beauford and Baldwin asked him to endorse it so that it could be used for the operation. Beauford did what he was told but was resentful since he did not want the operation.

In the clinic Beauford became Brer Rabbit. He locked the door of his room from the inside so that the nurses could not shave him for the operation—"I will not expose myself before a woman," he shouted. A locksmith was called and Beauford was shaved by a male orderly. On the morning of the operation, Beauford broke the necessary fast by eating a large breakfast he found on a hospital tray in the hallway, a meal obviously intended for someone else. The operation was rescheduled for the next day, but that morning Beauford managed to sneak out of the hospital for croissants and coffee. On the way out he had found a jar of thermometers, which he passed out as "gifts" to patients he met in the hallways. Bernard was called to retrieve him, his clothes were removed from his room, and finally the operation took place and a period of recuperation followed.

Since no alcohol was available in the clinic, Beauford's condition improved somewhat. He did a few pencil sketches, which he gave as gifts to the nurses and orderlies, who by now adored him. Only the surgeon was denied a painting because he had "hurt" Beauford in the pre-operation examinations and had invaded his privacy with a knife, no doubt with "evil intentions" toward his manhood.

The weeks that followed at the house in St. Paul were perhaps Beauford's last truly happy ones. He was feeling much better physically; Bernard was careful to see that he did not drink, so that he was reasonably lucid most of the time, and he was able to paint in the glorious sunshine of southern France in the spring and summer. Tria's children had been taken by relatives, some money had come into the household and with it good food, and Beauford was with the two people with whom he felt most at ease, Baldwin and Bernard.

In the early fall, however, Beauford insisted on returning to Paris, where it soon became evident that, although he was physically improved and trying to avoid excessive drinking, he could not cope with the details of everyday life. An American friend, Burton Reinfrank, who worked for the Office of Economic Development, had bought several paintings and often, with his wife, took Beauford on Sundays

Beauford at his Vercingétorix studio, 1973.

for picnics to Fontainbleau, was alarmed for his friend's safety when he discovered matches all over the floor in front of the gas heater.

By this time Beauford's condition was clearly complicated by what some said
was Alzheimer's disease. At various times he came to Charley Boggs to complain
that he had lost his passport and/or checkbook, that people had stolen his money.
Yet he would often have checks written by him that he asked Charley to cash, and
Darthea Speyer confirmed that she had deposited considerable sums directly into
his bank account. Beauford complained regularly about being "surrounded by
bad people," and if some of these people were aspects of his hallucinations, some
were not. Charley worried about the fact that the former "squatters" had keys to
the Vercingétorix apartment and that anyone could walk off with anything, especially when Beauford chose, as he often now did, to sleep in the loft of Charley's
atelier. Charley noticed that Beauford, who had always been careful about such
things, no longer bothered to shave. He sometimes offered to shave his friend and
Beauford seemed to enjoy being pampered in that way.

In October Boggs wrote an urgent letter to James Baldwin: "Our blessed Beauford is rapidly losing mental control," he wrote. "His memory-banks are practically
depleted." Baldwin agreed that Charley should take over Beauford's checkbook and
that some arrangement would have to soon be made to find permanent care for

The last days at 53 rue
Vercingétorix, 1975.

him. Some temporary relief came in the person of the young painter Clarence Hagins, who visited Beauford in December and spent many days, including Christmas 1973, with him. Jim and Bunny LeGros also helped by having Beauford visit Velizy as often as possible.

But by this time Beauford's deterioration had accelerated to the point that little could be done. Emery wrote another pleading letter from Knoxville. It had been over a year since the Knoxville family had received an answer to its many letters (January 7, 1974). Even in the coldest night of winter Beauford would be found wandering aimlessly through his neighborhood looking for his address, which he had forgotten. Madame du Closel had warned the police in the quartier and they sometimes took him home. In his apartment he fed and talked to the many mice that had invaded it. He allowed his beard to grow to such a length that people compared him to King Lear in his madness.

When Ruth Ann Stewart attempted to do an oral history interview with him she found him kind and gracious but disconnected and frightened. In a cafe he ate everyone's food at the table, drank a good deal of brandy, and disappeared.

Madame du Closel wrote to Knoxville describing Beauford's condition, and in September Imogene answered for her father and announced that someone in the family would come soon to evaluate the situation. Meanwhile, the urban renewal demolishers were coming closer to 53 rue Vercingétorix. Madame du Closel had interceded with friends in the government to allow Beauford to stay in his apartment as long as possible, but all around and even within the building there was a scene of destruction and walled-up doors. Beauford had become, in effect, a squatter. Realizing that he soon might require more care, Madame du Closel appealed to the Ministry of Culture for artist's medical insurance for her friend and coverage was granted in November 1974.

In the early spring of 1975 James Baldwin was informed by Barry Tompkins that Beauford had disappeared, leaving his studio unlocked. Someone had called to invite him for dinner, he had gotten dressed, left, and never come back. Afraid that Beauford would be deported when and if he was found, Baldwin immediately went to the American Consulate in Nice and declared himself the financially responsible party. He undertook future care for the disposition of the painter's estate to "insure that [it] . . . will be protected to the advantage of his family and heirs."

Meanwhile, Beauford had been found by the police collapsed in the street and sick, quite far from his home. He was hospitalized and then committed to St. Anne's Hospital for the Insane. Hearing of this, Baldwin went to Paris hoping to find a way of arranging for Beauford's permanent care. His first act was to find—at his expense—a new apartment for the storage of Beauford's paintings and for the painter's use should he recover. The apartment was in the rue d'Anglais, near an apartment Baldwin hoped to rent or buy for himself. Unfortunately, Baldwin neglected to inform Madame du Closel of his actions and she arrived at the Vercingétorix apartment to find it empty of Beauford and his things and occupied by two belligerent squatters, who said they were Beauford's friends and with whom there was, literally, an exchange of blows.

Madame du Closel visited Beauford several times at St. Anne's beginning in October 1975—sometimes with Darthea Speyer—and was convinced that he was "no longer there" mentally and was best off remaining in the hospital.

In December 1975 Baldwin went to New York and obtained a temporary and revocable notarized letter of authorization from Joe Delaney to act in the family's behalf in connection with Beauford. He also spoke by phone with Emery and urged the family to take charge of the situation. The family promised that Joe Delaney would come to Paris as soon as possible.

On January 26, 1976, a trusteeship for Beauford was formed by a French judge. After a careful examination of the situation, including an extensive interview with Madame du Closel, the judge determined who Beauford's closest associates

Beauford and Baldwin, 1976.
Photograph by Max Petrus.

were and appointed a panel of trustees consisting of James Baldwin, Bernard Hassell, Solange du Closel, James LeGros, Darthea Speyer, Ahmed Bioud, and Burton Reinfrank.

During his stay at St. Anne's Beauford had many visitors. Fortunately the hospital was in the Montparnasse area so it was convenient for Beauford's friends. One such friend was artist Bill Hutson who visited several times in early 1976. Hutson was able to converse a bit with Beauford once or twice, but usually the old man seemed either heavily sedated or mentally unfocused.

Painter Vincent Smith came together with Herb Gentry and his wife and took some photographs, which the hospital confiscated. In their place he did a few sketches. Beauford was wearing blue pajamas and a large straw hat given him by James Baldwin; he was walking in the hospital garden.

Max Petrus, a friend of Baldwin's, took several photographs, which the hospital did allow since Baldwin was the primary trustee. These photographs show Baldwin and Beauford standing together holding hands. Beauford seemed relatively happy that day; Baldwin was one of the few people—Bernard Hassell was another—whom Beauford apparently recognized. He did not recognize the LeGros or even Charley and Gordon Boggs. But even when he did not seem to know them, Beauford liked receiving visitors. He wore a constant smile on his face and always tried to leave with his guests. If they brought candies, which they often did, he would immediately devour them all. There was a fellow patient who walked arm-in-arm with Beauford and constantly tried to kiss people on the lips. As in the case of Beauford, whose hand and face movements were familiar to visitors, he probably retained gestures related to his former life, which had now become tragi-comic rather than meaningful. One young patient saw Charley Boggs bringing roses—Beauford had always loved roses—and warned him that Beauford would eat them. When Charley handed the flowers to his old friend he peeled off a petal and ate it. Beauford always had a special love for food. When the nurses had discovered he was a painter they had given him materials for sketching, but for the most part he seemed uninterested in using them. Beauford had simply stopped fighting. When he did so the voices left, but they also left an emptiness.

Joseph Delaney came to Paris in the summer of 1976 as the family's representative, presumably to take charge of his brother, perhaps even to take him home. Apparently, however, finding that Beauford was without memory but at least comfortable, he decided to leave matters in the hands of Baldwin and the court-appointed trusteeship.

Meanwhile, in the Montparnasse cafes ugly rumors began to circulate that James Baldwin and/or the psychiatrists had stolen Beauford's paintings and that he was being held under duress. According to one story Barry Tompkins and a sculptor called Msika—a drinking companion of Beauford—managed to convince the doctor in charge to release the painter into their care and according to another, sneak him out of the hospital on the floor of a taxi. Within twenty-four hours Msika and Tompkins realized how sick Beauford was physically as well as mentally and brought him to the Hôpital Cochin and placed him in the geriatrics ward.

The Hôpital Cochin judged that the patient would be better served at St. Anne's and returned him there, after sending a bill for treatment of an intestinal condition to Baldwin. Msika continued to believe that Beauford was mistreated in St. Anne's, that his paintings had been stolen, and that Beauford was in need of a rest home instead of the hospital. In July Msika formed a "Committee to Save Beauford Delaney" that for several months organized vicious newspaper attacks on Baldwin and the other friends who were genuinely and seriously concerned with Beauford's welfare. There were also threatening phone calls to various members of the trusteeship, prompting Baldwin to respond with a printed statement on July 28, outlining the events that had actually occurred and ending with a passionate defense regarding his treatment of his friend and mentor. Beauford was "one of the greatest men, and possibly the greatest painter, that it will ever be my privilege to know," he wrote. Those who dared accuse him of abandoning his friend or of "using his mighty and life-long effort to further my own ends—must take their case to court."

In the summer of 1977 Richard Long came to Paris to visit Beauford and collect some of the paintings that Baldwin had moved to the rue d'Anglais apartment. These would be taken to the Studio Museum in Harlem under the directorship of Mary Schmidt Campbell for a retrospective Beauford Delaney exhibition, which would remain in place for three months beginning in April 1978. The exhibition was the first in a projected "Black Masters" series at the museum and was sponsored by the Exxon Corporation and the National Endowment for the Arts. Long would edit the catalogue, which included his long biographical introduction, the 1945 Henry Miller essay, and the 1964 James Baldwin introduction to the Galerie Lambert exhibition. The show contained a few works from the New York years, but primarily was an exhibition of Delaney's Paris work—both abstractions and portraits. For many in New York this was the first exposure to the Paris work—essentially what had been shown in 1973 at the Speyer Gallery—and it was received enthusiastically. John Russell in the *New York Times* spoke of this "uninhibited colorist" who in his abstract paintings could make "a high-keyed slither of paint that led to Tobeyesque entanglements of color" (April 14, 1978, p. 20).

Friends who visited the Studio Museum show could not help thinking of the ironical fact that while it was going on—perhaps the most impressive exhibition ever of Delaney's work—the painter lay in a psychiatric hospital in Paris unaware of his own growing fame.

On March 21 James Baldwin was informed by the hospital that Beauford's physical condition was declining rapidly. Meanwhile Joseph Delaney attempted though UN Ambassador Andrew Young to arrange for more elaborate care for his brother. Young suggested that the American Embassy could help (letter to JD, October 18, 1978), but again it was decided that the care at St. Anne's was essentially good. Beauford lingered for a year in a state of semiconsciousness, recognizing no one. On March 26, 1979, he simply stopped breathing.

When he was shaved and washed in the hospital morgue, the hospital attendants, who had grown to love him, came to see him one more time. They marveled at the smoothness and beauty of his skin and at the gentle expression on his face.

Joseph and Ogust came to Paris for the funeral and to settle Beauford's affairs. This proved difficult as Beauford had left no legal will and the paintings that had been sent to New York for the Studio Museum show had not been returned to the French government, which had some claim on them. Joseph was able, however, to retrieve the paintings Baldwin had had placed in storage that had not been part of the New York exhibition. Eventually he had them sent to New York and then to Knoxville.

Obituaries praised Beauford Delaney as a great and neglected painter. *Le Monde* spoke of him as a painter of another age who thought little of glory. His portraits were direct and sincere, and his abstractions emanated a profound light (April 5, 1979). The *International Herald Tribune* quoted James Baldwin who had written that when we stand before a Delaney painting we "stand in the light . . . which is both loving and merciless" in its truth—in its insistence that we "confront ourselves" (April 6, 1979). Gerald Fraser in the *New York Times* saw Beauford as a man whose life seemed to "symbolize the mythical artistic existence of privation and relative obscurity" (April 1, 1979). Fraser ended his obituary by quoting from Richard Long's remarks in the Studio Museum catalogue: Delaney's "painterly statement evolved in a kind of luminous purity consonant with the feeling of exaltation and humility with which he approached his canvases, seeking not domination through strategy, but union with an ultimately ineffable ideal through unending research."

One of the saddest episodes of Beauford Delaney's saga took place during the days between his death on March 26 and his funeral on April 6. James Baldwin had wanted his friend buried in honor in Montparnasse Cemetery, but neither the family nor he at that time had the money to pay for the plot. As the head trustee in charge of the last years of Beauford's life and the painter's self-proclaimed spiritual son, Baldwin should at least have attended the funeral. It is true that he was in St. Paul sick with a serious case of flu; it is true that he was under a great deal of psychological stress both because of Beauford's passing— he had a horror of death—and other traumatic events occurring at that time in his life. It is also true that he was embarrassed at not being able to live up to his promise to have Beauford buried at Montparnasse. But in the weeks following the funeral, these facts were not sufficient to outweigh the simple guilt he felt at having missed the final passage of the person who, with the possible exception of his mother, had done more than anyone else to mold his views and his approach to life. He spoke of it later as his own "worst moment" and admitted to acting like a spoiled son somehow angry at his father for dying without his permission (conversation with DL, 1986).

The funeral on April 6th at 11 A.M. was presided over by the Reverend Scott Campbell at the American Church in Paris on the quai d'Orsay. It was a simple service with organ music, prayers, Beauford's favorite psalm, the 23rd—"The Lord Is My Shepherd"—and a message from Henry Miller about his friend's saintliness. The main reading was Beauford's favorite biblical passage, Chapter 13 of Saint Paul's First Letter to the Corinthians, which ends

> For now we see through a glass darkly; but then face to face: now I know in part; but then shall I know even as also I am known.
>
> And now abideth faith, hope, charity, these three; but the greatest of these is charity.

The preacher gave a moving eulogy. This was a "sacred gathering," he said—a "bond" that "will go with us from this place." Beauford's uniqueness was based in his seeing "not as the world sees." Everything "which came to him was passed through eyes of love, and in that very process of seeing differently his reality was transformed." Beauford, then, was a "great lover—and the cost was high" in this life. Yet "all of the brush strokes, all of the colors, all of the love have created in the eyes of heaven, a masterpiece." The preacher ended with a hymn, in which others joined him. It was always Beauford's favorite:

> Amazing Grace how sweet the sound
> That saved a wretch like me
> I once was lost, but now am found
> Was blind, but now I see.

There was a large crowd at the funeral and few left dry-eyed. Beauford was taken to a municipal cemetery—the Cimetière Monte Rouge—just south of Paris near the Porte d'Italie to be buried. It was not exactly the pauper's grave to which he had committed himself in the dark days of the Athens clinic, but it was one of those sites to which the occupant is granted only a limited number of years. At the simple graveside service were a very few of Beauford's closest friends—Charley Boggs, Jim and Bunny LeGros, Joseph and Ogust, and a mysterious young black woman whom no one recognized.

The final visitors at the grave remembered not so much the lost mind of the last years but the Brer Rabbit–St. Francis Beauford of Knoxville, Boston, New York, and Paris who could, as his friend Bill Hutson put it, "Hear with his eyes . . . see what you thought or said and look past your idea to its conclusion and essence" (letter to DL, January 15, 1995). They remembered the man of dignity who could say to his friend Ahmed Bioud, "An egg, a daily piece of bread—that goes well with the purity of inspiration." And they remembered the man whose suffering was transformed into the amazing light of his paintings.

Although buried in Paris, Beauford had somehow returned to Knoxville, too. Brother Emery wrote to brother Joseph that while he worked in the yard "Beauford speaks to me; today he seems nearer to me and that is why I go into the yard" (October 9, 1979).

And, of course, Beauford Delaney lives in the way he ultimately wanted to live—in the great works of art that are only now receiving the attention they deserve. In his painting, as Richard Long tells us in a poem dedicated to his friend, Beauford ascends to the realm of light and in so doing he takes us with him:

> The cycle. The Discovery. The Cycle
>
> All gathers, comes to growth, fuses.
>
> The yellow, the green. The white paper
> catching, refracting the sunlight.
>
> The palette fills with light and love.
> The spirit lifts, rises.
>
> The world floats, ascends.
>
> Ascension.
>
> Ascending.
>
>   (From "Ascending," 1975)

bibliography

African-American Art: 20th Century Masterworks, I–IV. Exhibition Catalogues. New York, Michael Rosenfeld Gallery, 1993–1997 (essays by Beryl Wright, Richard Powell, and Michael Rosenfeld).

Afro-American Artists Abroad. Exhibition catalogue. Austin: The University Art Museum of the University of Texas, 1970 (introduction by James E. Lewis).

Against the Odds: African-American Artists and the Harmon Foundation. Exhibition catalog. Newark, NJ: Newark Museum, 1989.

Atkinson, Bruce. *Once Around the Sun*. New York: Harcourt Brace, 1951.

Ashbery, John. *Art News International*, 31, (1966), 146.

Conger, Lesley (Shirley Suttles). "Jimmy on East 15th Street," *African American Review* XXIX, 4 (Winter 1995), 557–66.

Driskell, David C. *Hidden Heritage: Afro-American Art, 1800-1950*. San Francisco: The Art Museum Association of America, 1985.

Baker, Houston A. Jr. *Modernism and the Harlem Renaissance*. Chicago: University of Chicago Press, 1987.

Baldwin, James. Introduction to *The Price of the Ticket: Collected Non-Fiction, 1948-1985*. New York: St. Martin's Press, 1985

Bearden, Romare and Harry Henderson. *A History of African-American Artists: From 1772 to the Present*. New York: Pantheon, 1993 (esp. pp. 280–92).

Catalogue for *Beauford Delaney*. Paris: Galerie Paul Fachetti, 1960 (esp. introductory note by Julien Alvard).

Beauford Delaney. Exhibition catalogue. Paris: Galerie Lambert exhibition, 1964 (esp. short essay by James Baldwin).

Beauford Delaney. Exhibition catalogue. Paris: Galerie Darthea Speyer, 1973 (esp. commentaries by Georgia O'Keeffe, James Baldwin, James Jones, and Henry Miller).

Beauford Delaney. Exhibition catalogue. Paris: Galerie Darthea Speyer, 1992 (comments by Henry Miller and Darthea Speyer).

Beauford Delaney: A Retrospective [50 Years of Light]. Exhibition catalogue. New York: Philippe Briet, Inc. February–March 1991

Buffalo, Audreen, ed. *Explorations in the City of Light: African-American Artists in Paris, 1945-1965*. Exhibition catalog. New York: The Studio Museum in Harlem, 1996.

Campbell, Mary Schmidt, et al. *Harlem Renaissance: Art of Black America*. New York: The Studio Museum in Harlem and Harry N. Abrams, Inc., 1987.

Castro, Jan Garden. *The Art and Life of Georgia O'Keeffe*. New York: Crown Publishers, 1985 (pastel portrait of Beauford Delaney, p. 109).

Catalogue for group exposition at the Centre Culturel Américain, Paris, 14 January–11 February 1961 (esp. introduction by Julien Alvard).

Cederholm, Theresa Dickason, ed. *Afro American Artists: A Bio-bibliographical Dictionary*. Boston: Boston Public Library, 1973.

Chipp, Herschel B. *Theories of Modern Art*. Berkeley: University of California Press, 1968.

Contemporary Negro Art. Exhibition catalogue. Baltimore: Baltimore Museum of Art, 13–19 February, 1939 (esp. foreward by Alain Locke).

Davis, Stuart. "A Rejoinder to Thomas Benton," *Art Digest* 1 (April 1935).

Delaney, Beauford. Unpublished sketchbook journals, biographical notes, and correspondence, 1923–1975.

Delaney, Joseph. *Thirty-Six Years Exhibiting in Washington Square Outdoor Art Show*. New York: privately printed monograph, 27 March 1962.

Dover, Cedric. *American Negro Art*. Greenwich, Conn: New York Graphic Society, 1960.

Driskell, David C. *Hidden Heritage: Afro-American Art, 1800-1950*. San Francisco: The Art Museum Association of America, 1985.

Du Bois, W. E. B. "The Criteria of Negro Art," *The Crisis* 32 (October 1926).

Du Bois, W. E. B. "The Negro in Art," *The Crisis* 32 (March 1926).

Exhibition of the Productions by Negro Artists. Exhibition catalogue. New York: New York: Harmon Foundation, 1933 (esp. "The Negro Takes His Place in American Art" by Alain Locke).

Exhibition of the Work of Negro Artists. Exhibition catalogue. New York: Harmon Foundation, 1931 (esp. "The African Legacy of the Negro Artist" by Alain Locke).

Fabre, Michel. *La Rive Noire: Harlem à la Siene*. Paris: Lieu Commun, 1985.

Fabre, Michel and John A. Williams. *Way B(l)ack Then and Now*. Paris: CETANLA, 1992.

Fine, Elsa H. *The Afro-American Artist*. New York: Holt, Rinehart and Winston, 1973.

Fine, Elsa Honig. *Joseph Delaney*. Knoxville: McClung Museum, University of Tennessee Exhibition catalogue, 1970.

Fountain, Gary and Peter Brazeau. *Remembering Elizabeth Bishop*. Amherst: University of Massachusetts Press. 1994.

Freeman, Don. *Newstand*, April 1941.

Gardner, Paul. "They Followed their Muse to the City of Light," *Smithsonian* (March 1996), 106–12.

Gibson, Ann. *The Search for Freedom: African-American Abstract Painting, 1945-1975*. Exhibition catalogue. New York: Kenkelaba Gallery, 1991.

Handy, W. C. *Unsung Americans Sung*. Illustrations by B. Delaney. New York: Handy Brothers Music Co.,1944.

Hatch, James W. and Leo Hamalian, eds. *Artist and Influence 1987*, V. New York: Hatch-Billops Collection, Inc., 1987 (esp. interview with Ernest Crichlow, Bob Blackburn, et al. on the Harlem Artists Guild).

Hatch, James W. and Leo Hamalian, eds. *Artist and Influence 1994*, XIII. New York: Hatch-Billops Collection, Inc., 1994 (esp, interviews with Palmer Hayden and Ellis Wilson).

Heartney, Eleanor. "Whatever Happened to Beauford Delaney?" in *Art in America* (November 1994), 116–19.

Hess, Elizabeth. "The Undiscovered Art of Beauford Delaney," *The Village Voice* (26 February 1994).

Huggins, Nathan Irvin. *Harlem Renaissance*. New York: Oxford University Press, 1971.

Huggins, Nathan Irvin. *Voices from the Harlem Renaissance*. New York: Oxford University Press, 1976.

Hughes, Langston. "The Negro Artist and the Racial Mountain," *The Nation* 122 (23 June 1926).

Hyland, Douglas K. S., ed. *African American Art*. Exhibition Catalogue of the Harmon and Harriet Kelley Collection. San Antonio: San Antonio Museum of Art, 1994.

Jacques, Geoffrey. "Beauford Delaney's New York Years," *Race and Reason*, I, 1 (August 1994), 36–38.

Jenkins, Paul. "A Quiet Legend," *Art International* (December 1962).

Johnson, James Weldon. *Black Manhattan*. New York: Atheneum, 1968.

Leeming, David. *James Baldwin: A Biography*. New York: Knopf, 1994.

Lewis, David Levering. *W.E.B. DuBois: Biography of a Race*. New York: Henry Holt, 1993.

Lewis, Samella. *African American Art and Artists*. Berkeley: University of California Press, 1990.

Locke, Alain, foreword. *The Negro in Art*. Washington, D. C.: Associates in Negro Folk Education, 1940.

Locke, Alain L. *Negro Art: Past and Present* (1936). New York: Arno Press and the *New York Times*, 1969.

Locke, Alain L., ed. *The New Negro* (1925). New York: Atheneum, 1968.

Logan, Rayford W. and Michael Winston, eds. *Dictionary of American Negro Biography*. New York: W. W. Norton, 1982.

Long, Richard A. *Ascending and Other Poems*, Chicago: The DuSable Museum, 1975 ("Ascending" dedicated to Beauford Delaney).

Long, Richard A. ed. *Beauford Delaney: A Retrospective*. New York: Studio Museum in Harlem, 1978 (exhibition catalogue with articles by Long, Joseph Delaney, James Baldwin, and reprint of Henry Miller essay).

Long, Richard A. "Crisis of Consciousness," *Negro Digest/Black World* (May 1968).

McKinzie, Richard D. *The New Deal for Artists*. Princeton, N. J.: Princeton University Press, 1973.

Miller, Henry. "The Amazing and Invariable Beauford Delaney" in *Remember to Remember*. New York: New Directions, 1945.

Miller, Henry. "A Few Words of Homage to the Unforgettable Beauford Delaney." Unpublished, for evening dedicated to Delaney, Paris, 1969.

Morrison, Allan. "Twilight for Greenwich Village," *Negro Digest* (January 1949), 30–32.

Neely, Jack. No Greater Lover," *Metro Pulse* (Knoxville) V, 8 (April 21–May 5, 1995), 6.

Negro Artists: An Illustrated Review of Their Achievements. Exhibition catalogue. New York: Harmon Foundation, 1935.

"Negroes," *Life Magazine* (3 October 1938), 54.

Perry, Regenia A. *Free Within Ourselves: African American Artists in the Collection of the National Museum of American Art*. Exhibition catalogue. Washington, D. C.: The Smithsonian Institution, 1992.

Porter, James A. *Modern Negro Art*. New York: Dryden Press, 1943.

Powell, Richard J. *Black Art and Culture in the 20th Century*. New York: Thames and Hudson, 1997.

Rose, Barbara. *American Art Since 1900: A Critical History*. New York: Praeger, 1967.

Stein, Harry. "Patience, Virtue and Artist." *International Herald Tribune*, 14 March 1972.

Stewart, Ruth Ann. *New York/Chicago: WPA and the Black Artist*. Exhibition catalogue. New York: The Studio Museum in Harlem, 1978.

Stovall, Tyler. *Paris Noir: African Americans in the City of Light*. Boston: Houghton Mifflin, 1996.

Suttles, Shirley. See Conger, Lesley.

Thompson, Robert Farris. *Flash of the Spirit: African and Afro-American Art and Philosophy*. New York: Random House, 1983.

Who's Who in Colored America. New York: Christian E. Burckel, 1927, 1929.

Woodruff, Hale. *The American Negro Artist*. Ann Arbor: University of Michigan Press, 1956.

Wye, Pamela. "Beauford Delaney," *Arts Magazine* 65:71 (Summer 1981).